Community C

Vermont

||||| ||||||||| ||| ||||||| |||||||||||||||| ||
W9-BJV-202

Spri l

TIME AND CHANGE IN VERMONT

C.C.V.
Community College of Vermont
110 Front St.
Springfield, VT 05156

i

TIME AND CHANGE IN VERMONT
A Human Geography

Harold A. Meeks

VCTC Library
Hartness Library
Vermont Technical College
Randolph Center, VT 05061

The Globe Pequot Press

Old Chester Road
Chester, Connecticut 06412

Copyright © 1986 by Harold A. Meeks

All rights reserved. No part of this book may be reproduced or transmitted in any form by any means, electronic or mechanical, including pho-
tocopying and recording, or by any information storage and retrieval
system, except as may be expressly permitted by the 1976 Copyright Act
or in writing from the publisher. Requests for permission should be
addressed to The Globe Pequot Press, Old Chester Road, Chester, Connecticut 06412.

Library of Congress Cataloging-in-Publication Data

Meeks, Harold A.
    Time and change in Vermont.

    Bibliography: p.
    Includes index.
    1. Vermont—Economic conditions. 2. Land use—
Vermont—History.   I. Title.
HC107.V5M44   1985   330.9743   85-29271
ISBN 0-87106-883-4

Manufactured in the United States of America
First Edition / First Printing

Contents

Acknowledgments

For several years I have taught a course at the University of Vermont, part of it dealing with the subject of this book. That course on Vermont's geography has brought me face to face with students representing nearly every town in the state: students who were only too willing to point out things that I did not know or interpretations that were incorrect. I have tried to heed their advice, but I am sure that more errors will be called to my attention, especially because my students will have to buy this book for use in their classes. Leaving that caution aside, teachers always learn from their students and I am certainly no exception. As it should, much of my knowledge comes from my students, and to them, many thanks.

No work of this type could be written without the help and advice of colleagues and friends. At UVM, Canute VanderMeer, Andrew Bodman, Gardner Barnum, Ted Miles, and Daniel Gade, all of the Geography Department, provided help, and some read portions of the manuscript. Peter Shea, Eileen Driscoll, Jackie Tear, Louis Steponaitis, Steve Farrow, Allex Marshall, Peter Meyer, and Albert Pitt, as students wrote research reports that helped immeasurably. If I have forgotten some, I apologize.

Students also helped with drafting some of the maps. Jeff Burger, Peter Shea, and Gardiner Fraker must be specifically thanked, as should Northern Cartographic in Burlington, which executed some of the graphs.

Malcolm Bevins, Ray Tremblay, Dwight Eddy, and Al Gilbert helped in the chapters dealing with agriculture and recreation. Walter Cooley of the Vermont Department of Health was always able to provide me with population data when I needed it. Richard Overton of Manchester was a critical reader of the chapter on railroads, pointing out several manuscript errors and providing helpful advice on organizing the material. William Wallace of the Geography Department at the University of New Hampshire assisted me on early Vermont boundaries, and Kevin Graffagnino helped with materials from the Wilbur Collection at the University of Vermont. Gilbert Myers, Alan Overton, Charles Howe, Stanley Knapp, William Flanders, and Hazen Wood of Essex Junction are all personal friends who helped and gave encouragement.

Rowling Illick of Middlebury College introduced me to the field of geography, and much of this work reflects the teaching of a remarkable man. The chapter on evolution of dairy farming is taken from a paper I did while I was a student under Rowland in 1956; I hope he thinks the present account is better than the first!

I find it enjoyable to write, so long as someone can go over my miserably typed page and retype what I wrote so that it makes sense. Four people were able to do this chore for me: Pat Oliver, Cindy Valletta, and especially Rita Benjamin in the Geography Department, and at home, my long-suffering wife, Milly. She not only put up with me while this book was being written, but, with my children, Charles and Lany Ann, provided the encouragement to finish it.

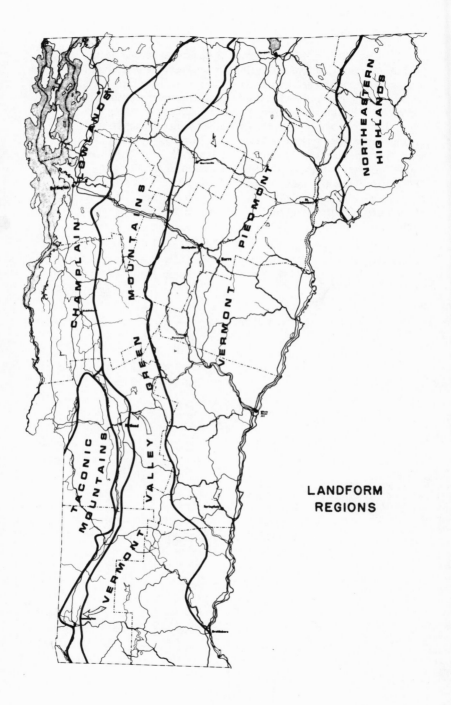

LANDFORM
REGIONS

Introduction:
Environment of Vermont

Vermont consists of 9,609 square miles, of which 342 are water. Many of the 9,267 square miles of land seem more vertical than flat. As Daniel W. Cady said in his *Rhymes of Vermont Rural Life*, "They say Vermont if rolled out flat, would equal Illinois in size; but primaries then would cost so much, the rich might win and not the wise, . . . "

Although most of the land slopes more or less, there is a pattern to the landscape that is fairly obvious to those familiar with Vermont. On the west, between the Green Mountains and Lake Champlain (the eighth-largest freshwater lake in the United States—490 square miles, with 322 in Vermont), lies the Champlain Valley, sometimes called the Champlain Lowland. Here the land ranges from gently rolling to flat, although occasional small mountains, such as Snake in Addison and Arrowhead in Milton, rise clearly above the surrounding topography. These and others mark distinctive geologic faults (or fractures) commonly running north and south through the region.

The Champlain Valley experiences most of the state's maximum summer temperatures and is also the largest area with long growing seasons. Burlington averages about five months without frost, and even longer frost-free periods are found elsewhere by the shores of Lake Champlain, especially in Grand Isle County.

As recently as 10,000 years ago, most of the lowland was an arm of the sea; before that, a series of freshwater lakes with levels far higher than that of present Lake Champlain covered everything between the Adirondacks and the Green Mountains. These glacial bodies of water, and the streams draining into them, are responsible for the high-quality sand, silt, and clay soils of western Vermont, soils far superior to the thin bouldry material covering most of the rest of the state.

1

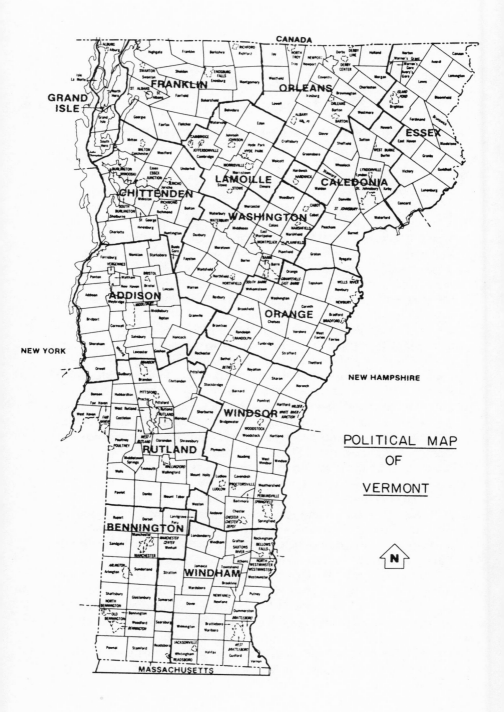

POLITICAL MAP

OF

VERMONT

With flatter land, warmer temperatures, and better soils, the Champlain Valley is Vermont's premier farm area. Franklin, Grand Isle, and Addison counties retain their agricultural importance. Chittenden County is less important for dairying because of suburban Burlington growth, but it is becoming more important for other, more diverse types of farming.

South of the Champlain Valley (or Lowland) lie two distinctive regions. The map shows the Valley of Vermont as a north–south linear region reaching from the Massachusetts border to Brandon. This narrow valley, in which Route 7 lies, supports some commercial dairy farms but is more significant for its role in Vermont's history. As a lowland passage from western Connecticut and Massachusetts it was a factor in the early settlement of western Vermont. Along its western edge, from Manchester northward, marble quarries for a hundred and fifty years have been making Vermont famous.

The true calcite marbles of western Vermont are most closely associated with the Taconic Mountains, a distinctive region astride the Vermont–New York border south of the Champlain Lowland and west of the Valley of Vermont. Geologically very complex, the Taconics may be the ancient tops of the Green Mountains that were thrust westward many millions of years ago. They are now thoroughly separate and form Vermont's second major north-south-trending mountain system.

Although some excellent farmland is found in the Mettawee and Poultney River valleys cutting through the Taconics, the chain's major influence upon Vermont has been the stones hacked from its bedrock, marble on the east and slate on the west along the New York border. With construction of Vermont's primary railroad network after 1850, these stones, along with granite, contributed much to Vermont's nineteenth-century economic development.

The Green Mountains form Vermont's backbone and give the state its identity. Composed of the same metamorphic rocks found everywhere except in the Champlain Valley, the system actually consists of two parallel and fragmented ranges. Route 100 follows the intermontane valley, linking major ski areas like beads on a chain, and providing one of the most scenic routes in the state. A few farms still remain on small, flat valley floors, but the region is best known for its recreation.

The Green Mountains south of Manchester are a plateau, cut by deep streams such as the Deerfield and West rivers, and surmounted

by scattered mountains, chief of which is Stratton. The plateau itself
is a unique old erosion surface called by geologists a "peneplain."
This surface not only has Vermont's highest church (in Woodford),
but is one of the two major wild areas in the state.

Most of the land east of the Green Mountains is hilly, forming
the classic image of hill farming and quaint villages in the valleys that
carve the topography. This section is the Vermont Piedmont or Vermont Hills, the largest of the physical regions. The same type of
landscape is found everywhere in New England, but to Vermonters
and others it seems to have a special quality. Pockets of commercial
dairying are scattered through the area, the most notable being in
Orleans County and around Randolph in Orange. Elsewhere, abandoned or restored farmhouses delight the eye as the land grows back
to mature northern hardwood forest.

Interrupting the uniformity of the hills are a few scattered high-
land areas, most composed of granite. Harder and more resistant
than the metamorphics, many of the granite masses have been quarried. Most famous of these is Barre, but Woodbury, Ascutney, and
other places have been important in the past.

The largest area of granite is not the Vermont Piedmont, but is
in the Northeast Highlands, a high and wild region that geologically
is an extension of New Hampshire's White Mountain mass. Here
isolated mountains reach altitudes of 3,000 feet or more without any
particular pattern. Soils are poor and thin, winter conditions are
rigorous, and most of the land is inaccessible except by logging
roads, which crisscross much of Essex County. This area is still
frontier Vermont and in fact some of the settlement here did not take
place until well after the Ohio country and much of the Midwest had
been settled. Most of the land today is owned by large lumber
companies.

Vermont then has six distinct regions, though they often grade
into each other without much change in landscape. Yet the core
characteristics remain and can be recognized without much difficulty.

This book is the story of the settlement and use of Vermont's
natural environment. It is mainly a historical geography, but with a
modern component. The book could probably serve as an economic
history of the Green Mountain State, for it is arranged by subject
and time rather than by geographic regions.

I

A Land-Use History

In every environment, depending upon its resources and its location, the land will be put to use in a succession of stages. In Vermont, certain periods are clearly defined, most of them ushered in by a change in transportation. Each of these changes connected the state more extensively with the larger New England region.

As settlement swept across Vermont after 1760, it occupied a New England frontier, and Maine and New Hampshire experienced the same type of development. This was the pioneer stage of occupance, and Chapter 1 examines this flow of settlement as it engulfed the state over a period of fifty years or so.

Initial settlement was uneven in its pattern and in its timing. In Chapters 2 and 3 we look at some factors responsible for this variation. Of great significance was the availability of improved transportation; the Crown Point and the Bayley-Hazen military roads were Vermont's two earliest improved highways. Both greatly influenced settlement of the regions through which they passed. Canals gave equally strong stimulation to economic development. The earliest of these was the short Bellows Falls canal, completed in 1802. The later Champlain canal of 1823 was even more significant.

The timing of this pioneer settlement was greatly influenced by Vermont's political instability, culminating in the state's brief existence as an independent Republic during the American Revolution. New York, New Hampshire, and even Canada claimed bits and pieces of Vermont's territory.

By about 1820, depending upon where one was in Vermont, goods began to be produced for export, always dependent upon the resources in the environment. Aided by canal construction, agriculture for the first time became somewhat commercial, with sheep providing wool for a developing local textile industry. In Chapter 4 we review land use in Vermont prior to the coming of the railroads.

Beginning in 1850 the Railroad era (Chapter 5) ushered in great changes in the state. Three major trends developed during the last half of the nineteenth century. In Chapters 6, 7, and 8 we trace the beginnings of a recreation industry, the change in farming from wool to milk, and the shift in population accompanying a rise in industry. Vermont was becoming a part of New England, thanks to improved accessibility provided by the iron horse and highways of steel.

As automobiles began to appear in the early years of the twentieth century, population and economic activity were no longer tied to the public transportation provided by the railroads. Vermont began to change again. Modern Vermont, culminating with the interstate highway system, is the subject of Part II.

1

Pioneer Settlement

Before a southern New England tide of settlement engulfed Vermont after 1760, Indian, French, and even Dutch groups were present. Yet on today's landscape, the imprint of these earlier cultures is hidden and elusive. Indian sites have been discovered, most commonly in the northern Champlain Valley, and a growing body of evidence suggests that Vermont was not solely an Algonquin and Iroquois hunting ground, or a territory to get across quickly for greener pastures elsewhere. Indians did live permanently in the state, although their density was low. They undoubtedly grew corn in the fertile intervales or *coos* of the upper Connecticut and elsewhere. Aside from numerous place names, however, nothing today reflects the Indian stage except possibly the ancient oak and hickory forests of the Champlain Valley, which may have been created by widespread Indian burning of the natural vegetation.

The first Paleo-Indian culture in the region that was to become Vermont probably dates from about 8500 B.C., when the environment was still glacial. Cariou were hunted, and as the climate gradually warmed with the melting of ice, the base of the Indian culture moved northward. These people may have been followed by an Archaic culture about 5000 B.C., again nomadic people whose livelihood was based on hunting, gathering wild plants, and fishing. The first plant cultivation probably occurred between 1300 and 1000 B.C., as the Woodland culture evolved from the Archaic. It is these people who left behind most sites, telling something of this occupance stage.

The Woodland peoples apparently divided into tribal groups, bonded by common language, and established territories in which

7

they maintained hunting privileges. In Vermont, the Connecticut Valley and the Champlain Valley became core areas, with the land between these a disputed ground. Algonquins dominated the eastern region and much of New England. The Mohegans, Pequots, and Narragansetts were members of the Algonquin family. In Vermont, smaller Algonquin groups were the Abnakis along the Connecticut River, and the Coaticooks a little farther north; the Nulheganocks centered in Island Pond; and even the Kenebekis around Canaan and the Connecticut lakes of New Hampshire. Differentiation among these Algonquin groups was probably more geographic than cultural, and in any case very small numbers were involved in A.D. 1600. In the early 1700s, seven hundred may have lived in the large area between Lake Memphremagog and Lake Winnepesaukee in New Hampshire.

On the other side of the state were the Iroquois, represented in Vermont by the Mohawks. It was the Iroquois whom Champlain encountered in 1609 on his venture to the lake that now bears his name. In the ensuing French and Indian Wars, the Iroquois (Six Nations) allied themselves with the English partly as a result of unfortunate incidents with Champlain and other Frenchmen. Their bitter foes, the Algonquins, allied themselves, as would be expected, with the French.

Simple division of Vermont into an eastern Algonquin territory and a western Iroquois territory is not strictly accurate. The unofficial boundary between the lands claimed by the two ran roughly from northeast to southwest through Vermont. Today a line drawn from near Westport, New York, northeast to the southern tip of Lake Memphremagog, would show the ancient territories. The Algonquins were generally to the southeast of the line, the Iroquois to the northwest.

A few miles north of Westport is Split Rock Point, so named for the deep cleft in the rock there. Tradition has it that this dominant physical feature separated the Algonquin and the Iroquois lands— Algonquins to the south and east, and Iroquois to the north and west. No Indian tales tell in which direction each claimed land from this point, but legend was sufficient to sanctify the place for the Treaty of Utrecht in 1713 as the official boundary between the French and English in North America. Even in 1760, the line from Split Rock to Lake Memphremagog was the fixed boundary between New York (and Vermont) and Canada. The line was also acknowledged as late as 1774, even after the Americans forged seventy-seven miles farther north to approximately the present Vermont–New York–Canada boundary line. The latter line was officially surveyed in 1772 (see Chapter 3).

Vermont Place Names

Today the ancient boundary lines are long gone, but Split Rock Point, Memphremagog, Monadnock, Nulhegan, Moose (Mozin), and even Ticklenaked Pond in Ryegate remind us of the Indian occupation of what was to become Vermont. Some of the place names are fascinating: Ticklenaked, despite the romantic image associated with the word, is probably from a Delaware Indian word meaning "beaver kittens here." You can believe that if you want.

Esther Swift, in her *Vermont Place Names*, gives the Indian origins for many of our common names. Most of her material comes from the noted Vermont historian and archaeologist John C. Huden. Here is a sampling of these:

Monadnock Mountain (Lemington)	Abnaki: "mountain which sticks up like an island"
Winooski City and River	Abnaki: "wild onion"
Passumpsic River	Abnaki: "clear sandy bottom"
Jamaica Town	Natic: "beaver" (from Massachusetts)
Nulhegan River	Abnaki: "my log trap"
Ompompanoosic River	Abnaki: "at the place of the mushy, quaky land"
Okemo Mountain	Abnaki: "a louse" Chippewa: "a chieftain"
Ottauquechee River	Natic: "a swift mountain stream"
Maquam (Swanton)	Abnaki: "a beaver"
Pico Peak	Abnaki: "a pass or opening"
Ascutney Mountain	Abnaki: "at the end of the river fork"
Ohio Hill (Bridgewater)	Mohawk: "big, or beautiful, river"
Sadawga Pond (Whitingham)	Mohawk: "swiftly flowing water" or a Mohawk chief called "Sadawga"
Shatterack Mountain (Jamaica)	Pocumtuck: "big mountain"

Abnaki names predominate, probably because the Abnaki were the most numerous Indians remaining in the territory with the coming of the white people, and the word sounds were recorded. Because the Abnaki possessed no written language, the transliterations make it difficult to be sure of the place-name interpretations. Recently, attempts have been made to prove that many commonly accepted Indian place names throughout New England actually have an ancient Anglo-Saxon or Celtic derivation and either were applied directly by Celtic peoples in the region or were learned by the Indians from much earlier European contacts than anyone had supposed. In Vermont alone, the names Quechee (and the Ottauquechee River) and Mt. Monadnock are both claimed to be Celtic in origin. In Gaelic, *cuithe* means "pit, trench, deep moist place," and *Otha-cuithe* is "the waters of the gorge." Similarly, the Gaelic *monadh* means "mountain," and *cnoc* a "hill, rocky outcrop." both are borrowed from Old English and are in Scottish mountain names to this day.

It would be a matter of great pride if Vermont and other parts of New England could claim ancient European settlement. Sites that have been identified as ancient stone borrow pits or nineteenth-century potato cellars have become popular. Excavations in coastal Maine, New Hampshire, and Massachusetts have indicated much earlier European visitations to the New World than previously accepted, but it requires considerable imagination to account for ancient celtic people in Tunbridge, Vermont. From a geographical perspective, one is hard pressed to imagine ancient peoples penetrating the cold, mountainous, and inhospitable regions of northern New England when coastal locations were abundant. Even the Champlain Valley would be a more logical site than the interior parts of Vermont, not to mention the miserable conditions that must have prevailed in the vicinity of Mt. Monadnock in the wilds of the Northeast Highlands. Whatever the reality, legends and authors of theories, newspaper articles, books, and scholarly works will continue to speculate on pre-Columbian European occupancy of Vermont.

The Indian imprint on Vermont's landscape is told mainly in place names. The early French left a more substantial legacy, although it was minor compared to the English wave of colonial settlement from the south that swept over the state after 1760. French place names occur in parts of the state, but chiefly in the northwest. A few structures still standing may have incorporated French-built walls. Vestiges of ancient French field patterns have been found along the shores of Lake Champlain.

A favorite Vermont story is about the naming of the Lemon Fair River, a tributary of Otter Creek in Addison County. Traditionally the early settler, dragging himself and his family through the infamous Addison County clay, surrounded by swarms of mosquitos, came upon a stagnant, murky channel of water blocking the path. "What a lamentable affair," cried the frustrated person, and in time that stream was known as Lemon Fair River. I doubt that the pioneer of the late 1700s knew the word "lamentable," and furthermore if the scene is right, the words would have been a lot more colorful. Perhaps the best explanation of Lemon Fair is the Yankee trying to pronounce the French word for "Green Mountains" (les Monts Verts). But then, the French phrase for "making mud" is "Limon Faire." Take your choice. The name Vermont itself derives from French, as does that of Montpelier, the State capital, but neither was named by early French visitors.

The Lamoille River was said to have been the "La Mouette," or a place where gulls are found; at least that is supposed to be what Champlain had in mind when he named it in 1609. The story is that a French mapmaker forgot to cross his t's, and it became Lamouelle, gradually changing to its present form over the years. Isle La Motte in Lake Champlain was chartered by the State of Vermont in 1779 as Isle of Mott, but the French form prevailed. It comes from Pierre de St. Paul, Sieur (Lord) de la Motte, who constructed Fort St. Anne in 1666 with its garrison of three hundred men. The fort and settlement lasted only four years, but the name endured, even after the local inhabitants in 1802 petitioned the Vermont legislature to change the name to Vineland.

Other names of French derivation dot the Vermont landscape. Some later French place names include Fayetteville in Newfane (from Lafayette), and St. Johnsbury (from Michel-Guillaume-Jean de Crèvecoeur, or J. Hector St. John, a somewhat eccentric character who urged wide use of French names in Vermont during the Revolution). The name Vergennes was bestowed by the Vermont legislature in 1788 to commemorate a former French minister of Foreign Affairs. The small place, originally of 1,200 acres, was carved out of the spot where New Haven, Panton, and Ferrisburg came together at the Falls of the Otter Creek. It is the only city in Vermont that was not chartered first as a town or village and as such is supposed to be the third-oldest "city" in the United States (after New Haven and

Hartford, Connecticut). Probably it is the smallest legally constituted city in the United States, with a 1980 population of 2,273.
Because the U.S. Census Bureau uses a cutoff of 2,500 to distinguish
rural from urban places, strictly speaking those who live in the city
of Vergennes are rural people.

French occupation of Vermont was transitory, but some place
names survive, suggesting the sphere of French influence. French
settlements were short-lived, and of a military character. Isle La
Motte was inhabited for four years, and off and on after that. Far-
ther south, the French built Fort St. Frederick on Crown Point, New
York, and had a smaller settlement on the Vermont side of Lake
Champlain at Chimney Point. There the French in the 1730s built
upon the ruins of a Dutch trading settlement of 1690 organized by a
Captain Jacobus D'Narm (or de Warm) of Albany. Both the Crown
Point and Chimney Point settlements were abandoned in 1759 when
General Amherst pushed north up the Champlain Valley, driving the
French before him. Chimney Point received its name from the chim-
neys standing in the area after the English occupation. Old cellar
holes can still be found, and at least one wall of the imposing stone
house on the point is probably of French origin.

Patterns on the Land

It is very likely that the early French occupied more of the Champlain Valley than we have written record of. One hundred and fifty
years elapsed between Champlain's exploration and the coming of
the English, a period during which the region was largely under the
arm of New France. Hints of early permanent agricultural settlement are suggested by ancient field patterns identifiable both in modern aerial photographs and on early maps of many valley towns. In
the Addison Town Plan accompanying the original charter by Governor Bennington Wentworth (see Chapter 3), the French Chimney
Point area is left unplatted with no lots laid out, suggesting previous
land divisions. Moreover, except for Chimney Point, the entire lakeshore of the town is divided into forty long, narrow lots, each numbered, a few yards wide and about a mile deep. The observant
traveler will see today the same field pattern throughout the Quebec
lowlands close to the St. Lawrence River. The long-lot system of land
division is a lasting imprint of French culture in the New World, and

Fields and farms along the upper Connecticut River in Lemington still reflect the original settlement grants. In parts of the Champlain Valley a similar field pattern might indicate early French land divisions.

the lots along the lake in Addison County may be a legacy. Similar land divisions can be found in Alburg, where aerial photographs clearly show the old field patterns in both towns, with the elongated fencelines stretching a mile or more back from the shore. The regularity of the long, narrow lots contrasts strikingly with the rough rectangles of most early Vermont field patterns. In Alburg, the long fields probably date from the 1740s, but often late nineteenth-century French Canadian settlers in the United States imported their field systems with them. The Acadian French used the same system widely up and down the Mississippi River, even as far north as Chester (Kaskaskia), Illinois.

Another point to keep in mind is that several seventeenth-century Massachusetts and Connecticut colonies were plotted with long, narrow strips back from the Connecticut River. Springfield, Massachusetts, and Wethersfield, Connecticut, are examples. The rationale there was the same as that of the French along the St. Lawrence, the

Mississippi, and possible Lake Champlain; equal access to the only easy means of transportation at the time: water. The combination of 150 years of time, French names on the landscape, and the commonness of enduring French field patterns all suggest more early French settlement than has been thought.

Long and narrow fields are not unique to the Champlain Valley. They are common along the upper Connecticut in Maidstone, Brunswick, Lunenberg, and Lemington. The first two towns are even laid out as long, narrow parallelograms from the river itself, but it is doubtful that these can be traced to early French influence.

Down in the extreme southwest corner of the state, the otherwise straight boundary with New York jogs around a bit in the town of Pownal (see Chapter 3). Although the details are not clear, the angles of the boundary conform to earlier property lines stemming from Dutch settlement in 1724. Here again aerial photos indicate a field pattern different from that typical of most of Yankee Vermont. Barns bearing a definite Dutch influence are common in Pownal, as well as Rupert, Castleton, and Poultney—all suggesting more settlement and cultural influence.

The Indians, the French, and in a small way the Dutch, have all left their print on modern Vermont. But the state is nearly all Yankee in its place names, its heritages, and its early settlement. Middle and late nineteenth-century immigration of many ethnic groups—French Canadians, Italians, Irish, Poles, Finns, Hungarians, Welsh, and Cornish—contributed to the rich culture that is Vermont's today, but until 1840, Vermont was Yankee Vermont. Nearly all settlement after 1760 was from southern New England. Architectural forms, words, pronunciations, farm practices, manufacturing technology, religions, and the people themselves came from Connecticut, Massachusetts, and New Hampshire, with smaller numbers from Rhode Island, New York, and Maine.

Yankee Frontier

The flow of settlement into the and that was to become Vermont began after 1760 with the end of hostilities between Britain and France. You will find in any good history the events of the French and Indian Wars, the deeds of Rogers's Rangers, and the failures of Jeffrey Amherst (see Chapter 2). The early history of Vermont settlement has been well covered, as has been emigration from the promised land beginning in the 1830s. Historians have commented, and probably they are correct, that if the Erie Canal (1825) had been opened fifty years earlier, Vermont to this day would not have been settled. Hilly land full of rocks, poor soils, miserable winters, Indian scalping parties, political instability, and difficult transportation, not to mention mosquitos, black flies, and other delights of the north country should have been enough to discourage even the most optimistic settler.

But after 1760, the southern New England farm boy and farm girl had no other place to go than north to Vermont. In those years, the only occupation was farming, and as Connecticut saw all but the highest mountain summits planted to corn and other crops, the family farms could not be subdivided further. Because most colonial families had a prodigious number of children (at least by today's standards), the sons and daughters had to move elsewhere. They should have gone to the Ohio country, but that was not available in the late 1700s, and anyway, there was no easy way of getting there. Salisbury and other areas in the hill lands of western Connecticut became important sources for settlers to Vermont. There the land was poor, no more was to be had, and Vermont was the promised land. The Taconic Mountain wall to the west was a barrier, the Erie Canal was unheard of, and in the desperate search for land, the staple commodity of existence, the only direction in which to turn was toward the north.

Connecticut had knowledge of Vermont. Many of the road builders on the 1759–1760 Crown Point Road (see Chapter 2) were from Connecticut, and word soon filtered through the region. Penetration into land that was to become Vermont began as a mere trickle in the late 1760s, and swelled to a flood over the next fifty years. From western Connecticut young people moved up the lowlands of western Massachusetts and western Vermont; from central and eastern Connecticut they moved up the Connecticut Valley. The U.S. Census of 1800 reported that two-thirds of the Vermont population were under twenty-six years of age.

Figure 1.1 is an isochronic map designed to show the timing of permanent settlement as it swept over the state. Using the recorded dates at which first settlement occurred in every town in Vermont, lines are drawn at four-year intervals. The Connecticut Valley and the Valley of Vermont (Route 7) show up as the earliest arteries of immi-

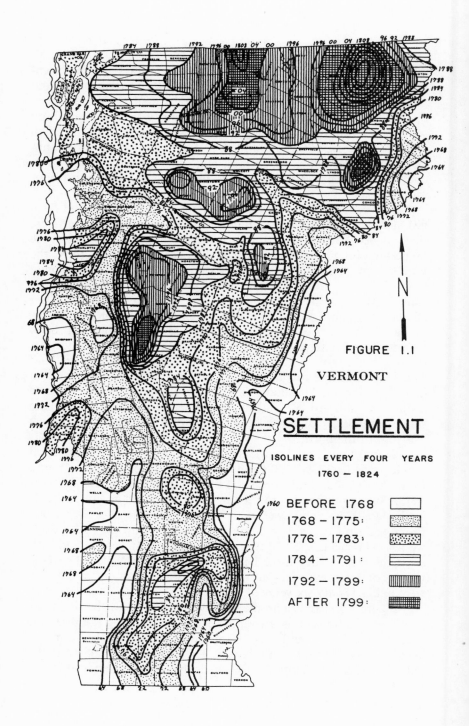

FIGURE 1.1

VERMONT

SETTLEMENT

ISOLINES EVERY FOUR YEARS
1760 — 1824

BEFORE 1768
1768 — 1775:
1776 — 1783:
1784 — 1791:
1792 — 1799:
AFTER 1799:

gration, but other valleys such as the West, the White, and the Winooski helped influence the early movement. Last areas to be occupied were the Green Mountains and the Northeast Highlands. Towns there did not receive their first inhabitants until 1824, when people were even entering Ohio. Relatively early settlement across the southern Green Mountains through Plymouth and Shrewsbury, and around Bridport and Shoreham along Lake Champlain, is related to Vermont's first important highway, the Crown Point Military Road. Settlement through Peacham, Cabot, Hardwick, and Greensboro was greatly influenced by the Bayley-Hazen Military Highway twenty-five years later (see Chapter 2).

Literally forced off the farms of southern New England, the young pioneers moved north into land that often was worse than that they had left behind. Between 1790 and 1810, the state of Connecticut increased in population from 232,734 to 261,942, an increase of 17 percent. In Vermont, meanwhile, the population went from only 85,425 to 217,895, or a twenty-year growth of 150 percent. This is not to say that everyone from Connecticut moved to Vermont in twenty years; many Connecticut people migrated into northeastern Pennsylvania, but a great many Connecticut people were certainly important in the early Yankee settlement of the state. Many scattered sources give us fascinating hints about where early Vermonters came from.

Old gazetteers often list the home state of the first settler or settlers. More than fifty towns in Vermont were first settled by people from Connecticut, twenty-seven from New Hampshire, probably thirty-four from Massachusetts, and another three from Rhode Island. Ryegate was settled directly from Scotland, Canadians were in Alburg, a Hessian in Highgate, and even one "Yorker" in Manchester. Eight towns saw first settlement by Vermonters who migrated north from the southern part of the state. The major region of initial Connecticut settlement was western Vermont, especially the Champlain Valley as far north as Colchester and South Hero. A secondary Connecticut grouping was in the so-called Connecticut Towns of Windsor County, including Norwich, Hartford, Sharon, and Pomfret. New Hampshire's initial settlement was in the White River region of western Orange County, and along the West River in Windham County. The only important Massachusetts concentration was in southeastern Vermont, including Whitingham, Halifax, Guilford, Brattleboro, and other towns in Windham County. Until

1740 this section of Vermont was a part of the Massachusetts Bay Colony (see Chapter 3), and some early first settlement predates later boundary adjustments.

Place names help little in determining where the first people in a town were from. Most Vermont towns were named by Benning Wentworth, sitting behind a desk in Portsmouth, New Hampshire. Frequently, he wanted to impress someone in England, or even himself, with Bennington in 1749! Rarely did the first settlers have the option of naming a town for someplace familiar to them. The only towns in Vermont definitely named for towns in Connecticut besides those listed already were probably Fletcher, Derby, Canaan, East Haven, New Haven, Roxbury, Hartford, Weathersfield, and Wallingford. In these towns, as in Wallingford, Connecticut, many of the first settlers were from that town in central Connecticut. But Middlebury, Vermont, often pointed to as a "Connecticut town" and settled early by Connecticut people, was named by Governor Wentworth because, of the three north–south towns chartered at the same time, it was in the "middle" between New Haven and Salisbury.

Of more interest to many is delving into old graveyards. Old marble stones often carry much more information than our modern granite memorials do. In the cemetery in Randolph Center is the stone of General John French. General French was born in Randolph, Massachusetts, and died in Randolph, Vermont. But Randolph, Vermont, according to Esther Swift, was a Vermont-named town (neither New Hampshire nor New York had claimed the land), and she states only that the town was named by a group who secured a character for the town of this name. It may be that General French's connections with the two Randolphs are a coincidence, but in place of a better explanation, a Vermont gravestone may tell us where Randolph got its name. But, to further confuse us, the old records state that at least the first settler was from New Hampshire, and there is a Randolph in that state as well.

Cemeteries in Barnet, Ryegate, and Groton are full of stones of lowland Scots, especially from around Paisley. The first settler in Groton, however, was Dominicus Gray, and his marble slab on top of a hill tells us he was born in Connecticut. Groton was a Vermont-chartered town, originally spelled Grotton, but somewhere along the line the second "t" was dropped. Esther Swift says the town was probably named for either Groton, Massachusetts or Groton, Con-

Sir Isaac Newton, the famous English physicist, is buried in Westminster Abbey. In South Wardsboro is another Sir Isaac Newton, bearing a name bestowed by his parents.

The portal of the Addison Railroad covered bridge across the Lemon Fair River in Shoreham. Long abandoned, this is one of the finest examples in Vermont.

necticut. Because of the weathered stone of Dominicus Gray, I opt for the latter. Gravestone searching can be rewarding and might unravel a lot of mysteries about the early settlement of the state.

The quest in discovering where Vermonters came from has taken us to a road map for place names, to graveyards for inscriptions on stones, and now to talking with the natives. Certain speech forms and words meaning certain things are handed down from generation to generation. If the language can be traced back to a place where the phrases are in everyday use, we have something to go on. For example, the thing we pull out every morning that holds clothes, in western Vermont is a "drawer," but in eastern Vermont, along the Maine coast, and around Boston, it is a "draw." In the same way, western Vermonters "park" their car, and eastern people "paak" their automobiles. In parts of Orange and Caledonia countries, an earthworm is a "mudworm," and in the old days in western Vermont, a serenade was a "horning." Mudworms are very common in southern New Hampshire, and hornings can be found through western Massachusetts and most of Connecticut. A "horning" was a nuptial celebration apparently originating in Connecticut. There in the wee hours of the morning, the wedding guests would surround the newlyweds' home with an assortment of clarinets, bugles, and other noisemakers. How the custom came to be called a serenade is anyone's guess.

These fascinating bits of local differences in dialect were recorded in the *Linguistic Atlas of New England*, put together in the 1930s. At that time, long before widespread radio and television, traces of the local vernacular still could be found. Small pockets in many parts of Vermont still have the regional speech forms, but they are harder to find.

Barns and Bridges

Early settlers, with nothing else to go by, would often build in the style of the area from which they came. Barns and houses bearing the imprint of other New England areas can be identified. The farmhouse connected to the barn is common in central and eastern Connecticut, and it occurs in eastern Vermont. Rarely west of the Green Mountains does that architectural style appear. Barns bearing a Dutch influence are found in southwestern Vermont, but nowhere else in the state. After the 1840s, with standardized builders' manuals available, structures do not show much regional differentiation: even the original covered bridges, built on the model of preexisting barns, became "patent" bridges, built according to patents issued New England builders.*

The first bridges built across Vermont streams, if they were not too wide, were "stringer" bridges. They were made of two substantial trees felled across the stream, with boards nailed crosswise and lengthwise for the traffic. The trouble was that these early bridges would sag and quiver alarmingly toward the center as one got farther from the support at both ends. To cross a wider stream, some sort of trusswork was necessary so that the weight in the center of the span could be transmitted to the ends without the center's collapsing.

The simplest sort of support involved pilings, but with the tools of the time the labor of building supports upward from the stream bed to the underside of the stringers was more than most could cope with.

The first and easiest truss was the kingpost design (see Figure 1.2), the same sort of truss used to hold up the roof of early barns of the pole type. Any good carpenter could fashion a kingpost truss, and many covered bridges still standing show this method of construction. An improvement was the queenpost ordinarily used for a slightly wider stream. Many of these also survive, and in fact Vermont has more homemade kingpost and queenpost covered bridges than any other state. Of the 118 bridges now standing, 51 are of these methods of construction; this is the highest percentage in the United States. Although Pennsylvania has more covered bridges (347), fewer are of the homemade variety. The other important covered-bridge states, Oregon (106) and Georgia (44), also have fewer that are so constructed.

After about 1820, various patent bridges were invented by Theodore Burr, Ithiel Town, Willis Pratt, William Howe, and others. Bridges such as the Burr Arch and the Town Lattice became popular and in most areas dominated covered-bridge construction, but in Vermont kingpost and queenpost designs were built right up to 1900.

A tradition of native bridge building lasted in Vermont far longer than anywhere else, but as to all else, changes came. The last

---

*Bridges were "covered" to protect from rot the structural timbers holding up the span. As long as plenty of low-cost wood was available, it was a sensible precaution.

A

B

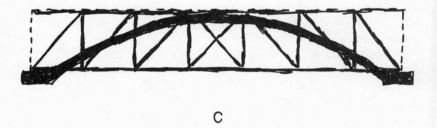

C

Figure 1.1. Covered bridge designs: (a) is a kingpost truss, (b) is a queenpost. Both are very common in Vermont. Example (c) is a patent bridge, in this case a Burr arch, patented in 1805. After Richard S. Allen, *Covered Bridges of the Northeast.*

covered bridges in the state were built shortly after 1900 as the age of steel and iron came to the Green Mountains. Bridge-building companies from out of state put up contracted bridges practically overnight at far lower cost. Guaranteed for an indefinite period and impervious to rot, the iron bridge came into its own. Few things are more graceful than the old iron bridges on the byways of the state, but even they are now passing from the scene as they are replaced by steel culverts.

Bridge construction was only one of the problems that the first newcomers overcame with patience, ingenuity, and a lot of fortitude. The means of communication were gradually improved as the wilderness was subdued with the axe and with the plow.

The river valleys were the migration routes of the sons and daughters of southern New England. The Crown Point Road and the Bayley–Hazen Road were important, the former especially for Connecticut settlers. In 1771 the estimated population of the area that was to become Vermont was only about 7,000, mostly hunters, trappers, and the military. During the Revolutionary War, settlement just about ceased, especially in the Champlain Valley. Some places like Charlotte, south of Burlington, were abandoned, only to have people return in 1784. By 1780 probably 30,000 were in the territory, and the first U.S. Census, with debatable accuracy, reported a total of 85,000 in 1790.

Because Vermont's Revolutionary War and French and Indian War hostilities were chiefly in the Champlain Valley, settlement in the Connecticut Valley and in southeastern Vermont was far more substantial and lasting. Halifax, Guilford, Dummerston, Putney, and Westminster all saw their maximum population before 1810; in both 1790 and 1800, Guilford was the most populous town in Vermont.

Settlement of what was to become Vermont was a tide of short duration. By 1810, Vermonters were thinking of going West, and after the Erie Canal was completed in 1825, the dream became a reality. Settlers in the towns of northern Vermont were mostly Vermonters, or their offspring, who had settled in other areas twenty years earlier.

The shape of the land more than anything else determined the course of earliest migration, as the map of early settlement superimposed on a map of river valleys shows clearly. But two nonphysical factors had great bearing on initial settlement: the military highways and early roads, and the unstable political situation. The early high-ways provided a means of access outside of the easy valleys; the latter discouraged settlement because of uncertain land claims.

2

Military Highways, Turnpikes, and Canals

Crown Point, New York, is a small neck of land constricting Lake Champlain to a few hundred yards in width. At this strategic narrowing of the waters, the French in 1731 began constructing fortifications to enhance their control of the lake. Soldiers were given small farms in the typical French fashion: 550 feet wide and 7,400 feet long. Settlement spilled over onto Chimney Point on the Vermont side as the permanent population continued to expand to around 1,500. The name Chimney Point itself is attributed to the stone chimneys found by the British on their advance "down" the valley a few years later. (Down and up are confusing terms in the Champlain region. Technically, because the lake drains northward, going north in the valley means going down the lake, and going south means going up. For today's armchair traveler, visualizing north as "down" requires considerable effort.)

With the completion of Fort St. Frederick on the New York side, the French in 1756 began constructing Fort Carillon (later Ticonderoga) at the strategic confluence of Lake George and Lake Champlain, a day's march to the south. All this activity goaded the English into action, and after two attempts they took Fort Carillon and advanced toward Crown Point in 1759. Vastly outnumbered, the French followed a scorched-earth policy, demolishing their fort and the associated agricultural settlements, and retreated northward.

Lord Jeffrey Amherst and his troops arrived at Crown Point on August 4, 1759. He was supposed to push on after the French and catch them in a pincer movement between his forces and those of

25

General Sir James Wolfe, who was attacking Quebec City. Amherst, however, forever cautious no matter what the song says, felt it best to solidify his position. He was, of course, worried about French naval superiority on the lake. Deciding not to try to rebuild Fort St. Frederick, the demolished French fortification, he had the remains leveled, as much as he could, and put his troops to work constructing the largest colonial fort ever built in North America. Three years of work resulted in an enormous fortification enclosing a parade ground of more than six acres, and eventually an English settlement of considerable size sprang up outside the walls, again spilling over into Vermont across the lake. Its cost at the time was two million pounds sterling, or more than $10 million, an incredible amount of money in 1760.

The Crown Point Road

Amherst's eagerness to solidify his position must have been paramount, because on August 8, 1759, only four days after securing the position, he wrote to Governor Benning Wentworth of New Hampshire:

> Since I have been in possession of this ground one of my particular attentions had been to improve the advantages it gives me of most effectually covering and securing this country and opening such communications as will render the access between the provinces and the army easy, safe and short; accordingly I sent to explore the Otter River, in order to erect posts on each side of it as will obstruct all scalping parties from going up that river to annoy any of His Majesty's subjects that may now choose to come and settle between N. 4 and that. And for easier communication of your two provinces [New Hampshire and Massachusetts] with this post, I have already for these some days past had a number of men in the woods that are employed in cutting a road between this and No. 4 which will be finished before you receive this. [Letter from General Amherst, Crown Point, New York, to Benning Wentworth, quoted by Walter H. Crockett, *History of Vermont*, Vol. I (New York, 1921), pp. 168–69.]

Amherst certainly was no slouch. At the same time as he was occupying the site, he had sent out a detail to survey and start constructing the route that has become known as the Crown Point Military Road (Figure 2.1).

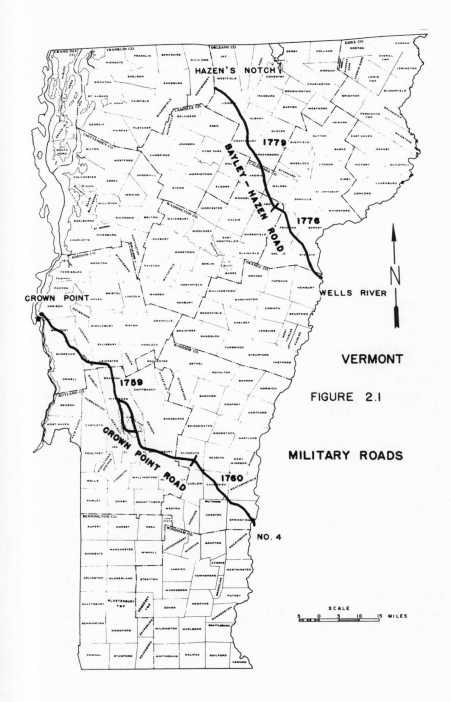

HAZEN'S NOTCH

BAYLEY – HAZEN ROAD

1779

1776

WELLS RIVER

CROWN POINT

1759

CROWN POINT ROAD

1760

NO. 4

N

VERMONT

FIGURE 2.1

MILITARY ROADS

SCALE
5   0   5   10   15 MILES

No records of collusion between Amherst and Wentworth remain, but it is easy to speculate that Wentworth had a lot more to do with authorization for the road than he is given credit for. There is little doubt that he stood to gain financially from its construction, and his immediate granting of towns along the route in 1761 was hardly accidental (see Chapter 3).

Fort Number 4 had been constructed by Massachusetts and had borne the brunt of several Abnaki Indian excursions in the Connecticut Valley. It had been built in 1740, twenty-five miles north of Fort Dummer, Vermont, and there in 1747 it was successfully defended by Captain Phineas Stevens against a marauding band of French and Indians. In fact, so heroic was Captain Stevens's defense that Sir Charles Knowles, then commodore of the British Navy in Boston, presented the Captain with his sword as a token of admiration. Henceforth the town was known as Charlestown, New Hampshire. And this place was to be the beginning or end (depending upon how the map is held) of the Crown Point Road.

After the attacks of 1747, the pace of Indian incursions in the Connecticut Valley diminished, the last raid occurring in 1754, with the famous "Captive Johnson" episode, when Mrs. Suzanne Johnson was hauled northward as a prisoner but lived to tell her tale of trials and tribulations. Most standard Vermont history books tell of the Johnson affair. Mrs. Johnson is best known for giving birth to a daughter while a prisoner, probably in the town of Cavendish. In an advanced stage of pregnancy, she had been given a horse by her captors, and it is possible that the jouncing brought on the event. In any case, daughter Johnson was named "Captive," and Captive Johnson has become a part of Vermont folklore.

Mrs. Johnson was being taken back to territory that is now Canada on the old Indian Trail or Indian Road. This was one of several traditional Indian routes across Vermont to the settled areas of Massachusetts to the south. One called the French Road (or Trunk Line) came down from Canada by way of Lake Champlain, up the Winooski Valley, across the height of land into the White River tributaries, and then down into the Connecticut Valley. Another entered Vermont through Lake Memphremagog and also crossed the height of land, one branch connecting with the Winooski River route, the other dropping down into the Connecticut River Valley north of Newbury. The Indian Road itself, the one most used, followed Lake Champlain, went up Otter Creek, over the mountains in

Shrewsbury and Mount Holly, and down the Black River Valley to the Connecticut. A branch followed the present Route 4 across the mountains east of Rutland and along the White River to the Connecticut where White River Junction now lies.

The Indian Road, now closely followed by Routes 103 and 131, was chosen as the route of the Crown Point Road, which had been thought about for several years, In 1756, three years before road construction began, the legislature of Massachusetts had commissioned a survey of the region, but Colonel Israel Williams went only as far as the present town of Mount Holly. Williams, however, did gather some material on the proposed route and submitted with his report a letter from Captain Humphrey Hobbs, who had traveled the Indian Road from Fort Number 4 in 1748.

> From Number 4, up the river, on the east side about a mile to avoid crossing the Black River; then cross the river, deep still water, good landing on the banks, to the northward of northwest to the foot of the mountains called Ascounde [perhaps Ascutney?] about 2 miles, the land white oak and pine, sandy and course full of gullies, at the foot of the mountain, struck into the Indian Road, which followed to Otter Creek, left the mountains to the northward, the land much the same but inclined to oak and beech, tolerably level, steered about west-north-west four days and came to Otter Creek, which is inclined more to beech and sugar maple tree, called it 60 miles but do not think it is so much, thence down the river, on each side of which interval land about a mile wide and continued after this sort to the Great Falls [Proctor]. I am very confident a good wagon road may be made hitherto . . . . [Letter from Captain Humphrey Hobbs to an unknown recipient, probably Colonel Israel Williams, September 18, 1756, quoted from *Topographical Descriptions of Such Parts of North America as are contained in the Map of the Middle British Colonies, etc., in North America, by T. Pownall, M. P. Lake Governor of his Majesty's Provinces of Massachusetts Bay and South Carolina*, Printed for J. Almon (London, 1766), as found in Mary F. Charlton, "The Crown Point Road," *Vermont Historical Society Proceedings* (Montpelier, 1931), p. 169.]

This is nearly an exact description of where the road was eventually to go.

Under the command of Amherst when he stopped at Crown Point were two companies of Rangers, one commanded by Captain

The western end of the Crown Point Road was Amherst's fortress at Crown Point, New York, now a state park. This photograph shows the ruins of the old French fort in the foreground, and the chimneys of Amherst's Fort Crown Point in the left background.

John Stark of New Hampshire, the other by Major Robert Rogers. Amherst decided that Rogers would attack the Indian village of St. Francis, and Stark would be relegated to a road-building detail. The task was probably not to Stark's liking, and his efforts have been forgotten in time, though not the exploits of Rogers and his Rangers, told in *Northwest Passage*, by Kenneth Roberts. Stark left Crown Point with his party of 200 Rangers, probably on August 5, 1759, and returned with his party on September 8, a few days before Rogers departed northward with his contingent. Stark probably still wanted to go with Rogers, but many of his men were sick and hungry.

In retrospect, Stark was probably happy that he and his men did not accompany Rogers. After traveling down Lake Champlain to the head of Missisquoi Bay, the Rangers went overland to St. Francis on the St. Lawrence River and successfully attacked their objective.

Rather than returning to Crown Point, the group was to proceed via Lake Memphremagog and the Nulhegan River to the Connecticut River, and thence down the Connecticut to the "Coos" (river meadowlands) at the present site of Newbury. There they expected to pick up food and supplies waiting for them before proceeding down the river to Number 4.

Hounded during the retreat by the pursuing French and their Indian allies, the Rangers suffered horribly. Splitting into two parties soon after leaving Memphremagog, one group followed the planned Nulhegan route, the other struck off on a more direct route through the present towns of Victory and Granby. With less than half their original force left, and on the edge of starvation, the Rangers regrouped at the Coos, only to find that the expected supplies had gone back downstream to Number 4. The force had left Crown Point on September 13, and finally managed to reach Number 4 on October 31.

While all this was going on, the fortunate Stark, with his company, had blazed a trail for the road from Crown Point across the mountains to Number 4. The Indian path had been widened and improved, but no bridges had been built and many stumps remained to impede wagon traffic. No one knows how long Stark and his men stayed at Number 4 before the return journey, but it could not have been very long. He certainly was worried about deserters, and also wanted to get back to Amherst before Rogers left. Rivers being at their lowest ebb and small brooks easily fordable in September, it appeared that they did not need bridges. Stark's work was a rush job, and he reported that the route as he measured it was seventy-seven miles, but "could be much shortened."

After Stark got back, Amherst sent a detail under the command of Major John Hawks to begin improving the road and building necessary bridges as well as laying corduroy (logs) over wet spots. The road detail worked under sometimes terrible conditions until the middle of November 1759, when they rushed on to Number 4 over the road blazed by Stark. They had completed a good wagon road to Otter Creek or a little beyond, and had improved the trail to Plymouth before they ran the rest of the way. Upon arriving at the fort, they were paid off and dispersed to their homes, most of them to Connecticut. A record of much of the construction was kept by Sergeant Robert Webster, and his entry of November 6, 1759, is typical of the troubles faced by the soldiers:

Tues. 6 Nov. This is a pleasant morning. We killed two cattle. Our bread is just gone. We haven't had but one bisquit a day this four or five days. Yesterday we came to Otter Creek and there are still. We are very hungry. We sent forty men after bread [to Crown Point] which we expected was on the road coming to us. This day we lay still whilst just night and then went to work without any bread to eat. Ammedown killed a beaver with my hatchet.

It took the detail five days to erect a bridge over Otter Creek; Webster's remarks were made on the second day of the encampment.

For the sake of the historical record, and to clarify some of the Daughters of the American Revolution markers that presently dot the route of the old road, Webster's diary often refers to Major Stark. What probably happened was that Stark was promoted to Major for his early trailblazing efforts, and either accompanied Hawks or took over command of the detail from Hawks during late fall of 1759. No one knows the exact circumstances, which is why some of the monuments erected later appear to contradict one another.

As the Vermont winter descended, work on the road halted. A reasonably good wagon road had been constructed from Crown Point (actually Chimney Point, Vermont) as far as Otter Creek in Pittsford, and an improved trail extended beyond. Plans were made for the eastern end to be worked on as soon as the weather broke, and Colonel John Goffe and his regiment of New Hampshire men were selected for the task. Although most of Hawks's Provincials had been from Connecticut, and were now happily home telling others the wonders of Vermont, the 1760 construction was to be strictly a New Hampshire affair. Goffe's men mustered at Litchfield, New Hampshire, between Nashua and Manchester, and marched, eight hundred strong, to Number 4 during late May and early June 1760. Because there was no road, they got an early taste of what was in front of them, and Goffe was a great organizer. The construction was to be a lot more professional than the hit-or-miss proposition of the year before. Seventy-two men were assigned as scouts, a hundred carpenters were to build the blockhouse at Wentworth's Crossing on the Vermont side of the Connecticut River, and an additional 192 men were placed under the command of Captain John Hazen (not Moses Hazen of the Bayley-Hazen Military Road) to protect the actual road-building crew. The remaining 400 men drew tools and were ready to start by the middle of June 1760. By this time Amherst was becoming a bit impatient, but Goffe maintained that this was to be an efficient expedition and was not to be hurried. On June 18, the entire regiment, including the baggage train of supplies and a drove of cattle destined for the garrison at Crown Point, crossed the Connecticut on flatboats two miles north of Number 4 and began their work. The carpenters set to with a will to build the blockhouse at the ferry crossing.

Work officially began on June 20, in the midst of the blackfly season, on the route first referred to as Atkinson's Road after Theodore Atkinson, Benning Wentworth's brother-in-law. Within two weeks, the road was being referred to as Goffe's Road. Wentworth's interest in the construction, however, was fairly obvious. The trail left by Stark, following for the most part the Indian Trail, was widened to twenty feet, and at the end of July the road builders reached the point where Hawks had left off the past year at the Twenty-six-Mile Encampment at the north end of Lake Amherst. The men had built a good road, twenty-six miles in length, with culverts, bridges, and corduroy, in a little more than a month in the hottest part of a Vermont summer. It was an achievement paralleling the heroics of the previous November. There were the normal desertions and the occasional flogging; several men died and are buried just east of the road in Springfield.

This eastern section of the road was far better engineered than the western portion. Keeping to the highlands, swamps were avoided, which meant far less corduroy; also, streams could be crossed at their headwaters, so that smaller bridges would suffice. Besides the Twenty-six-Mile camp on Lake Amherst, a major camp and supply base were located on Twenty-Mile stream in Cavendish. Here, on July 16, 1760, Goffe wrote an angry letter back to Lieutenant Parker, in command of the Wentworth Ferry Blockhouse, to get on with sending supplies up to the front. "It is strange to me that we have not the Provision that is with you," wrote Goffe.

From the head of Lake Amherst to Pittsford, the regiment improved the road hastily constructed the year before. During late July, the first contingent of troops destined for Crown Point overtook Goffe's people. Regiments from Massachusetts and Rhode Island were on their way, and soon long lines of baggage wagons and packhorses were winding their way westward with needed supplies for Amherst's forces. Goffe's regiment itself finally struggled into Crown Point July 31, 1760, now only 665 in number.

As originally completed, the Crown Point Road was about eighty-five miles long. Many parts of it are obliterated, abandoned as later roads sought the valleys, or as the homesteads on the uplands were abandoned in the nineteenth century. Many markers trace the old route, but some are in the wrong places. Sections of the old road were too steep to be navigated by Henry Ford's tin lizzie and were left to grow up to weeds, then forests, in the early years of this century.

The Crown Point Road was never too important as a military highway. In 1759, 7,782 soldiers and artisans were at work on Amherst's Crown Point fortress (a larger force, incidentally, than that employed at the IBM plant in Essex Junction in 1980!). That complement generally continued through 1761. Of the workforce, 3,640 were from Connecticut; 47 percent of the garrison. The remainder were from, in order, Massachusetts, Rhode Island, and New York. The number of troops from New Hampshire are not recorded, but Goffe's detachment means that some were there. In 1760, 1761, and 1762, a great deal of traffic flowed along the road to supply the garrison, but with the Treaty of 1763, when peace between England and France finally became a reality, the road lost its military function.

For the Crown Point Fortress itself, work ceased in 1762, before the structure was completed, but many of the large garrison remained in the area when paid off. Others went home to tell of the Champlain Valley and to swell the tide of later settlement. In 1769, New York colonial administrators took steps to establish local town government for the community about the fort. A few years later they went further and granted New York patents to Vermont lands east of Lake Champlain. Then on April 21, 1773, the fort, now decaying, suffered a major blow. On that date, a Mrs. Ross, while cooking some pork and beans, set fire to a sooty chimney; the fire soon spread throughout the barracks and eventually into the powder magazine. Crown Point as a functional fortress ceased to exist, and the dreams of Amherst literally went up in smoke. It played no role in the Revolutionary War, the British seeing no sense in rebuilding or garrisoning the structure.

Although official peace between English and French did not occur until 1763, Wentworth was busily granting land along the route of the road, beginning in 1761, the year after it was completed. A letter from Wentworth to a William Sharp records that some "provincial colonels" desired to obtain tracts of land between Number 4 and Crown Point. Many of the first settlers along the road were members of military companies that tramped its route and saw what excellent possibilities parts of the region offered. Captain Ephraim Doolittle of Shoreham, Gideon Cooley of Proctor, and John Coffeen of Cavendish were all first settlers in their respective towns who had traveled the route at one time or another. Captain Doolittle built a grist mill in Shoreham on Prickly Ash Brook in 1776, and the house he built still stands on the hillside overlooking the cellar hole of the old mill and the Military Road on which it was located.

Portions of the road were changed from time to time to suit the needs of the settlers, whose cabins were strung along its length. Centers of population sprang up at sites with water power, of which Springfield is a good example. Pittsford grew up at the point easiest to ford on Otter Creek, although a bridge had been built there in 1759. A local historian records that in 1772, of the twenty-six families in the town of Springfield, most were still located along the route of the old road.

Until the eve of the Revolution, the road was primarily a settlement route. It was the best highway in Vermont. In 1772, Ira Allen contemplated purchasing tracts of land in Hubbardton with his brother Zimri. Allen proposed to build another road from those lands to connect with the Military Road, "so that it might induce settlement in Hubbardton." With the war, Ticonderoga and Crown Point again became a center of attention and troops once more began crossing Vermont. Though it could never be construed as a busy highway, parts long in disuse and overgrown awakened to the tramp of armies. New branches were constructed as necessary in western Vermont, the most important being the Hubbardton Military Road. Early in 1777, three New Hampshire regiments, commanded by Nathan Hale, Joseph Cilley, and Alexander Scrammel, traveled the route. Following the Crown Point Road as far as Whiting, the troops then turned west to Orwell and Mt. Independence, across the lake from Ticonderoga. Other troops, rushing to repulse Burgoyne, started over the road, only to turn back when it was learned that Ticonderoga had fallen to Ethan Allen and his Green Mountain Boys. Allen's greeting at that time, "Open in the name of the Great Jehovah and the Continental Congress," has become an important part of Vermont folklore. What he really said was probably a lot more profane and colorful.

At the close of the Revolution the road was kept in improved repair and not allowed to sink into neglect as it had after 1763. It was not until 1791 that a long road was built between Bennington and

Vergennes, which could rival the old military road in quality. With minor changes, it was the route selected for the Rutland and Burlington Railroad in 1849. Taverns proliferated, as did settlement. Timothy Dwight, who did not particularly like Vermont anyway because most Vermonters did not share his political and moral views, described a local tavern scene in 1829:

> We lodged at an inn, where we found, what I never before saw in New England, a considerable number of men, assembled on a Saturday evening, for the ordinary purpose of tavern hunting. They continued their orgies until near two o'clock in the morning; scarcely permitting us to sleep at all. Early the next morning, these wretches assembled again for their Sunday morning dram. [Timothy Dwight, *Travels in New England, and New York* (New Haven, 1829), Vol. 1.]

Today roughly two-thirds of the old road lies unused, bypassed by modern highways. Much of its route is correctly marked and can be followed by a hiker armed with maps and compass. Very old bridge abutments, dating from 1760, can still be found, as well as the rotten remains of stretches of corduroy road. In the settlement of Amsden in Cavendish, the original eleven-mile marker still sits alongside a paved and still-used section of the old highway and is probably the oldest inscription on stone left by the English in Vermont. In its time, the Crown Point Road was a vital settlement route from the Connecticut Valley into the Champlain Valley. It was the only road across the mountains for many years, and though its military significance was small it still was more important than the ill-starred Bayley-Hazen Road in northern Vermont, which, though built for military purposes, never saw that use.

The Bayley-Hazen Military Road

On May 10, 1776, two months before the Declaration of Independence was signed, the U.S. Congress, meeting in Philadelphia, voted "That as the road recommended by Gen. Washington between the towns of Newbury on the Connecticut River, and the province of Canada, will facilitate the march and return of troops in that quarter, the gen'l be directed to prosecute the plan he has formed respecting such road." By June 1776, only one month after Congressional approval (and funding), Colonel Jacob Bayley of Newbury had pushed a well-built road from Wells River into the town of Cabot, using 110 road builders at $10 a month and a liberal amount of rum.

Newbury and its sister town, Haverill, New Hampshire, shared some of the widest floodplain in the upper Connecticut Valley. The remarkable stretch of fertile flatland had long been known and for many years before the white man came had served as a site for Indian encampments, where corn and other crops were tilled. Robert Rogers and his Rangers, on their return from the raid on St. Francis in 1759, were making for the Coos Intervale, and it was here that Wentworth granted the town of Newbury to Jacob Bayley and seventy-four others in 1763, although the first settlement by Samuel Sleeper had commenced a year before. Sleeper's own son, Moses, was killed and scalped by Indians at the Hazen Road blockhouse in Greensboro eighteen years later.

Bayley had considerable influence with Wentworth because the Coos Intervales were some of the best land in the New Hampshire Grants, and the town granted to Bayley was much larger than most of the Wentworth grants. When granted and settled, Newbury, along with Haverhill, was a remote outpost in the north some sixty miles from the nearest settlement at Number 4 in Charlestown. For several years the early settlers shipped their grain down the river in canoes to that place to have it ground. Colonel Bayley from Newbury, Massachusetts, was successful in persuading Wentworth to name the town for the one of same name in his home state, no mean feat when Wentworth was often more interested in bestowing names that might do him some good in London political circles.

The good Colonel, later promoted to General, foresaw Newbury prospering as it became the departure base for the north, where he had additional landholdings. A road into the wilderness would bring a flood of settlers up the Connecticut or over the Great Road in neighboring New Hampshire. He took the initiative by writing to General Washington in April 1776, urging construction of a road, and enclosing a report of a survey he had commissioned Colonel Thomas Johnson, another of the original grantees to do. Johnson, between March 26, 1776, and April 8, 1776, had marched the proposed route to St. John, Quebec, blazed a trail, and estimated the mileage. As proposed, the road would follow the subsequently constructed route through Hazen's Notch in Westfield, descend the Missisquoi to Swanton, and turn north there to St. John. At that time no settlement lay between Newbury and Swanton, although the route followed by Johnson combined several trails often followed in past years by Indian parties on their way southward.

Washington was impressed, and even before Congress acted, he wrote Bayley to go ahead and start work, promising him 250 pounds sterling as a first instalment. By the time Bayley had heard from Washington, he had already started. James Whitelaw of Ryegate surveyed the route, and Bayley followed with his road-building crew.

The original idea behind the road, or at least the idea sold by Bayley to Washington, was a military road to St. John, Quebec, to enable American forces to bypass the Champlain Valley in attacking and perhaps gaining control of that portion of Canada. The route proposed would have to be built through ninety miles of virgin forest. In 1776, Peacham was the advanced edge of settlement in northeastern Vermont, and a trackless wilderness stretched north from that outpost.

Work on the road came to a grinding halt in the middle of June 1776, after construction six miles north of Peacham (Center) in the vicinity of the place now called Cabot Plains. The cause was a letter to Bayley from Washington informing him that Benedict Arnold's planned invasion of Canada up the Champlain Valley had fizzled, and cooler heads were thinking that the road, if completed, might just be an excellent way for the British to invade northern New England through the back door.

Through 1777 and 1778, the road sat, completed as far as Cabot, awaiting further work. There is some confusion as to just where Bayley stopped work on the wagon road. A tablet at the beginning of the road in Wells River in the north part of Newbury informs anyone interested that in 1776, Jacob Bayley built the road as far as Cabot. But another monument on Hardwick Street in Greensboro, just south of Caspian Lake, indicates Bayley's work went only as far as Peacham. What probably happened, as in construction of the earlier Crown Point Road, was that a finished road was actually built as far as Elkins Tavern in Peacham (Center), and preliminary work had been done six miles farther on into Cabot.

In 1779, Burgoyne's army had been defeated at Saratoga, France was an ally of the United States, and thoughts again swung to an invasion of Canada. In April 1779, work began once more on the road; this time the militia used were under the command of Colonel

The Bayley-Hazen Military Road never had any military importance, but was an important artery for settlement in northeastern Vermont. Peacham Inn in the background.

In the early 1800s most of the trade of eastern Vermont was oriented toward southern New England, thanks in part to the first canal built in the United States. Western Vermont, on the other hand, tended to look northward to Canada for its markets because that was the direction in which Lake Champlain drained. The opening of the Champlain Canal in 1822 and 1823 linked the Champlain Valley to the Hudson River, and trade with Canada declined after that.

(later General) Moses Hazen, another man with considerable interests in the region, some not military at all. Over the years as Bayley's work was forgotten the route came to be called the Hazen Road, and some original markers along the way indicate only the latter name. Hazen did build the road another thirty-five miles to Hazen's Notch in 1779, far more than the twenty miles that Bayley had managed three years before.

As Hazen continued the road from Cabot, he erected forts and blockhouses along the way. One was just west of Caspian Lake in Greensboro, where two sentries, Constant Bliss and Moses Sleeper, were killed by Indians in 1781. The final camp was where the village of Lowell is now found, and in late fall 1779 a rough wagon road had been built as far as the ledges overlooking Hazen's Notch. That is as far as Hazen and his troops got. The British, although defeated earlier, were still strong, and pushing the road much farther north could have invited disaster. And so as the winter snows began to fall in 1779, Moses Hazen had stopped work on the road started by Jacob Bayley in 1776. As completed from Wells River to Hazen's Notch in Westfield, the total length was about fifty-four miles. Until the late 1960s there was not a straighter road in Vermont. Moses went from point A to point B by the shortest possible route. The Hazen Road is like a beeline and contained when built some of the longest stretches of Vermont roads without a curve.

Many miles of the old road were abandoned in this century, some portions marked as a "Trail," protecting the local selectmen from lawsuits. Also, early in the 1900s, many farms began to go downhill as more opportunities developed in the valleys; stretches of this and many other upland Vermont roads were abandoned as families moved off the higher land.

Today the Bayley-Hazen road is well marked with state signs and more than two-thirds of the original route is still in use. An Atlas of the old highway is available from the Northeast Vermont Development Association in Lyndonville, and, with but a couple of small errors, it accurately traces the road. The only major problem is the route through part of Craftsbury, the Atlas showing the road between Little Hosmer Pond and Great Hosmer Pond, and local tradition insisting that the road went through the Center of Craftsbury Common and East Craftsbury. Actually the road may have done both, having been relocated soon after construction.

The road's influence on early settlement was dramatic and clear. Although through most of Vermont the initial settlement followed the river valleys, here the first occupance was upland settlement along the route of the road. Even first settlement in the Passumpsic River Valley to the east took place after that in the Bayley-Hazen towns. Peacham was first in 1775; Danville, in 1784; Cabot, in 1785; and Walden and Hardwick, in 1789. The delay between completion of the road in 1779 and the first settlements some years later was caused by raiding parties from the north, which continually used the route and occasioned the need for the blockhouses. In Hardwick, the actual first settlement was in 1782 along Hardwick Street, but the land was abandoned for seven years before people again arrived. North of Hardwick, settlement of Greensboro commenced in 1789, and in Craftsbury in 1788. North of there the road was unimportant through Albany and across the Lowell Mountains. Albany saw its first settlement in 1799 and Lowell in 1806. Both of the latter towns had different names then: Albany was Lutterloh and Lowell was briefly called Kelleyville.

Turnpikes

In general, Vermont's initial settlement followed the easiest routes of access into the territory. The river valleys were first; the Bayley-Hazen Road and the Crown Point Road, as the first roads capable of handling wagons, were extremely important. As soon as the wilderness areas began to experience this settlement, an internal need was generated for communication. Early road networks were established haphazardly as one town hooked up with another town without much rhyme or reason. No state coordination, construction, or maintenance of highways took place until 1898.

Actually, most early settlers were more interested in keeping their own bodies and souls together than in broadening their horizons to the next town or the next valley. Little but primitive trails between the clearings marked the first roads. But soon, potash was being produced, more grain was being grown than could be consumed, new houses used cut lumber rather than logs, and the need for wagon roads was evident. The local Surveyor of Highways was saddled with the job of getting the populace to build these roads, which was probably the most hated job in town. Each able-bodied male (except for ministers, college students, and college professors) was expected to donate four days of free labor. Townspeople grudgingly did their work, but always sought an easier way. The toll turnpike came into existence as early as 1796, and toll roads were to provide the best long-distance roads in Vermont for almost a hundred years. People were more willing to shell out their hard-earned cash at innumerable tollgates than they were to donate labor. Although complaints about tolls were common, they were nothing compared to the yelps over forced labor for the town roads.

At least thirty-one toll roads existed at one time or another; one source lists fifty. The list here is reasonably complete:

1796–1801

Searsburg Turnpike and Windham Turnpike	Bennington to Brattleboro
Green Mountain Turnpike	Clarendon to Bellows Falls
Royalton and Woodstock Turnpike	Royalton to Woodstock
Woodstock and Windsor Turnpike	Woodstock to Windsor
White River Turnpike	White River Junction to Royalton
Center Turnpike (the two above were connected by turnpike)	Middlebury to Hancock
Elijah Paine Turnpike	Brookfield to Montpelier
Connecticut River Turnpike	Bellows Falls to Norwich

1802–1807

Weathersfield Turnpike	Cavendish to Weathersfield
Hubbardton Turnpike	Poultney to Sudbury
Fair Haven Turnpike	Fair Haven to Bridport
Rutland and Stockbridge Turnpike	Rutland to Stockbridge
Randolph Turnpike	Randolph to Royalton
Waltham Turnpike	Vergennes to Middlebury
Winooski Turnpike	Burlington to Montpelier
Passumpsic Turnpike	Wells River to St. Johnsbury
Danville Turnpike	St. Johnsbury to Danville
Williamstown Turnpike	Williamstown to Brookfield
Mt. Tabor Turnpike	Manchester to Mt. Tabor

After 1807

Stratton Turnpike	Arlington to Newfane
Peru Turnpike	Manchester to Peru
Shelburne Turnpike	Shelburne
Goshen Turnpike	Brandon to Goshen
Panton Turnpike	Lake Champlain to Vergennes
Warren Turnpike	Warren to Lincoln
Strafford Turnpike	Norwich to Chelsea

Mt. Mansfield Turnpike	Mt. Mansfield Toll Road
Lamoille County Turnpike	Waterbury Center to Hyde Park
Bristol Turnpike	Vergennes to Bristol
Glastenbury Turnpike	Woodford to Glastenbury

Geographically, most of the later toll roads were in the north, or filled in gaps in the southern road network. Wherever these were, locals continually grumbled about the high tolls and at the same time shunned local roadwork. In 1815, it cost a single passenger in a wagon drawn by two horses $2.75 to pass between Bennington and Brattleboro. Animals on the hoof were assessed proportionately. In the 1970s on the Ohio Turnpike the toll was fifty cents for the same distance for a passenger car. Rates were exorbitant, traffic was light, and the era of turnpikes rapidly came to a close after 1850. In retrospect, the expense of traveling any distance in Vermont may have contributed for many years to the Vermonter's narrow horizon—the encircling green hills. It was just too expensive to leave home. Rather than giving greater mobility to the population, Vermont turnpikes probably had just the opposite effect. It's a wonder that anyone could afford to migrate west after 1810; but then, once across the Hudson, it cost a lot less than it did to get to the Hudson.

Canals

With the difficulties of internal transportation it is hard to imagine how Vermont was able to become an exporter of raw materials. Yet as soon as the self-sufficient early settlers had enough to keep themselves in one piece, Vermont began to export foodstuffs and wood products to both the north and south. This progress was made possible by flowing water on both sides of the state.

In eastern Vermont, the Connecticut River flowed south, carrying products to New England markets. The earliest canal in the United States was completed in 1802 to bypass the falls at Bellows Falls, and other "canals" were constructed in 1810 just north and south of White River Junction, allowing boats to get as far as the Wells River. Barnet, the goal of steam navigation later in the nineteenth century, was an impossible achievement because of the shallowness of the river. Connecticut River flatboats were said to be able to float on dew, and certainly Captain Morey's first steamboat in

1791 must have done so. Navigation on the upper Connecticut was a curiosity.

The canal and flatboats of the Connecticut River tied many Vermont towns east of the Green Mountains to the growing urban centers to the south. In the same way, the geography of western Vermont was influenced by the waters of Lake Champlain as it drained northward through the Richelieu River into Canada. Notwithstanding the Jefferson Embargo of 1808 (which prohibited trade with Canada), and even the War of 1812, lumber and other products continued to go to the traditional northern markets. Smuggling flourished. Burlington became an important lumber city in this era, developing into the nation's third most important sawmilling center in the 1870s.

Canal fever swept the United States after 1800, and though the small canal at Bellows Falls was the first, it was insignificant in the scheme of things. Of much greater influence on Vermont was the construction in 1822 and 1823 of the Champlain Canal in New York, joining the southern end of Lake Champlain at Whitehall with the Hudson River, connecting two years later with the Erie Canal (1825) across New York State. Vermont not only had a low-cost water link with New York City, it also had a route to the growing West, soon to be used by Vermonters leaving their rocky hillsides.

With the completion of the Champlain Canal, the trade of western Vermont quickly oriented itself toward markets to the south, something that even the War of 1812 had not been able to do. For the first time, both sides of the state were completely integrated into a United States market, and trade with Canada declined steadily.

Water transport mattered so much in the era before good roads and, later, the railroads, that a cross-Vermont canal was even proposed and some serious surveying was done. The difficulties were enough to discourage even the most ardent canal supporter, a Mr. Araunah Waterman of Montpelier.

Mr. Waterman was, if nothing else, a Vermont visionary. On his urging, John Quincy Adams in 1824 sent into Vermont a topographical party to investigate a possible canal between the Connecticut River and Lake Champlain. Such a venture would ultimately connect Boston with the West across the "minor" obstacle of the Green Mountains, and would certainly negate the trade advantages New York City had with its own Erie Canal. At the time, the heights of the Appalachians were about to be ascended by the Allegheny Portage Railroad at Altoona, Pennsylvania, which was built to raise canal boats over the Allegheny Front. At Honesdale, Pennsylvania, a gravity railroad was being built to haul anthracite coal over the Poconos to the Delaware and Hudson Canal. This line used the first steam locomotive on American railroads.

In Vermont, survey parties worked intermittently from 1826 to 1829, each year bringing more bad news about the possibilities, in spite of the optimism embodied in the Onion River Navigation and Tow Path Company, incorporated in 1825. That company issued a circular soliciting public subscription. There is no record of how much money was subscribed, but one person (James Whitelaw, former Surveyor General of Vermont) sent three dollars, along with a note that this would probably be the biggest subscription from his town, Ryegate. But with federal funding and survey parties, the routes were surveyed, Mr. Waterman himself on occasion rescuing parties of surveyors who had either gotten lost or trapped in bogs along the height of land.

Everyone agreed that the Winooski River was the obvious route through the western section of the region. Regardless of the problems presented by the major falls at Bolton and Hubbell's Falls (Essex Junction), the question of how to get from the Winooski to the Connecticut was paramount. Five routes were proposed and surveyed. Two might use the White River tributaries, two would have used the Wells River, and a third would connect via the Waits River. The routes using the White River were long, but proponents argued that these would need fewer locks. One would use the Second Branch, north from Royalton, and ascend through Williamstown Gulf to a summit elevation of 910 feet, from there dropping via Stevens Branch into the Winooski. The survey parties rejected this route, as did Charles Paine twenty-five years later when the Vermont Central Railroad was being built. The other White River route would have utilized the Third Branch via Bethel, but locking through the flats at Roxbury at more than 1,000 feet before the quick drop of 525 feet via the Dog River to the Winooski at East Montpelier was discouraging to a canal builder. Apparently it was easier for a railroader, because the final route of the Vermont Central followed the old canal survey (see Chapter 5).

Mr. Waterman, guiding canal surveyors and rescuing parties, totaled his own expenses at $18.64 and decided that it was money down the drain. Surveys had been done, and some of the country had been mapped for the first time. The Connecticut Valley and the Champlain Valley were to be forever separated, but their waters continued to play a vital role in the historical geography of Vermont.

3

Boundary Disputes:
The Origin of Vermont

As the Green Mountain State was settled, the river valleys were vital in channeling the flow of people. The military highways greatly influenced the areas that they traversed. These were major conduits, but they were less significant in influencing *when* that settlement took place.

In a general way, Vermont was settled when it was because it was a nearby piece of frontier land at a time in American history when the West was not yet available. But it was also a battleground and no-man's-land with, first, English and French forces contesting the region, and later American and British armies, during the Revolution. Because it was a disputed political territory, probably many potential immigrants had second thoughts about locating their families in such a place. Charlotte and Hardwick are examples already mentioned of towns where settlements were abandoned during the Revolutionary War, only to be commenced again after peace was signed between Britain and the United States.

But even peace among nations did not bring peace to Vermont, because New York and New Hampshire took up where Britain and America had left off. In the following pages we look at the evolution of the state through the conflicting boundary and territorial claims advanced by those who felt they were entitled to a piece of the Green Mountains.

The Southern Border

According to the charter of the Massachusetts Bay Colony of 1629, the northern border of its territory was defined as a line three miles north of the Merrimack River, running westward to the South Seas. The South Seas at the time were an unknown body of water lying far to the west, and no one really knew much about the Merrimack River, either. Massachusetts Bay Colony was stripped of its charter in 1684, and a new charter was given in 1691. That charter also referred to "all that parte of New England in America lying and extending from the grete River commonly called Monomack, also Merrimack on the Northpart and from three miles Northward of the said River to the . . . Western Sea or Ocean . . . . "

Modern maps show the Merrimack River ending in Franklin, New Hampshire, the name changing there to Pemigewasset. At the time of the original charters, however, its source was considered to be Lake Winnepesaukee, where the present village of Weirs Beach is now located. A line drawn westward from a point in the lake three miles north of Weirs Beach would have passed through the present White River Junction and just a few miles north of Rutland. This line is shown as Number 1 in Figure 3.1. See this illustration for all references to Vermont's borders.

Seeking protection for settlements farther south in the Connecticut Valley, Massachusetts erected forts along the Connecticut River north of the present Massachusetts border. The first was Fort Dummer (1724), in the extreme southeast corner of Brattleboro Town. It became the first permanent New England settlement in land that was to become Vermont. Today the remains of Fort Dummer lie beneath the backwater from Vernon Dam, built in 1908 and 1909. Fort Sartwell and Fort Bridgeman were in existence in Vernon before 1738, and Fort Hinsdale in Hinsdale, New Hampshire, was constructed in 1743. Massachusetts also laid out the so-called Equivalent Lands in 1713, encompassing most of the present towns of Brattleboro, Dummerston, and Putney. The lands were so named because, in the confusion of deciding on the boundary between Massachusetts and Connecticut, Massachusetts might have taken more than its share. These lands then were to go to Connecticut if subsequent studies of the disputed border showed that Massachusetts had done so.

Establishing a presence north of the present boundary, Massachusetts laid out four towns without names along today's New Hampshire side of the Connecticut River in 1735 and 1736. They were numbered 1, 2, 3, and 4 from south to north. Number 4 (subsequently to be rechartered by New Hampshire as Charlestown) was

VERMONT BOUNDARY ORIGINS

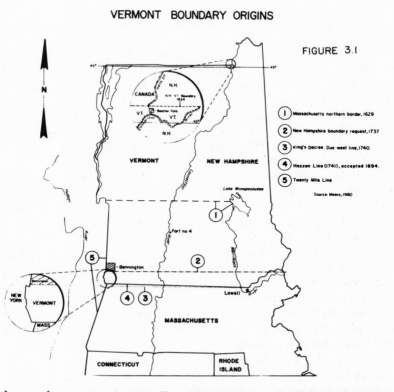

FIGURE 3.1

① Massachusetts northern border, 1629

② New Hampshire boundary request, 1737

③ King's Decree. Due west line, 1740.

④ Hazzen Line (1741), accepted 1894.

⑤ Twenty Mile Line

Source: Mees, 1980

the northernmost outpost. Fort Number 4 was built in Charlestown in 1740 and was later the terminus of the Crown Point Military Road.

During this activity, the Province of New Hampshire was becoming increasingly nervous as it appeared that Massachusetts was effectively blocking westward extension of New Hampshire. New Hampshire requested that its southern boundary be affirmed as a straight line running due west from a point at sea three miles north of the mouth of the Merrimack River (Figure 3.1). That line would have crossed through Vermont in the towns of Dummerston, Newfane, and Dover, and along the south line of Bennington. Massachusetts, of course, claimed the boundary line of the charter of 1691. They were unable to agree, and so the dispute went to a Royal Commission that met in Hampton in 1737. The Commission submitted a recommendation to George II, and in 1740 the King declared in Council that:

the northern boundary of the province of Massachusetts be a
similar curved line, pursuing the course of the Merrimack River,
at three miles distance, on the north side thereof, beginning at the
Atlantic Ocean, and ending at a point due north of Pawtucket
falls (now Lowell), and a straight line drawn from thence, due
west, till it meets with his Majesty's other Governments.

This line translates to the present north border of Massachusetts, and today's maps show the border with New Hampshire curv-
ing in a series of arcs three miles north of the Merrimack River, and
then a straight line from just north of Lowell westward. This 1740
line subsequently became Vermont's southern boundary and was
first surveyed and marked in 1741, but not without considerable
disagreement.

New Hampshire must have been pleased, and probably surprised as well, because the specified line gave it a strip of land at least
fifty miles long and of varying width in excess of that which had been
requested. It must have been very awkward for Mr. Belcher, who at
that time was governor of *both* the Provinces of New Hampshire and
Massachusetts Bay. He was asked to get the respective Assemblies
together to agree on running and marking the line of the decree. The
Assembly of Massachusetts Bay wanted no part of establishing the
line, and so New Hampshire proceeded alone. George Mitchell and
Richard Hazzen were appointed by Governor Belcher to survey the
line. It was run in 1741, with Hazzen carrying the line across the
Connecticut River all the way to the Hudson.

Subsequently, Hazzen's Line was found to run a little north of
west, and, upon calculations made in 1774, to cause New Hampshire
to actually lose 59,872 acres, or almost 94 square miles. Hazzen had
not allowed enough for the magnetic declination of the compass
needle. It is also reported, however, that Hazzen was operating under
orders of Governor Belcher, who had instructed him to run the line
west 10° north. The actual line is about west 8° north. A surveying
party struggling over uninhabited terrain in 1740 can certainly be
excused for a small (94-square-mile) error. New Hampshire did not
think it amusing at all, and Benning Wentworth, who became governor of the province in 1741, refused to accept the Hazzen Line
because of the loss of territory it implied. There was no agreement
on the line for eighty-five years after it was run. Massachusetts,
which stood to gain, apparently was in favor of the Hazzen survey,
but New Hampshire wanted nothing to do with it. The vagueness of

the line, however, did not prevent Governor Wentworth from granting the string of towns across the southern border of Vermont. But he was careful to place their southern borders on the Hazzen Line, and not on the "due-west" line that had originally been claimed farther south. The Hazzen Line became generally accepted through common use, but in 1825, commissioners from the states of Massachusetts and New Hampshire were unable to agree on the line, and so in 1827 the Massachusetts legislature went ahead alone and had the Hazzen Line officially marked.

This resolution, of course, was unacceptable to New Hampshire, and the whole matter dragged along until 1894, when a joint commission of Massachusetts, New Hampshire, and Vermont finally agreed to maintaining the Hazzen Line as the official boundary. The line was retraced and remarked and small granite monuments were set between 1894 and 1898, although some were added later. The initial point of the survey was the southeast corner of Vermont. A witness marker, however, is inaccurate, in that it refers to the corner of Vermont as the west bank of the Connecticut River; a U.S. Supreme Court decision in 1933 moved the official spot to the mean low-water mark on the Vermont side of the river.

The Western Border

Governor Wentworth had been upset at losing 94 square miles but was nonetheless pleased with the decree of 1740, which he interpreted as giving him all the land westward to a line some twenty miles east of the Hudson River, or a northward continuation of the western boundaries of Massachusetts and Connecticut. This assumption led to many years of bitter wrangling between New Hampshire and New York over what was to become Vermont.

Historians have debated whether Wentworth honestly thought that New Hampshire extended as far west as he claimed, or that in fact that he knew he was acting illegally in granting the territory in land that was to become Vermont. These are the circumstances:

The Province of New York, under charters of 1664 and 1674, claimed title to all lands lying west of the Connecticut River. That description originally included all the lands west of that river in both Connecticut and Massachusetts. The earliest dispute over this title arose in Connecticut, and commissions met in 1665, 1683, and 1725

Small granite markers like this one were placed along the Vermont–Massachusetts boundary in 1895 and 1896 after final agreement to accept the old Hazzen Line. A few have been added since.

George Pratt of Pownal helped guide me to the remote Three Corner Marker where Vermont, New York, and Massachusetts converge. This granite block is three fourths of a mile and 1,000 feet lower than the Southwest Corner Marker.

and finally agreed on the western boundary of Connecticut as it now stands: a line approximately twenty miles east of the Hudson River. By 1725, the question of the border had been reasonably well settled, although some minor changes occurred during the nineteenth century.

In Massachusetts the same question arose. After many attempts, the present western boundary of that state was established in 1773, as a line twenty miles east of the Hudson River. With the Revolutionary War in progress, the line was not surveyed or marked until 1787. Subsequently, Vermont's western boundary was to become a northern extension of this twenty-mile line, but not without a lot of debate and litigation.

It seems odd that, after 1740, Benning Wentworth claimed to within twenty miles of the Hudson River, when at the same time Massachusetts and New York were debating the Connecticut River as the western border of Massachusetts. The Twenty-Mile Line was not accepted between those two states until thirty-three years later, and long after Wentworth had granted many illegal towns in land that was to become Vermont. Wentworth in 1749 even wrote to the governor of New York, stating his legal claim to the area west of the Connecticut River and citing the King's 1740 decision. At the same time (1749), Wentworth made his first grant in the Vermont territory: the Town of Bennington, with its western border carefully placed twenty-four miles from the Hudson River, or at least Wentworth so thought. Actually the line is between nineteen and nineteen and a half miles from the Hudson.

In Figure 3.1, an enlargement shows the irregularity of the state line in Pownal, the town immediately south of Bennington. The boundary line skirts older Dutch patents, some possibly dating back as far as 1728. This section of the boundary was disputed for some time, and even the original 1760 charter map of Pownal refers to the "supposed" New York line and the "supposed" southwest angle of the Province of New Hampshire. There are reports of friction with Dutch settlers in the area when the line was first surveyed and marked in 1812. This and the whole western boundary, was for a time a no-man's-land. In 1781, the Vermont Legislature even passed an act to incorporate into Vermont all the New York towns lying on the east side of the Hudson River.

Later, on June 22, 1781, the Vermont Legislature appointed three delegates to go to Philadelphia to arrange for admission of

Vermont into the Union. The admission was delayed, but Congress resolved, as one of the preliminaries to admission, that Vermont should accept the following western boundary:

> Beginning at the northwest corner of the State of Massachusetts, thence running twenty miles east of the Hudson's river, so far as the said river runs northeasterly in its general course; then by the west bounds of the townships granted by the late government of New Hampshire, to the river running from South Bay to Lake Champlain, thence along the said river to Lake Champlain, thence along the waters of Lake Champlain to the latitude of 45 degrees north, excepting a neck of land between Missiskoy Bay and the waters of Lake Champlain.

In the final settlement in 1789, the boundary was made final generally as stated above. The only change was that the Alburg Peninsula (the neck of land) was incorporated into Vermont and the line specified as following the "deepest channel" of Lake Champlain. In 1876 Vermont ceded a small patch of land to New York in the town of Fair Haven when the Poultney River changed its course.

After New York recognized Vermont in 1790, things were quieter and the boundary was rather generally defined in official acts, but there were still questions. On June 8, 1812, the New York Legislature agreed to survey the disputed line, and Vermont followed on November 6. At that time, the entire border was marked only by thirty-three permanent markers, and both states felt it appropriate to resurvey and remark the line. The survey, carried out in 1814, accurately defined the boundary, but placement of permanent granite markers waited until the 1890s, when the present granite shafts were emplaced. In checking the accuracy of the 1814 survey, one change involved moving the southwest corner fifty-eight feet west. In 1903, the boundary line was again checked, and some monuments were replaced or anchored in concrete.

The starting point for the survey and final demarcation of the New York–Vermont line was the northwest corner of Massachusetts, where the Tri-State Monument today is deeply buried in the forest. It is a granite post eight feet tall and fourteen inches square, set five feet deep in the ground, with the faces toward the respective states labeled, "N.Y., 1898; Mass., 1896; and Vermont, 1896." The flat top is also grooved appropriately. A copper bolt once set there has long since disappeared and a hole remains. The marker is also well cov-

The pocket knife lies along the Vermont boundary on top of the Tri-State Monument. The hole once possessed a copper bolt. Massachusetts is the angle in the background.

Along the New York–Quebec boundary the original cast-iron monuments were replaced by granite ones in 1902 and 1903. These markers are identical to those along the New York–Vermont border.

A simple wooden post marks the boundary between the uninhabited Township of Lewis and the Town of Brighton in Essex County. Most of the land is owned by large lumber corporations.

ered with graffiti, frustrating when you consider the remote location. According to the agreement reached in 1789, the line was run from this point in 1814, first almost due west 3,300 feet (50 chains) to the New York–Vermont corner (the southwest corner of Pownal). From here the line runs north along the western border of the Vermont towns to the Poultney River.

The New York–Vermont corner sits at an elevation of more than 2,000 feet along the spine of the Taconics and is accessible by a trail northward from Petersburg Pass two miles south. The marker here is similar to all those along the entire line, a granite post, pointed at the top, extending about five feet above ground level. Some are placed in concrete with appropriate notations in the concrete base, others simply rise from the earth. They are the same as those which mark the New York–Quebec boundary. In the forest, both the Massachusetts–Vermont line and the New York–Vermont line are well marked with yellow paint blazes. Fish and Game department signs are placed appropriately, but many are defaced or weathered.

Wentworth Grants

While New York and Vermont were having a problem (which would last into the twentieth century) about placing boundary monuments, Benning Wentworth was having his own problems in the 1760s, but those were not keeping him from granting land to applicants, between the Connecticut River and the Twenty-Mile Line. After Bennington was granted by Wentworth in 1749, he issued 134 more grants of land between January 1749 and October 1764, covering about three million acres or roughly half the present state of Vermont (Figure 3.2). One hundred and twenty-nine of the grants were for towns, most of which exist today with but minor changes. There was an attempt to make each town about thirty-six square miles (six miles on a side), but survey techniques in the wilderness left much to be desired and only a few Vermont towns are a reasonably exact thirty-six square miles. Most were laid out in blocks from the Connecticut River, Lake Champlain, or the Twenty-Mile Line, their north and south boundary lines at right angles to the particular reference point. As the shoreline of Lake Champlain and the course of the Connecticut change direction, however, towns from those reference points rarely have due east–west north–south boundaries. The most regular

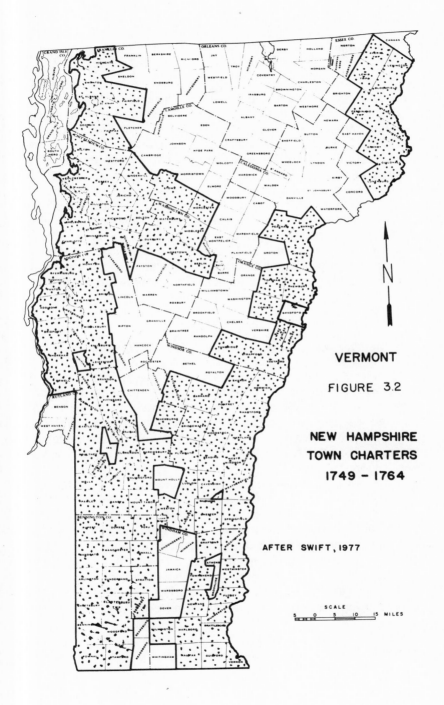

VERMONT

FIGURE 3.2

NEW HAMPSHIRE
TOWN CHARTERS
1749 - 1764

AFTER SWIFT, 1977

SCALE

5   0   5   10   15 MILES

Vermont towns are those in the southwest, where the straight north-south Twenty-Mile Line was used as the principal meridian.

Wentworth's grants all followed the same format, the only differences being the names of the grantees, the area of the town, and the description of its boundaries. The charters provided for town meetings, fairs, markets, lots for the Society for the Propagation of the Gospel in Foreign Parts (an influential group in London), one parcel for the Church of England, and one for the first settled minister. After 1760, the charters reserved a lot for a school as well. All the charters provided a five-hundred-acre lot in each town for Wentworth himself, and in many towns that lot was in a good corner. By claiming a lot in the northeast corner of one town, the southeast corner of another, the southwest corner of a third town, and the northwest corner of a fourth, a plot of land 2,000 acres in extent could be fashioned. This procedure was commonly done, and is shown in Figure 3.3 for the Town of Lemington. (See the illustration in Chapter 1.)

Vermont Gores, Grants, and Townships

Many of the grantees were friends or relatives of Wentworth, or people whose support he wished. Few ever settled on the lands granted; rather, they sold or assigned their grants to young settlers or even land speculators. Sometimes the entire town was granted to one person, as with Lemington (1762) in Essex County, where the recipient was one Samuel Avery, whose name still appears on the map in Avery's Gore.*

Avery was a wheeler-dealer. He was born in Groton, Connecticut in 1731, and was educated as a lawyer. Sometime before 1780, he had purchased large tracts of New York-patented land, mainly in western Vermont, land formerly part of the John Henry Lydius Mohawk Tract. The total ownership was something more than 52,000 acres of probably rather poor farmland, although one writer mentions Avery's ownership of "some of the most fertile portions of the Otter Creek Valley in the Middlebury area." A 1779 New York map shows that land as owned by a McLure and Company.

---

*"Gores" were pieces of land left over when imprecise town boundaries were surveyed. "Patents" were New York grants to groups and individuals, commonly military veterans.

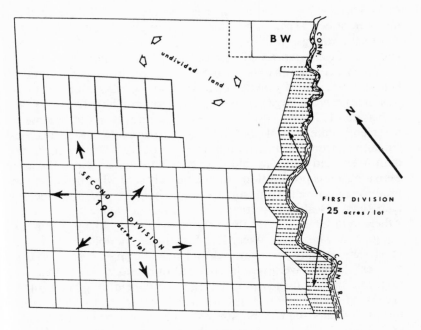

FIGURE 3.3

LAND ALLOCATIONS
LEMINGTON VERMONT
1786-87

In any event, by 1782, Samuel Avery was a well-respected citizen of Vermont and was deputy sheriff and keeper of the jail in Westminister. When Vermont became a Republic (1777), one of the first acts of the young country was to declare all previous land claims null and void. Avery petitioned against this decision, and as a respected man in his community the Legislature sought to restore to him the land that he rightfully owned through legal purchase. But the trouble was that no more large chunks of land were available for Avery, and so between 1791 and 1796 the state Legislature (Vermont became the fourteenth state in 1791) gave him eight separate parcels of unallocated land as reimbursement, totaling about 62,000 acres, or more land than Avery had under his old New York patents. To Avery, the lands were a business proposition, and he quickly sold what he could, and tried to collect rents from squatters on what he could not. The only land that was already settled and was not completely wild was in Athens and Grafton, and there the settlers refused to pay him anything. Where he could, Avery sold his lands for a dollar an acre, and most were quickly incorporated into neighboring towns. The eight "Gores" of Mr. Avery were reduced to only two by 1948, and since then one has been incorporated into Bakersfield and Montgomery (1963); the other remains in Essex County, capped by Gore Mountain. Originally there were Avery's Gores in Granville and Lincoln (8,744 acres), which was divided between those towns in 1833 and 1847 respectively, and Troy (more than 11,000 acres), which, along with another grant to John Kelley, became the town of that name in 1803. In 1794, another Avery grant became part of the towns of Huntington and Hinesburg in Chittenden County.

The only other gore on a modern Vermont map is Buel's Gore at the southern tip of Huntington. Major Elias Buel (or Buell) was a land speculator and Connecticut resident. In 1780, so the story goes, he settled in the Gore to establish his own town of Montzoar. He bought up all the land titles in the 2,240-acre parcel, but apparently did not bother to have his titles recorded. Neither did he pay his taxes. The parcel of land is said to have been sold for $11.02 to satisfy the tax assessment. Buel's Gore still exists, with a population of five people, and someone should find out the exact sequence of events that produced this narrow finger of land pointing south from the town of Huntington—clear on all Vermont maps.

Besides the various gores of Avery and Buel, several other miscellaneous pieces of uncharted Vermont land remain. In Essex

County, in Vermont's northeastern corner, are Ferdinand, Lewis, and Averill Townships, as well as Warren's Gore and Warners Grant. They usually show up on modern Vermont maps as blank spaces, or with N.D. (no data) over them.

Averill was granted by New Hampshire in 1762 to Samuel Averill of Connecticut. Previously Averill and his associates had been granted the towns of Brunswick, Ferdinand, Wenlock (later divided between Brighton and Ferdinand), Maidstone, Bloomfield (originally Minehead), Lemington, and Lewis. Averill was another land speculator, and probably never set foot on any of the enormous Vermont parcels that he was granted. Perhaps he knew better than many, because the maximum population of the town of Averill was reached in 1880, when forty-eight residents were enumerated by the U.S. Census Bureau. Ferdinand attracted even fewer settlers than Averill, the only count of people being made when lumber mills were in existence for a short time after 1881, and again from 1918 to 1923. Today the traveler on logging roads through the area will see yellow log posts signifying the town lines, but there is no permanent population, most of the land being owned by lumber companies. Lewis, as far as is known, never attracted even one permanent settler.

Warren's Gore is one of the three remaining gores in Vermont. It was chartered by Vermont in 1789, ostensibly to make up for the small amount of territory in the town of Warren in Washington County that had been granted by Vermont in 1780. Because the residents of Warren were never able to settle or use the land in the Gore, and because probably no one from that town ever set foot on the place, it is no surprise that the isolated piece of land had no permanent residents until 1970, when the U.S. Census Bureau recorded one person, possibly a fugitive from Earth's Peoples Park in Norton, a few miles to the north.

Warners Grant was a piece of land given to the widow of Seth Warner by the grateful Vermont Legislature for his heroic deeds at the Battle of Bennington. Mrs. Warner was never able to interest anyone in the property, and she probably had no idea where it was. Destitute Hester Warner saw no profit from the land, and it remains an area without roads, virtually untouched, in the northern wilderness of Essex County.

Down in southern Vermont are two unorganized towns, Glastenbury and Somerset. Both once had small populations. Glastenbury finally was incorporated in 1834, and its fifty people sent a representative to the Vermont Legislature. After the Civil War the demand for charcoal was great, and a railroad, the Bennington and Glastenbury, was built to the kilns. In 1873 the town had a postoffice, but it was closed in 1877, and by 1889 the boom, if there ever was one, was over. By 1930, a member of the sole surviving family was filling every town office, even to representing the town in Montpelier. In 1937, the town was disenfranchised and its current residents are several vacation homeowners.

About the same thing happened to Somerset across the line in Windham County, although in 1850 the town had three hundred widely scattered people. A post office was opened in 1870 and closed in 1916, when the last residents seem to have disappeared. As with Glastenbury, the 1937 Vermont Legislature disenfranchised Somerset. Today the only population of the town, most of which is Green Mountain National Forest, is the family of the New England Power Company employee who lives by the dam at the south end of the reservoir, and who dutifully records the National Weather Service readings for Vermont's highest official station.

Residents and landowners of Vermont's sparsely inhabited gores, grants, and townships are overseen by State Supervisors, whose duties are to inspect the properties, make sure the roads are taken care of, and, of course, collect the necessary taxes, which are then distributed to neighboring towns; these then assume the burden of road repair, education, and provision of other services.

The Connecticut River Border: Independent Vermont

Retracing our steps again, we left Benning Wentworth writing to Governor Clinton of New York and, at the same time, granting Bennington land as far west as he thought he could legally go. Clinton replied that Wentworth was obviously wrong and that the eastern boundary of New York was along the Connecticut River. He also demanded that Wentworth surrender the charter of Bennington, and suggested that they jointly submit the problem to the King for a decision. Wentworth ignored Clinton and relentlessly continued to grant charters. Had not hostilities with the French intervened in 1754, Wentworth would probably have granted most of Vermont.

No charters were granted between 1754 and 1760, but in 1761 alone, after the French and Indian Wars and Lord Jeffrey Amherst

Part of downtown Bellows Falls lies below the top of the west bank of the Connecticut River, and as such was taxed by New Hampshire before the matter was settled by the U.S. Supreme Court in 1934. Now the boundary between the two states is officially the low-water mark on the Vermont side. The hydropower plant is the brick building in the background.

had secured the Champlain Valley, Wentworth issued sixty grants, which were readily snapped up. The hostilities did much to make the area better known, for most military personnel were from southern New England. The lands in the fertile Champlain Valley were nearly all granted in 1761, including the towns of Addison, Bridport, Brandon, Cornwall, Leicester, Middlebury, New Haven, Panton, Pittsford, Rutland, Salisbury, and Shoreham. The towns along the Crown Point Military Road (see Chapter 2) were also granted in that year: Springfield, Cavendish, Reading, Ludlow, Shrewsbury, and Clarendon. Mt. Holly was left out, probably because its location across the heights at 1,300 feet was not too tempting. That town was subsequently granted by Vermont in 1792. In 1760, Wentworth granted only one charter, to Pownal, probably to protect his southwest flank.

While all this activity was going on, New York was firing off protests to both New Hampshire and London. Wentworth's reputation was no longer of the best, notwithstanding his naming of some towns for influential people, possibly including the King himself (St. George, 1763). That St. George was probably the smallest town

Wentworth chartered may have been more insulting than beneficial, as George III saw it. The blow fell at the Court of St. James's on July 20, 1764:

> Whereas there was, this day read at the board, a report made by the Right Honorable the Lords of the Committee of council for plantation affairs, dated the 17th . . . relative to the disputes that have some years subsisted between the provinces of New Hampshire and New York, concerning the boundary line between those two provinces—His Majesty, taking the same into consideration, was pleased . . . to approve of what is therein proposed, and doth accordingly, hereby order and declare the western banks of the river Connecticut, from where it enters the province of Massachusetts Bay as far north as the forty fifth degree of northern latitude, to be the boundary between the two provinces. . . .

Wentworth can perhaps be excused for issuing a military grant to Andrew Phillips for a part of Readsboro on August 11, more than three weeks after the King's decision, but communications must have been unusually slow to justify another military grant to John Walker, in Wardsboro on October 17, 1764, three months after the royal decree. Wardsboro was chartered later by Vermont, and so apparently John Walker, if he knew of the illegal grant, never pressed for it. It was the last piece of paper that Wentworth signed relating to Vermont lands.

But by no means was the granting of land in Vermont over. New York began where New Hampshire left off, regranting most of the New Hampshire towns and in addition issuing patents and town charters to lands that had escaped Wentworth. Three New York counties, Albany, Gloucester, and Cumberland, were established. New York eventually issued 107 patents for tracts of land that could be considered town-sized parcels. Many smaller tracts went to retired military men. Esther Swift reports that twenty-four of the larger New York grants went to individuals or families and were not given town names. Another twenty apparently duplicated New Hampshire grants. Fifty-eight large patents were for unsettled lands, and little if any settlement ever commenced on those lands under New York. Only five Vermont towns (Londonderry, Bradford, Readsboro, Royalton, and Whitingham) owe their identity solely to New York grants. Royalton's New York patent (1769) says:

. . . among other things, that there was a certain tract of land situate on the west side of the Connecticut River within our said Province, which the Petitioners had discovered to be vacant and unpatented. . . . And therefore the Petitioners for themselves and their associates humbly prayed that as the aforesaid Lands never were granted under our Province of New Hampshire . . . would be . . . pleased . . . to grant unto them and their associates . . . the aforesaid tract of land containing thirty thousand acres; And that the same might be formed into a Township by the Name of Royalton. . . .

Figure 3.4 shows the approximate coverage of New York grants on a modern map of Vermont.

Curiously, the King's decree of 1764 specified only that the boundary was *to be* the Connecticut River. It did not specify that it *had been*. This point is important, because it meant that the New Hampshire grants were legal after all. Those in Vermont who owned land under the Wentworth grants were quick to point this reading out; the only difference was that political control had shifted from the Province of New Hampshire to the Province of New York. The settlers took their case to court in New York, and that province acknowledged that it would confirm the title to any land settled and worked under a New Hampshire grant, but would not recognize the claims of those who had never set foot on the disputed land. New York had its own anxious speculators just as had New Hampshire. New York also set a small fee for recognizing New Hampshire titles, a source of irritation to many larger landowners in the New Hampshire Grants, as Vermont was then being called. In general, the small settler with his family was satisfied. The fee was small, his land was legally his, and he cared little who the great power might be.

Land hunger probably would have been quieted and Vermont a perpetual part of New York had it not been for New Hampshire land speculators, large landowners, and vocal individuals like Ethan Allen, Seth Warner, Remember Baker, and others who became leaders of the Green Mountain Boys. In retrospect, Vermont would not have had its colorful history, its period as an independent republic, and its folk heroes had communication been better and had not certain individuals with a gift of oratory been able to persuade the multitudes to a Cause. The story of Vermont's development first as a republic, and then as the fourteenth state in 1791, in time for an inaccurate U.S. Census, has been repeatedly told.

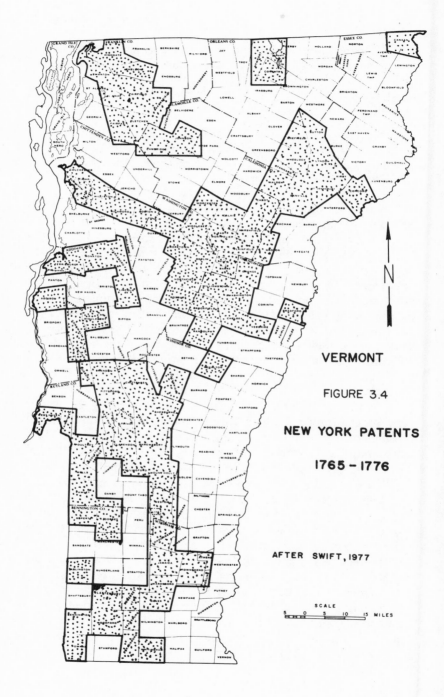

VERMONT

FIGURE 3.4

NEW YORK PATENTS

1765 – 1776

AFTER SWIFT, 1977

N

Those who opposed New York control, probably in the minority, held protest meetings at several places in southwest Vermont, that place closest to New York. The Allen family, especially Ira and Ethan with large landholdings, were rabidly against New York. Specific incidents of New York surveyors' appearing to mark off generally unworked Vermont lands sparked additional resentment. Edmund Fuller, in *Vermont; A History of the Green Mountain State*, emphasizes that most of the settlers in the New Hampshire Grants were unwilling to be under New York authority. That interpretation may or may not be accurate. In any event, those in direct opposition to New York were certainly a minority of the population, but repeatedly history has shown that a vocal and active minority can determine the course of a quiet and passive majority.

Active Vermonters had their say, first at Westminster on January 17, 1777 (at a time of year when travel was most difficult), where a declaration of independence was ratified by only sixteen towns, ten of which were on the New York side of the Green Mountains. The declaration specified that the new republic was to be bounded "South on the north line of Massachusetts Bay, East on Connecticut River, North on Canada line; West as far as the New Hampshire Grants extend." There was still some confusion about Vermont's western boundary.

The declaration further specified that the "State hereafter be called by the name of New Connecticut, alias Vermont." The delegates then adjourned until the following June, when another meeting was held, this time in Windsor, with a much better representation of towns. There, seventy-two delegates representing forty-eight towns reaffirmed the action taken in the previous January and officially adopted "Vermont" as the name.

Another meeting followed on July 2, 1777, also in Windsor, at which time a constitution was adopted, essentially the same as that of the State of Pennsylvania. Vermont expected immediately to become a state, and in fact, in the declaration of independence adopted in Westminster, the words "soverign state" are used. But such was not to be. New Hampshire and New York were both unwilling to accept Vermont as a state. Massachusetts acknowledged the existence of Vermont in 1781, New Hampshire in 1782, but New York prevented the young republic from becoming the fourteenth state until 1791. During the Revolutionary War, Vermont fought along with the American colonies, but as an independent country, a situation lasting fourteen years.

The reason for Vermont's delay in being accepted as the fourteenth state was partially a result of the intervening war, which prevented Congress from taking up the problem, but it was also the result of continued friction among Vermont, New Hampshire, and New York. This contention was sparked by the request on the part of a few New Hampshire towns on the *east* side of the Connecticut River, which asked for inclusion in the new republic in 1778. This request came at a time when, of all things, New Hampshire was willing to recognize Vermont's existence, which New York continually opposed. To accept the towns on the east side of the Connecticut into Vermont would have alienated New Hampshire; wisely, in 1779, the proposed union was dissolved.

To further strengthen its cause for admission to statehood, the small republic did two things. Vermont began to grant land not previously granted by New Hampshire, as well as granting all the land at one time covered by New York patents, except for the five legally chartered towns of Royalton, Bradford, Londonderry, Readsboro, and Whitingham. In all, Vermont issued 128 original charters for parcels of land not previously legally chartered or owned. The original Vermont towns, grants, and gores are shown in Figure 3.5. Nearly all were granted, often to influential people, before admittance to the Union in 1791. Only Goshen (1792), Jay (1792), Johnson (1792), and Sheffield (1793) were towns chartered after Vermont became a state. With the exception of a few gores and grants, the remainder of Vermont-granted towns date from the brief period of independence between 1777 and 1791.

Second, a few influential Vermonters participated in the Haldimand Negotiations, referring to Swiss-born Sir Frederick Haldimand, who was a British general and colonial governor of Quebec. These secret exchanges of correspondence, mainly involving Ira Allen, explored a possible alliance with and political incorporation of Vermont into Canada. Vermont's show of independence in granting land, plus the threat of the Canadian negotiations, was enough to produce some uneasiness in Congress, and these events probably hastened Vermont's becoming the fourteenth state.

Out of a bewildering array of claims and counterclaims, Vermont emerged as a hodgepodge of political units. Many towns changed their names over the years, others split off or annexed portions of neighboring towns. The gores disappeared as they were incorporated into adjoining towns. For almost two hundred years,

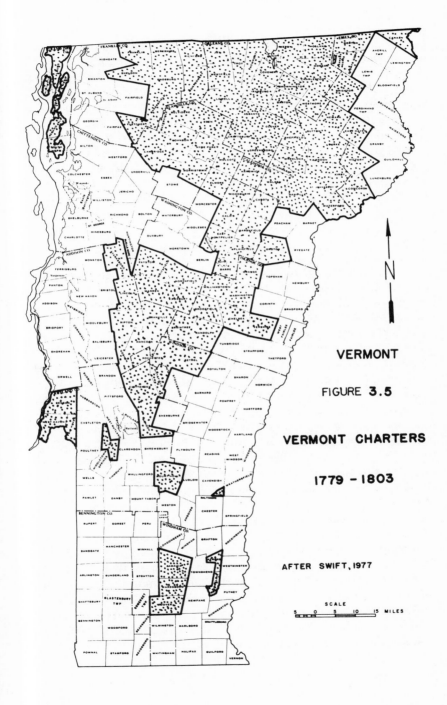

VERMONT

FIGURE 3.5

VERMONT CHARTERS

1779 - 1803

AFTER SWIFT, 1977

SCALE
5 0 5 10 15 MILES

the political units in the state have been evolving into the present map of Vermont. Vermont now has 237 towns. To this number, we add three townships (Averill, Lewis, and Ferdinand), two unorganized towns (Glastenbury and Somerset), three gores (Avery, Warren, and Buel), one grant (Warners), and nine legally incorporated cities (St. Albans, Burlington, Winooski, South Burlington, Barre, Montpelier, Vergennes, Rutland, and Newport). This list comprises 255 towns, grants, gores, and cities. Add in forty-nine incorporated villages (1980), such as Essex Junction, Swanton, Enosburg Falls, Proctorsville, North Troy, Perkinsville, and Morrisville, and the totals become much greater.

The Connecticut River Boundary

While all this organizing was going on, the Connecticut River became well established as the border between Vermont and New Hampshire—but where? The west bank? The center of the river? In the early days it didn't make much difference, but as towns began to grow and bridges were thrown across, and as canals and power dams were built, the question began to assume importance. The whole question was not resolved until 1933, what the U.S. Supreme Court ruled on a suit brought by Vermont against New Hampshire in 1915. Vermont claimed "the thread of the channel" of the Connecticut River for its entire course, except in the town of Vernon, where it "is the west bank of the Connecticut River at low water mark." All quotations are taken directly from the 1933 decision.

New Hampshire replied with the assertion that the boundary was "at the top or westerly margin of the westerly bank of the Connecticut River and the east branch thereof." The east branch referred to is Halls Stream in the town of Canaan (see Figure 3.1).

Vermont based its arguments on the fact that Wentworth, in granting the towns along the river, had followed the English practice in using the centerline of the watercourse as the normal boundary, but unfortunately, papers were discovered showing that in 1782 the Vermont Legislature had "relinquished any claim to jurisdiction east of the west side of the river, at low water mark." The 1782 action had followed a congressional resolution of 1781 that prescribed terms under which Vermont would be admitted to statehood. Thus the question really boiled down to whether the line was the low-water mark on the Vermont side, or the top of the bank, as claimed by New Hampshire. "In other words, whether New Hampshire acquired and retained jurisdiction of a narrow ribbon of land of varying width on the west side of the Connecticut River, extending along the entire eastern boundary of Vermont, which at some stages of the river is submerged and at other left uncovered by the water."

To support its claim, New Hampshire went back to the 1764 decision, in which "western bank" was mentioned. But without further clarification than that, the case appeared to be pretty weak for claiming the top of the west bank. The court decision went on for some ten pages, examining every aspect of Vermont and New Hampshire relations that had a bearing on the case. New Hampshire taxation of Vermont property was an issue, for it was not until 1909 that New Hampshire began to do apply this tax. From 1909 to 1927, New Hampshire taxed the Vernon Dam power structure on the west side of the river. From 1916 to 1927, Vermont was taxing the same thing. Long usage, however, indicated general acceptance of the low-water mark on the Vermont side by the towns and people up and down the river, and the actions of New Hampshire in taxing properties on the west side did not particularly impress the Supreme Court. The best example came in 1912, when New Hampshire "taxing authorities taxed seven corporations, three partnerships, and persons unknown having structures located on the Vermont bank of the river near Bellows Falls at a valuation in excess of $1,000,000. The same property appears to have been taxed by Vermont, the record of taxation of some of it belonging to the Bellows Falls Canal Company, going back to 1820." It was this action that precipitated Vermont's suit to get the boundary settled once and for all. "The fact that in the period of over a century following Vermont's admission to statehood this is the first well authenticated instance of an effort on the part of New Hampshire authorities to tax property located on the west bank of the river is of substantial weight in indicating the acquiescence of New Hampshire in the boundary line restricting her jurisdiction to the river at the low water mark."

Adding weight to the low-water-mark boundary were the circumstances surrounding the placing in 1897 of the Witness Marker and Corner Boundary Marker in Vernon. The Witness Marker states only that "The southwest corner of the State of New Hampshire and the southeast corner of the State of Vermont . . . is at a point on the west bank of the Connecticut River."

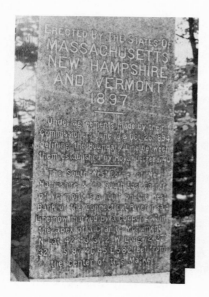

The "Witness Marker" for Vermont's southeast corner. Placed here in 1897, before the 1933 Supreme Court decision relating to the Vermont–New Hampshire boundary, the information is not correct. In part, the description states: "The South West Corner of New Hampshire & the South East Corner of Vermont is a point on the West Bank of the Connecticut River . . . now marked by a copper bolt in the apex of a Granite Monument . . . 582 feet from the center of this Marker." Notice that the description refers only to the west bank, not to the top or the bottom of it.

This small painted concrete monument was once claimed by New Hampshire as marking Vermont's southeast corner. It sits on top of the bank of the Connecticut River. In reality it is only a reference marker referred to as "Belden" in the 1934 Supreme Court decision. The actual marker is some fifteen feet lower and covered by the muddy waters of the river.

The written agreement provides further information, and the facts were supported by the testimony of many witnesses. A small granite monument was placed on top of the west bank as a reference point (called "Belding"), and the actual corner monument, "marked by a copper bolt in the apex of a granite block set upon a stone pier and sunk in the shore of the western bank of the Connecticut River," was actually placed seventeen feet below and 36.5 feet east of the Belding marker. And so the actual corner marker is buried beneath the silts and sands and water of the Connecticut River for most of the year.

During the hearings, many witnesses were called to corroborate the placing of this monument "at low water," set at an "opportune time" when the river was "very low." The monument was buried eight feet deep, with the apex level with the surface of the sand so as to avoid ice and other things "running down the river." New Hampshire claimed that the Belding monument was the true corner, but expert testimony and written evidence all pointed to the existence of the other marker, then submerged.

This is the famous Mud Turtle monument that was finally unearthed at precisely 11:00 A.M. on October 26, 1969, by the volunteer digging of Mr. Ernest Murray, the landowner, his son, and a Mr. Willis Parker of Northfield, Massachusetts. At the time it created quite a local stir of interest, and today, Vermonters and others can rest well, knowing that the corner monument is still there and still serving its function.

Vermont, when it brought suit, was primarily irritated by recent New Hampshire taxation on the western side of the river. It claimed the center line for the sake of argument, but that was quickly thrown out. The decision as rendered substantiated the long usage of the low-water mark on the western side of the Connecticut River as the boundary between the two states. New Hampshire's defense was weak, and the claim of using Halls Stream rather than the Connecticut River in the Town of Canaan was not even mentioned in the Court's decision. There a few square miles of Vermont lying between Halls Stream and the Connecticut River would have been lopped off had the Supreme Court accepted the arguments. Up in northeastern Vermont the boundary stayed where it always had been, along the low-water mark on the west bank of the Connecticut. Here, in "The Gore" one can drive north into New Hampshire rather than into Canada (Figure 3.1). It was only between 1915 and 1933 that Vermonters living east of Beechers Falls were not too sure whom they belonged to, but, as in the past, this little portion of Vermont still exists. Another granite witness marker on the Vermont side of the river marks the boundary between Vermont and New Hampshire, calling attention to the low-water mark on the west side of the Connecticut River.

How Vermont's southern, western, and eastern borders were established is a history of the evolution of the state itself. Yet those lines on the modern map separate Vermont only from other states; the line to the north is an international boundary, and although its evolution played no part in the beginnings of Vermont, negotiations over that thin line involved not only Vermont, but also Britain and the United States. As could be expected, the determination of the border was more complex and lasted many more years than the rest of the lines encircling the Green Mountain State.

The Northern Boundary

A close look at most maps shows that the boundary between Vermont and Quebec is anything but a straight line. Rather, it goes in a series of straight-line tangents, deviating a good bit from a true east–west direction. Although much may be imagined from the original bill submitted by the surveyors, which included 20 percent of the "sundries" for rum, brandy, and wine, the real reasons are equally fascinating.

Official descriptions of Vermont's eastern and western boundaries specified that the borders extend north to the forty-fifth parallel, or forty-five degrees north latitude. Furthermore, in 1763 a Royal Proclamation partially defined the southern border of the newly formed province of Quebec as: "from whence the said line crossing the River St. Lawrence and the Lake Champlain in 45th degrees of North Latitude. . . . " For once there was no disagreement. All parties involved agreed on something, a rarity in the conflicting boundary claims of the eighteenth and nineteenth centuries.

Yet the observant traveler today on Interstate 89 in the town of Highgate will pass a sign indicating 45° N, "halfway between the equator and the north pole." The traveler will then continue northward about a half mile before the international boundary is reached, with its attendant customs formalities. Something is obviously

Fort Montgomery ("Fort Blunder") as seen from the causeway linking Alburg and Rouses Point, New York. This southern exposure of the fortress is in good shape, but the rest of the structure is sadly neglected.

The North East Corner Witness Marker, which also marks the town line of Canaan, Vermont, and Pittsburg, New Hampshire.

An original cast-iron monument on the Vermont–Quebec border before repair in 1906. Now embedded in concrete, the markers are also covered with aluminum paint. U.S. Government photograph.

wrong. For most of its length across Vermont, the border is anywhere from a quarter of a mile to more than a mile north of where it was supposed to be, and where it was early agreed that it should be.

It all started back in 1766 when New York, then "owner" of Vermont, wanted to fix the northern line. After an exchange of correspondence with newly formed Quebec, surveyors representing both provinces met in the vicinity of Windmill Point in Alburg, and a point was agreed upon as being the forty-fifth degree of north latitude. It was subsequently agreed that from that point, a line should be surveyed and marked east to the Connecticut River and west to the St. Lawrence. In 1771 and 1772, Thomas Valentine of New York and John Collins of Quebec ran the line that was to become Vermont's northern boundary. In 1773 and 1774, the line was extended across northern New York to the St. Lawrence. The line was run through a virtual wilderness, and in the Vermont–Quebec portion over very difficult topography, with tree blazes serving as markers. The expenditures for alcohol were certainly justified.

The Revolutionary War followed, and the question of a precise boundary was far from the thoughts of the antagonists. When the hostilities concluded with the Treaty of Paris in 1783, Article II of that treaty again reaffirmed the forty-fifth parallel as the boundary between the United States and Canada. Article II further specified that the border would follow from "the northwesternmost head of the Connecticut River; thence down along the middle of that river, to the forty-fifth degree of north latitude; from thence, by a line due west on said latitude until it strikes . . . [the St. Lawrence River]." A long controversy ensued as to what was the northwesternmost head of the Connecticut River, it finally being decided as Halls Stream.

Valentine and Collins in 1771 and 1772 had run their line to the Connecticut River, following their instructions. At least one writer has told of an 1842 (Webster Ashburton Treaty) international monument actually east of Halls Stream on the Vermont–New Hampshire line. I can find no record of that monument, and in fact have been unable to find it. Soon after the War of 1812, the boundary had been well established at Halls Stream rather than the Connecticut River, and so the reference remains a mystery.

The Treaty of Paris (1783) had spelled out the boundary that was to exist between the United States and Great Britain.* But it was

---

*The Treaty of Paris (1763) brought the Seven Years War between France and Great Britain to a close. The Treaty of Paris (1783) ended the American Revolution.

an imperfect definition at best. No maps were included, and even the place names used did not agree as to their location. No mention was made of the earlier Valentine-Collins line; apparently it was still thought to be the forty-fifth parallel. It was up to the two countries to agree on the line as spelled out, and that was easier said than done. Although commissions met in 1796, 1797, 1798, 1803, and 1807 to try to determine the St. Croix River boundary between Maine (then part of Massachusetts) and New Brunswick, no agreement was reached. For more than forty years no one appears to have paid any attention to Vermont's northern border, and the tree blazes left by the early survey were rapidly disappearing.

That situation abruptly changed with the Treaty of Ghent (1814), which brought the War of 1812 to a close, but the indefinite boundary must have delighted the many smugglers who did so well during the war. Article V of the treaty provided for two commissions, which were to "cause the boundary . . . to be surveyed and marked, and . . . make a map of said boundary."

Apparently the peacemakers were unaware of the old Valentine-Collins survey, although the fact was well known in Vermont and Quebec. Suspicion had been growing locally that the line was in the wrong place.

The commissioners appointed as a result of the Treaty of Ghent were Thomas Barclay for Great Britain and Cornelius Van Ness for the United States. They in turn appointed agents to act for them: William Bradley for the United States and Ward Chipman and Ward Chipman, Jr., representing the other side. The agents were responsible for organizing the field surveys and determining the boundary, and for the Vermont–Quebec and New York–Quebec boundary, one of the first items of business was to ascertain 45° North Latitude. For that task, Dr. J. Tiarks for Great Britain and F. R. Hassler, the first director of the U.S. Coast and Geodetic Survey, were appointed as surveyors. Tiarks independently had earlier ascertained where the forty-fifth parallel was, where it intersected the Connecticut River. He and Hassler in 1818 discovered that the original determination of the critical latitude on the shore of Lake Champlain in 1766 was in error, some three-fourths of a mile too far north. The discovery was not made public at the time, but was reported to the commissioners only because the United States had commenced the construction of Fort Montgomery ("Fort Blunder") north of 45°, but just south of the Valentine-Collins line.

To guard against further British incursions up the Champlain

Valley, the soldiers in the Plattsburgh Barracks had been put to work in 1816 to construct a fortress just north of Rouses Point on the New York side of the lake's outlet. This structure was to be known as Fort Montgomery, but work ceased in 1818, when it was discovered that the site was just north of 45°, which meant, depending on negotiations, that the fortifications just might be in another country. Fort Blunder became locally famous, and it was not until 1843, a year after the final settlement of the boundary question, that work was started once more. Fort Montgomery was completed, and was manned by a small force through the Civil War until 1870, when it was abandoned. It was partially dismantled in 1908, some of the stone (from the Isle La Motte quarries) going into the present causeway across the lake, and other stones appearing in buildings in the village of Rouses Point itself. Today the south wall of the old fort is still in good shape, and can clearly be seen from the Rouses Point bridge, but the rest of the fortification is badly deteriorated.

About the boundary line, two primary questions were to be answered. One was whether the Valentine-Collins line or the forty-fifth parallel was the border. The other was the determination of what was the "northwesternmost" head of the Connecticut River. This problem definition primarily affected New Hampshire.

A long, confusing exchange of correspondence and several meetings between the commissioners and the agents developed over these questions. Discussions continued for ten years, but no agreements were reached. Charges and countercharges flew back and forth between Van Ness and Barclay. Even the two Americans, Van Ness and Bradley, could not agree. The old tree blazes continued to disappear.

One of the provisions of the Treaty of Ghent was that if the two countries could not mutually agree, the dispute would be submitted to a neutral party. The neutral party was the King of the Netherlands, and in 1830 the whole problem was dropped in his lap. The boundary disputes had occupied countless politicians, surveyors, and workmen for more than ten years, with little agreement on either side. Voluminous reports were generated. In 1827, the United States and Great Britain agreed on one thing, a "Convention Providing for the Submission to Arbitration of the Dispute Concerning the Northeastern Boundary." In the text of that document, Article II is actually amusing:

The reports and documents, thereunto annexed, of the Commissioners appointed to carry into the execution the 5th article of the treaty of Ghent, being so voluminous and complicated as to render it impossible that any Soverign or State should be willing or able to undertake the office of investigating and arbitrating upon them, is hereby agreed to substitute, for those reports, new and separate statements of the respective cases. . . .

In 1831, the King of the Netherlands (King William) handed down his opinions on the boundary in question. Nothing said that his decisions were binding arbitration, and therefore, as could be expected, few agreed with the findings. For the Vermont segment of the international border, the King completely supported the British position that the westernmost stream entering the Third Connecticut Lake was correct, and that the geographically determined forty-fifth parallel should be the boundary. Because of the Fort Montgomery construction at Rouses Point, north of 45°, however, he suggested that

it will be suitable to proceed to fresh operations to measure the observed latitude in order to mark out the boundary from the river Connecticut along the parallel of the 45th degree of north latitude to the river St. Lawrence, named in the Treaties . . . , in such manner however that, in all cases, at the place called Rouses Point, the territory of the United States of America shall extend to the fort erected at that place, and shall include said fort and its Kilometrical radius.

The King's decision therefore would have a straight line at 45° along Vermont's northern border, and a bubblelike circle of one-kilometer radius around Fort Montgomery. If the northern border of the United States had conformed to the recommendations, a small circle along the line in question would have looked very odd. But that was not to be done. The United States refused to accept the award, although the British were willing. No surveying or marking was done, and for the next ten years, various United States and British commissions met with proposals and counterproposals, but to little avail. In 1836, the British even withdrew their offer to accept the decision of the King of the Netherlands when the United States began to push for the boundary as earlier specified in the Treaty of Paris (1783). In 1837, the president of the United States informed Congress that after long meetings and negotiations, the British indicated that it would be impossible to figure out the boundary as specified in the 1783 treaty.

It is probable that the conventional line awarded by King William might have been accepted in the late 1830s had it not been for the strong objections to compromise coming from the new State of Maine, which continued to maintain that the line of 1783 should be the border. Feelings had been so strong in that state that boundary disputes with New Brunswick led to the brief "Aroostook War" in 1838. Similarly, in 1836 troubles developed in the Indian Stream boundary region of New Hampshire, and the "Indian Stream Territory" briefly existed as an independent republic. In 1838, the United States proposed formation of a new commission to start fresh. Great Britain agreed, and for two years negotiations on its composition and constitution took place. During this period, the British also had two surveyors and their parties at work along the Maine, New Hampshire, New Brunswick, and Quebec borders; their findings were published in 1840. Maine refused to recognize those surveys in 1841. In 1840, the United States appointed a commission to go over the territory the British had surveyed. To no one's surprise, a considerable difference of opinion was discovered. Finally, in 1841, Daniel Webster, Secretary of State, proposed to the British government that a final attempt be made to settle the entire Canada–United States boundary through direct negotiation rather than by the commission approach. The British agreed to try this method, and appointed Alexander, Lord Ashburton, who arrived in Washington in April 1842. Negotiations began at once.

Surprisingly, Ashburton agreed to both the Halls Stream boundary and the "old line" of the forty-fifth parallel, and mutual agreement was present at least for that portion of the boundary which was later to affect Vermont. The major hang-up, at least in the northeastern United States, was the question of the Maine border, Webster pushing for more land, Ashburton adhering to a boundary considerably farther south and east. All the deliberations were done through direct communication and public meetings. Finally, the two met in private and came to an agreement, which was formalized in the Webster-Ashburton Treaty of August 9, 1842, ratified on October

13 of the same year. No one knows the exact way in which the disputed border was finally settled.

The original wording of the Treaty of 1842 as it affects the Vermont border is:

> to the head of Halls Stream; thence, down the middle of said stream, till the line thus run intersects the old line of boundary surveyed and marked by Valentine and Collins, previously to the year 1774, as the 45th degree of north latitude, and which has been known and understood to be the line of actual division between the States of New York and Vermont on one side, and the British province of Canada on the other; and from said point of intersection, west, along the said dividing line, as heretofore known and understood, to the Iroquois or St. Lawrence River.

Article VI specified that commissions were to be appointed by both governments, and the line surveyed and marked according to the directions in the treaty. The method of survey, monumenting, and other details were to be left to the appropriate commissions. The boundary was surveyed and marked between 1843 and 1847, and a detailed description of the work was submitted by the joint commission under the signature of Albert Smith of the United States and Lieutenant Colonel I. B. Bucknell Estcourt of Great Britain, whose names can be found on the present monuments. Determination of the boundary and marking commenced at the head of the St. Croix River and proceeded west to the St. Lawrence River.

Marking the Boundary

From Monument 1, the boundary runs 490.79 miles over land and another 179 miles through water, and was originally marked between 1843 and 1847 with 773 cast-iron markers and two wooden posts, which were replaced in 1916. The Vermont-Quebec line is 90.3 miles in length from the center of Halls Stream to the center of the deepest channel of Lake Champlain as it becomes the Richelieu River, and along that stretch 126 cast-iron monuments were placed in 1845. Curiously, in 1849 it was reported that Monument 560 in the village

An 1845 monument about to be filled with concrete during the 1906–1907 restoration. U.S. Government photograph.

A renewed cast-iron marker and freshly cut boundary vista. U.S. Government photograph.

Monument 621 at Morses Line in the town of Franklin before and after the 1906 restoration. U.S. Government photographs.

of Beebe Line, Vermont, had been moved from its original location. Lieutenant Colonels Graham of the United States and Ord of Great Britain were dispatched to rectify the problem. They returned the monument to its original location and, while there, placed four new monuments in the area. These four 1849 markers were square, flat-topped granite posts with an east–west groove cut into their top surfaces. They were the only granite markers on the original line as surveyed and marked according to the Treaty of Washington, although emplaced four years after the first cast-iron marker.

The original hollow cast-iron markers were of two types. Thirteen were cast in three sections with a total length of ten feet. The remaining 760 were six feet in length, cast in two sections. The larger ones were placed at more important reference points, in Vermont on the west bank of Halls Stream, and on the shore of the Richelieu River in Alburg. None were used in New York State. All the cast-iron monuments bear the same inscription, cast into them in raised letters when manufactured. On the side facing the United States, "ALBERT SMITH U. S. COMssr."; on the side facing Canada, "LT. COL. I.B.B. EST-COURT H.B.M. COMssr." That took a good bit of squeezing. On the other sides are the words, "TREATY OF WASHINGTON," and "BOUNDARY AUGst 9th, 1842."

I have seen two reports about the manufacture of the original markers. One states that the work was done by a Boston firm, the other that at least the old monuments along the Vermont line were fashioned in the Troy and Boston ironworks in Troy, Vermont. Considering the weight and the problems of transportation, the latter explanation appears very likely. As the name implies, the iron furnace at Troy was controlled by Boston capital.

In marking the boundary, a "vista" twenty feet in width was cut through the forests, and the markers were set so that one could be seen from another. More than 370 miles of opening were hewn by axmen attached to the boundary parties. The hollow monuments themselves were thrust upon cedar posts and the posts buried in the ground. The expenditure of time and labor in the undertaking was tremendous and the logistical problems formidable. Most supplies were hauled to the line during the winter months when the snow was on the ground, at which time large supply depots and camps were established for the summer schedule. In the winter of 1844–45, a British party of eighty men started into the woods at Halls Stream, hauling the cast-iron markers on toboggans, and "after enduring great hardships and exposure, finally came out on Kennebec Road, having deposited the monuments at intervals as they progressed."*

The surveying party of 1845 had a formidable task in trying to figure out the old Valentine-Collins line because it was marked only by tree blazes. Seventy-five years of growth had occurred, forests were where fields had been, trees had been removed, and once-small saplings with a blaze were now full-sized trees. Yet the surveyors were able to retrace the line by finding the old blazes. In the words of the official Report of 1847:

> Upon cutting into those blazes it was seen that deep seated in the tree there was a scar, the surface of the original blaze, slightly decayed, and upon counting the rings [which indicate each year's growth of the tree] it was found that the blazes dated back to 1772, 1773 and 1774. . . . The coincidence of the date of the blazes with those of [the Valentine-Collins line], confirmed by the testimony of the people of the country, satisfied the undersigned that the line they had found was that mentioned in the treaty.

By 1847, the commissioners had finished their work and the final report was submitted, along with all the detailed maps called for. Two years later, Graham and Ord did their repair work and monumenting in Vermont, and final peace descended on the long-contested boundary.

The 1906 Remarking

Because the original cast-iron markers had been set on cedar posts, over the years they gradually deteriorated. Along the Quebec–New York section of the boundary, by 1900, only thirty-seven monuments were in good condition. Of the remaining, thirteen were broken off, eight had fallen entirely, five were cracked, thirty-nine had been heaved by frost action, and twenty-four were leaning. A formal treaty was concluded in 1908 between Great Britain and the United

*All quotations about the Vermont–Quebec border, and much other information, are from: International Boundary Commission, *Joint Report Upon the Survey and Demarcation of the Boundary Between the United States and Canada From the Source of the St. Croix River to the St. Lawrence River* (Washington, D.C.: U.S. Government Printing Office, 1925), 512 pp.

States to completely renew and remark the entire length of the international boundary. Renewal of the Vermont section, however, took place in 1906 and 1907 before final signing of the treaty.

The iron monuments that are now along the Vermont–Quebec border are those which were repaired in 1906 and 1907, and are the original 1845 markers. The restoration involved filling each of the old markers with concrete, then firmly placing them in a base of concrete, beveled on all four sides, and with additional inscriptions (RENEWED 1907, No. . . .). Twenty-seven were moved varying distances east or west, up to the 5,684 feet that monument 537 in Norton was relocated. Movement took place because some were on steep slopes where there was a danger of caving, other on stream banks. Still others were moved to more conspicuous places or away from areas of poor drainage that did not permit a good concrete foundation to be poured. In all, 111 of the original 130 monuments were accepted as marking the true boundary, and most of the others were restored to their original positions. About 110 new markers were added between the originals to better define the boundary and mark more important crossing places, such as the "line houses." These monuments were either granite or concrete blocks, ten inches square, extending sixteen and one-half inches above beveled concrete bases. The inscription is on the base. Many have been whitewashed, often making it impossible to tell which are granite and which are concrete, although the granite is of a rougher texture, and nearly all are granite along the Vermont portion of the boundary. These intermediate monuments are numbered with the number of the original monuments immediately to the east; for example, 556, 556A, 556B. For unexplained reasons, the numbering of intermediate monuments 519, 522, and 527 use the system 519A, 519A2, 519A3, and so on. Any monument emplaced after 1849 does not have the word "renewed" on its base.

And so have the lines on modern maps evolved. The story of Vermont's internal boundary lines, especially those of the counties, has not been touched upon here because that is another story. The establishment of the Hazzen Line as the Vermont–Massachusetts border, the "Twenty-Mile Line" with New York, and the Connecticut River boundary are a part of the state's evolution. With the demarcation of the international border with Canada, Vermont finally had its complete territorial identity, although despite the long disputes over that line, the Connecticut River boundary with New Hampshire was the last to be finally settled.

Small whitewashed granite posts mark intermediate points along the Vermont–Quebec border. They were placed during the remarking of 1906–1907.

Once Vermont knew what it consisted of, it was time to settle down and make a living off the 9,267 square miles of land area and the 342 square miles of water now making up the political area of the state. Even though the area of Vermont, then, is only 9,609 square miles (forty-third in the United States), the history of the state's developing land use is as fascinating as that of any other small political unit in the world. With meager land resources, Vermonters managed to fashion a profitable, functioning economy with lots of rocks, trees, and thin bouldry soils. The saga of that development makes up the remainder of this book.

4

Grain, Sheep, and Wool: 1820–1850

With transportation to the outside world improved by canals on both sides of the state, Vermonters got down to the serious business of making money selling locally produced goods in outside markets. The economy that develop after 1820 consisted of exporting raw materials, an economic orientation that was to last well into the twentieth century. Potash was the first exportable good, followed by lumber, then grain, then livestock and wool, then stone, and finally dairy products. These were the exports for which Vermont was best known, although not necessarily always in that order in the nineteenth century and the early twentieth century. After about 1830, people too were a leading export, and long did the hill farmers mourn the departing young in heart who were not satisfied to harvest rocks.

An attempt in the 1820 Census to list occupations had sparse results. Not until 1850 do we find good material on what Vermonters were doing. For what they are worth, the figures say that in 1820, 50,951 were engaged in agriculture, 8,484 in manufacturing, and only 776 in "commerce." The report gives no definitions, accounts for only a few more than 60,000 of the population of 235,966, and lists only adult males. The statistics do suggest that probably 85 percent of Vermonters were living on scattered farms and raising crops, rocks, and children.

Grain

The main crop raised for sale was grain, especially wheat, buckwheat, oats, rye, and barley. Grains could be shipped easily without

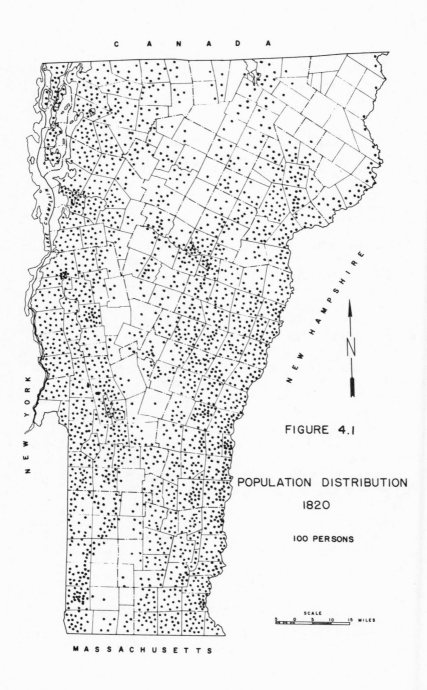

CANADA

NEW YORK

LAKE CHAMPLAIN

NEW HAMPSHIRE

N

FIGURE 4.1

POPULATION DISTRIBUTION

1820

100 PERSONS

SCALE
5 0 5 10 15 MILES

MASSACHUSETTS

spoilage, and appetites among the horses and mules assigned to the canal towpaths were enormous. Much grain from western Vermont ended up as fuel for moving canal boats on the Champlain Canal. Vermont farmers supplied both feed and the animals to consume it. Horses, mules, oxen, and cattle were all raised and sent out under their own power. Sheep came later and greatly swelled the economy.

We have very little information on what was going on in Vermont before the sheep era. Harold F. Wilson, in *Hill Country of Northern New England* probably the most substantial book on nineteenth-century land use for the region, has only twelve pages for the four decades from 1720 to 1830, and most of these deal with population changes. We can't even be sure that the state passed through a brief "grain stage," and if it did, the crop must have been restricted to the better lands in the Champlain Valley and the scattered intervals up and down the Connecticut. In most of the state the inhabitants were probably too busy eking out a self-sufficient existence to worry much about trade with areas outside the encircling hills.

With the completion of the Erie Canal across New York in 1825, western New York became the granary for the eastern seaboard. Vermont farmers rapidly lost their market, if they ever had one, and had to look for alternatives. The Erie Canal, though it perhaps did away with cash grain farming in the state, had a far greater effect on Vermont, for it allowed the westward migration to begin, a movement that was to continue for almost 140 years.

Westward Migration

Much has been written on the wholesale drift of New Englanders westward. In an era when nearly all employment was in farming, better lands were alluring and young Vermonters answered the call, as did their counterparts throughout the region. Exactly how many packed up and sought the promised land is unknown. After 1830 a trickle swelled to a flood. By 1850, 145,655 native-born Vermonters were living outside the state; by 1900 they were 168,000, and by 1960 184,600 people born in Vermont had gone to distant pastures.

The major reason for the westward migration was the same as for the migration to Vermont a few decades previously. After 1760 little good land was left in southern New England, and the only place to go was northward (see Chapter 1). After 1820, as Vermont filled

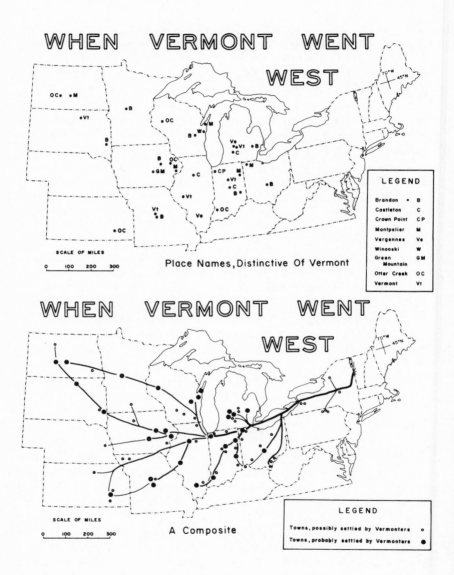

Figure 4.2. *Westward Migration from Vermont.* These two maps, prepared by Vincent Malmstrom, are from the *Vermont Geographer*, No. 2, 1975. They illustrate an interesting technique: using place names as an indicator of migration.

up, the lack was felt there too. In this still agrarian society, land meant wealth, and good land was spoken for. Figure 4.1 shows an almost totally rural population in the early 1800s, and little settlement in the early 1800s, and little settlement in northeastern Vermont. Most of the northern Vermont towns were settled after 1820 by Vermonters, not by people from Connecticut, Massachusetts, or New Hampshire. This was the last surge of New England frontier settlement, and it could accommodate few people.

West they went in great numbers; usually the sons and daughters of hill farmers. Most used the Erie Canal, proof of which is the common place name "Albany" in the Midwest. Albany was the jumping-off place. These names tell us where many young Vermonters went. Often the first settlers beyond the Appalachians, they were far in advance of Scandinavian and German groups. Towns are named Vermont in Missouri, Illinois, Indiana, Michigan, South Dakota, and Wisconsin. Vermontville, Michigan, just outside Lansing, has an annual maple-sugar festival. Otter Creeks turn up in North Dakota, Wisconsin, Indiana, and, of all places, Kansas. These may not be named for the one in Vermont, but otters are not found in Kansas, suggesting the possibility. Montpelier lies not only in Vermont, but also in Ohio, Indiana, Iowa, and North Dakota. And we can find a Winooski in Wisconsin! Figure 4.2 shows the possible migration routes of Vermonters, based on place names.

Not all Vermonters moved west. Many contributed to a reverse flow toward southern New England and New Hampshire, where non-farm jobs were plentiful. In 1890, 172,769 Vermonters were living elsewhere. Of that total, about 75,000 were in neighboring states, and the rest were scattered westward—11,345 in Illinois, 9,500 in Michigan, 5,800 in California, and nearly 5,000 in Nebraska, Ohio, and Kansas. Significant numbers were in Wisconsin, Indiana, Ohio, and Iowa. Every American state or territory at the time had native-born Vermonters. Many yearned for the home state, but knew that it could not provide a decent living. Societies like the "Sons of Vermont of Iowa" and the "Nebraska Sons of Vermont" sprang up all over the country, at least twenty-five of them. Annual meetings were held with native Vermonters in attendance, perhaps even the governor, and a gathering in Brooklyn, New York in 1914 was graced by the president of the United States.

The Vermont State Bank building in Vermont, Illinois, population 970. Settled in 1835, the town was named by an Abraham Williams from Vermont, who won the right by donating a bottle of whiskey.

The Sheep Era

Meanwhile, at home, the folks remaining were trying to keep body and soul together. William Jarvis of Weathersfield can be credited with keeping the state running for more than twenty years. Jarvis, American consul in Lisbon, Portugal, brought two hundred Merino sheep to Vermont in spring 1811. An enterprise that began as a hobby eventually thrust the state into the forefront as a wool producer and put the rocky uplands to use. Sheep, having a cleft lip, can graze on just about everything. Thousands of acres of really poor Vermont hill land were probably cleared in the 1830s and 1840s to feed the ever-forgiving sheep. Most accounts give the 1870s as the period of maximum land clearing, but it may have been before 1850;

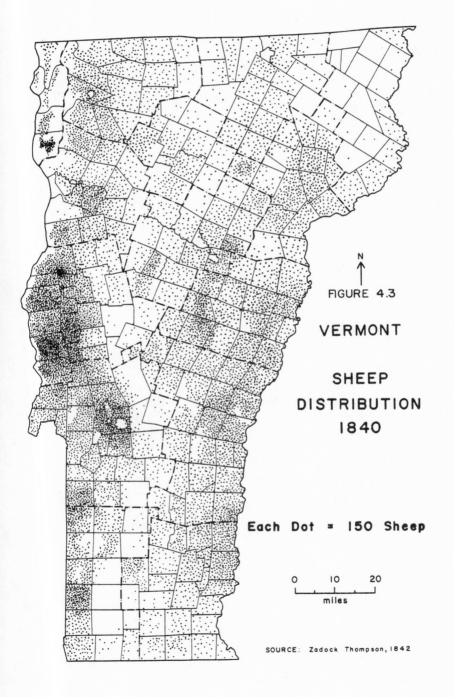

N

FIGURE 4.3

VERMONT

SHEEP

DISTRIBUTION
1840

Each Dot = 150 Sheep

0   10   20
miles

SOURCE: Zadock Thompson, 1842

TABLE 4.1

Sheep and Cows per Square Mile, 1840–1850

County	Sheep 1840	Sheep 1850	Cows 1850	Adjusted Sheep Distribution, 1850[a]
Addison	332	240	14	48
Bennington	159	106	10	21
Caledonia	164	49	19	10
Chittenden	208	107	24	21
Essex	21	11	4	2
Franklin	133	88	25	18
Grand Isle	357	228	16	47
Lamoille	86	32	12	6
Orange	226	104	16	21
Orleans	65	38	11	8
Rutland	292	201	19	40
Washington	157	46	17	9
Windham	144	75	18	15
Windsor	243	198	18	40
Total	1,681,819	1,014,122	146,128	

[a]For a discussion of this column, see text.

Source: Calculations from U.S. Bureau of the Census.

no record remains. Merino sheep covered Vermont, although greatest densities were on the better lands.

Sheep raising reached its peak in the middle 1830s, declining consistently thereafter. A map of the distribution of sheep in each Vermont town in 1840, when the state had almost 500,000 fewer sheep than two or three years earlier, shows how both good and poor lands were being intensively grazed (see Figure 4.3). The 1840 and 1850 data (Table 4.1) show concentration on the better lands of the Champlain Valley. The leading counties in sheep density are Addison and Grand Isle. Rutland, Orange, and Windsor counties, with their high proportion of hill lands, were certainly being overgrazed; erosion was a problem, and much topsoil from many Vermont hills disappeared in the 1840s.

Two factors set off the decline in sheep farming. One was the lowering of protective tariffs in the 1840s, which depressed the price of wool (it was selling for 57 cents a pound in 1835 and only 25 cents in the late 1840s); the other was growing competition in the West—a familiar Vermont story. Historians of the sheep industry report that the average annual cost of keeping a sheep in the "East" was between one and two dollars a head, compared to a cost in the "West" of 25 cents to a dollar. Such generalities are bothersome, but whatever the figures, farming certainly was more costly in Vermont. Also, midwestern growers in the Ohio country could use the Ohio and Pennsylvania canal systems to advantage and were therefore almost as "close" to market as were Vermont producers. Faced with depressed prices and growing competition, many farmers reduced their herds, replacing stock with cattle; others sold out entirely. Cheese production increased as well went down. The number of sheep in the state decreased by nearly a third between 1840 and 1850, and the trend was established.

Surprisingly, by 1850 Vermont was probably just as important as a dairy state as a wool-producing area; see the last two columns in Table 4.1. The third column suggests that cows were far less important, but this is not at all true. A rule of thumb is that it takes as much land and feed to care for one dairy cow as for five sheep; to find the relative importance of the animals in the economy, divide the number of sheep by five, as in the fourth column of Table 4.1. Regardless of total numbers, in *eight* Vermont counties cows were in fact more important than sheep even this early. Furthermore, except for Windham County, all the "dairy" counties were in the north: Franklin, Orleans, Caledonia, Essex, Chittenden, Lamoille, and Washington. Conversely, the "sheep" counties were Grand Isle and Addison in the fertile Champlain Lowland, Bennington (influenced by the woolen industry in Bennington itself), Rutland, Orange, and Windsor.

To reinforce this conclusion, Figure 4.4 shows the distribution of an estimated 150,000 dairy cows in 1840. This figure is equivalent to about 750,000 sheep, or nearly half of the 1.7 million sheep reported in that year. The maps of sheep and cow distribution can readily be compared because each dot represents the same number of animal units (30 cows equal 150 sheep) with respect to the carrying capacity of the land.

The growth of Vermont's dairy industry was therefore well under way at the turn of the century, and though sheep farming continued in Addison County for many years, the trend toward milk was well established.

The Woolen Industry

The earliest nonagricultural pursuits were retailing and working for the local grist or lumber mill. All such nonfarm activity was geared

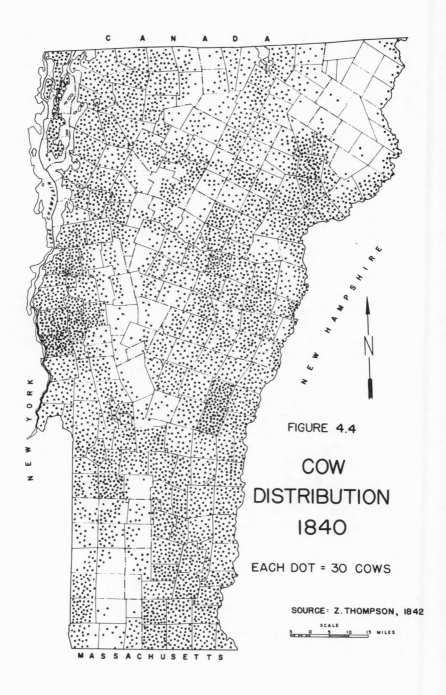

FIGURE 4.4

COW

DISTRIBUTION

1840

EACH DOT = 30 COWS

SOURCE: Z. THOMPSON, 1842

to the farming community, and products manufactured were for local consumption. Early paper mills using rags were typical of local industry employing local people for a local market. Even the first foundries and forges produced the implements and household items required on a frontier, and only as transportation improved and manufactured products were produced in excess of local demands did Vermont industry become more than a local curiosity. As nonagricultural employment began to develop, it was based almost exclusively on the processing of native raw materials.

As sheep spread, so too did industry based upon them. Carpenters built the barns, loggers cut the forests, and mills sawed the timber. Tanneries were started to take care of the skins, and most important, other mills followed to take care of the wool. The merino was a wool-producing animal; its major contribution to Vermont has to be considered the woolen industry that grew along with the increase in sheep.

The earliest textile operations taking place outside the home were fulling or cleansing mills. They provided a needed local service by washing the cloth brought to them from the handlooms throughout the region; in the fulled material, shrinkage could be controlled and the cloth was much smoother than rough, greasy homespun. Following the fulling mills came carding mills, although in manufacturing, carding actually comes before fulling in woolen textile preparation. Carding mills, beginning in the early 1790s, took the lumpy mass of wool as it came from the sheep and combed the material so that it was suitable for spinning into yarn. Spinning was a home occupation for many years, along with looming of the spun yarn into homespun cloth. The cloth then went to the fulling mill for improvement. Carding and fulling mills were separated by two basic steps (spinning and weaving) in manufacturing the final product. True textile factories did all the processing under one roof, and, after 1850, began to do away with much of the home manufacturing that characterized the early years.

By 1809, Vermont had twenty-eight carding mills and fifty-eight fulling mills. These early mills were small, and like the local forges and sash and blind mills, were producing a local product for a local consumer. Often the mill operator would be paid in grain or some other product the customer made that would later be resold to someone else for cash. Whether it was a fulling or a carding mill, or even a combined operation, the one major requirement was water and waterpower. We can see in these early mills and those which came later how much a source of energy mattered. Energy was taken from running water, streams were always in valleys, and the downhill movement had begun.

After 1820, as more Vermonters began to raise sheep, the small fulling and carding mills came to mean more than a supply of well-prepared wool to the hundreds of Abigails, Esthers, and Elizabeths who, with their looms, graced the landscape. The carding mills became suppliers for the woolen factories that were gradually developing. The system sounds simple, but because "factory" and "mill" were and are used indiscriminately in textile operations, it is often hard to know what one is speaking of. Technically, a mill prepares fiber; this work includes fulling, carding, dyeing, scouring, and other operations. The factory takes the spun yarn and, on mechanical looms, waves it into cloth, after which it may go through another fulling or cleansing, depending on the raw material delivered to the factory. Some factories (and even some "mills") took the cloth they made, and went on to the next step, fashioning (or knitting) the cloth into items like blankets, overcoats, union suits, and sweaters.

As the number of sheep grew, so too did the industry. Between 1810 and 1820, the number of fulling and carding mills increased by 300 percent, generally following population and sheep distribution. Factories also increased significantly, ten of them opening in 1812, but they were often small and inefficient affairs. Many disappeared after 1820, when normal trade resumed. Fulling and carding mills continued to expand, because they were based on local rather than out-of-state demand. These mills reached a peak in the late 1820s, declining thereafter as larger mills were built. Improved technology required more capital, and more factories arose to take over some of the operations. By 1900 the state had only two carding mills and one fulling mill. Figure 4.5 shows the pattern of fulling and carding mills in the years 1820 to 1829.

Replacing the small fulling and carding operations located in nearly every community were the larger factories, originally not doing fulling and carding operations; but as the smaller mills disappeared, becoming complete operations doing everything from preparation of raw wool to turning out the finished product. Although the small mills employed only a few local citizens, the factories employed scores and even hundreds. Vermont's first industry was being created. In the late 1830s there were eighty textile factories. One, in Colchester (later Winooski), employed more than a hundred,

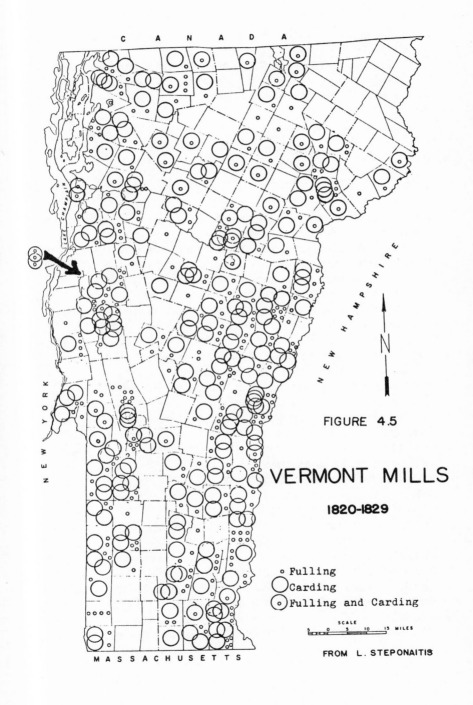

CANADA

NEW YORK

NEW HAMPSHIRE

N

FIGURE 4.5

VERMONT MILLS

1820-1829

○ Fulling
◯ Carding
◉ Fulling and Carding

SCALE
5 0 5 10 15 MILES

FROM L. STEPONAITIS

MASSACHUSETTS

and there were twenty-five employing between ten and ninety-nine persons.

We cannot know exactly how many workers were employed in the growing industry. Census material is highly questionable, but in 1840 it was reported that Vermont's workforce was engaged in these numbers:

Agriculture	73,150
Commerce	1,303
Manufacturing	13,174

Manufacturing employment was 18 percent of agricultural employment, whereas in the 1820 period, it had been a bit over 16 percent. The figures refer only to adult males and therefore do not show the large numbers of children and women working in the mills and factories. Their exact number will never be known.

In the early 1830s, the largest Vermont woolen factory employed about eighty workers. At least twelve operations in Massachusetts employed more than three hundred. In one New Hampshire mill more than five hundred worked. Statistics of the period are a real problem, but Vermont was certainly not yet a manufacturing state. In fact, even in 1850 and 1900, no Vermont community was listed among the top fifty New England manufacturing centers.

A word about using the U.S. Bureau of the Census as a source of data. Besides the population count, Congress tried to gather information for 1810, 1820, and 1840. The returns in both 1810 and 1820 were so poor that no attempt was even made to do anything in 1830. Inexperienced enumerators, in some cases hardly knowing what precisely constituted "manufacturing," were asked to gather data without benefit of instructions or questionnaires. Many mill and factory owners, upon being approached by the enumerator, refused to give any information, considering the intrusion unwarranted and likely to lead to tax assessment. Poorly trained clerical employees made many errors in tabulating the results. The only reasonably accurate statistical material before 1850 is an accurate sheep count taken in the 1830s and the McLane Report, a census of manufacturers in the United States taken in 1831, but not as an integral part of the 1830 census. Congress used this census in attempting to weigh the effects of tariff restrictions and did not intend it as a census document at all, but even so, it has become the most valuable pre-1850 documentation available on early manufacturing in this country.

Vermont's textile industry developed rapidly during the 1830s and early 1840s, the factories becoming supreme, the smaller fulling and carding mills disappearing as the factories took on those operations. The word "mill" continued to be used for factory operations. Between 1831 and 1849, the number of wool factories increased from sixty to ninety-seven. Two-thirds of these new operations were located in central Addison County, especially Middlebury; in Chittenden County; and on the Passumpsic in Barnet in Caledonia County. In southern Vermont, most of the best water sites were already taken. Bennington operations were using the Walloomsuc, and the Black River was a string of mills and factories from Ludlow to Springfield, with a major concentration in Proctorsville in Cavendish. Bellows Falls in Rockingham relied upon the Connecticut and the water flowing through the canal. The new factories, like the old, were small. Of forty-one new firms over twenty years, about thirty-five employed fewer than ten persons.

Growth slowed in the late 1840s. Although total employment was probably a little more than 2,000 in all phases of the textile industry, and wool was plentiful, Vermont was still remote from most markets. The production of local factories could easily take care of home demand, but larger mills in southern New England were better situated in relation to the consumer. Raw wool, being light and valuable, could be transported for finishing and manufacture outside the state, and most went south to Providence, Lowell, Springfield, and the mill towns of the Blackstone Valley. The industry was important in Vermont, but it was insignificant in the region, and the major period of the Vermont textile industry was still to come. Figure 4.6 shows Vermont's early textile industry just before a period of maximum expansion that came with the railroads after 1850.

In the 1840s, "shoddy" mills came to Vermont. Three are shown on the map. Rueben Daniels of Woodstock invented a machine to rework used wool, rags, felts, and other used products such as mill scraps. It was the only wool-textile invention to emanate from Vermont, and the Hartford firm of A. T. Dewey and Company was the first shoddy mill in America. The first knitting mills were also in existence, and the one in Swanton employed more than a hundred. Others were in St. Albans and Chelsea, but these were very small

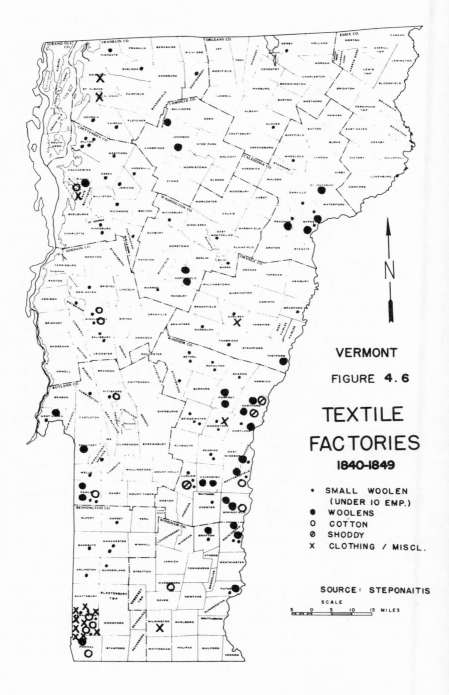

VERMONT

FIGURE 4.6

TEXTILE
FACTORIES
1840-1849

- SMALL WOOLEN
  (UNDER 10 EMP.)
- WOOLENS
○ COTTON
⊘ SHODDY
X CLOTHING / MISCL.

SOURCE: STEPONAITIS

SCALE

5   0   5   10   15 MILES

operations. Bennington in the 1840s was credited with nine "miscellaneous textile operations."

Even with the incomplete 1850 vintage data, it is possible to make some generalizations about the textile industry at the turn of the century. Vermont had 156 types of textile operations, nearly all working with the local woolen resource. By measuring output and some reports of employment, we find that about 2,300 people were employed.

In the Census of 1850 is a table listing all "Professions, Occupations and Trades of the Male Population," which documents an awesome 174 occupations, even to "one Feather Dresser, one Hosier, one Pipe Maker, one Flax Dresser, one Carver, one Author, and one Last Maker." The tabulations do indicate that 123 males are in cotton factories and another 800 are in woolen factories. Thus the estimate of 2,300 workers (including women and children) in the textile industry in 1850 may be reasonably good. This figure represents 16 to 20 percent of the manufacturing employment in that year.

In employment, Bennington was probably the largest center, followed by Colchester (Winooski), Springfield, Cavendish (Proctorsville), Middlebury, Bethel, Northfield, Pawlet, and Waterville as major centers. The data on Waterville are suspect, but in 1850 it was reported to have John Herron's Wool Factory, employing thirty-two men and eighteen women and purchasing 100,000 pounds of wool and 24,000 pounds of cotton to produce 374,400 yards of flannel, valued at $82,268. The factory was destroyed by fire in the winter of 1852.

Wool was *the* Vermont product, being carded, fulled, washed, dyed, recovered, and woven, but cotton too was being produced for local consumption. Raw-cotton bales were being imported up the Connecticut River and through the Champlain Canal to destinations in both eastern and western Vermont. In 1850, cotton was being manufactured into cloth in Burlington, Hartford (White River Junction), Mendon, Middlebury, Pawlet, Pittsford, Springfield, Weathersfield, and Wilmington. Besides cotton and wool, other textile products were linen made from flax, and hemp for rope. Like cotton, and most of the woolens produced, before 1850 nearly all production was locally consumed. The coming of the railways dramatically changed the agricultural land use of the state, from nonperishable wool production to perishable dairy products; it also led to expansion of industry; textile manufacturing increased greatly in the

TABLE 4.2

Vermont Population Growth, 1790–1850[a]

Year	Population	Net Change	% Change	U.S. % Change
1790	85,425			
1800	154,475	69,040	80.8	35.1
1810	217,895	63,430	41.1	36.4
1820	235,981	18,086	8.3	33.1
1830	280,652	44,671	18.9	33.5
1840	291,978	11,296	4.0	32.7
1850	314,120	22,172	7.6	35.9

[a]This information continues in Table 8.1.
Source: U.S. Bureau of the Census.

latter years of the nineteenth century. The marble and granite industries became important. Springfield became world renowned as a machine-tool center, and many other industries developed to satisfy local demand, and also to export Vermont-made products all over the United States and the world.

During the first half of the nineteenth century, Vermont built a manufacturing base based upon its raw materials.

Population change involved both the western migration and another movement into northern Vermont and the poorer mountain towns. After an initial surge of settlement when the state was the New England frontier, immigration slowed, ceased, and then reversed itself. By 1850, 43 percent of native-born Vermonters were living outside the state. Table 4.2 illustrates Vermont population trends between 1790 and 1850.*

Everyone yearned for the railways, which were to bring Vermont into the mainstream of New England economic life. Hill farms were going to flourish, jobs were to be created, and the young were going to stay at home.

> Vermont is with many advantages blest,
> Which they should consider who long for the West;
> Our clime is salubrious, fruitful our soil,
> Yielding ample reward for the husbandman's toil;

*Vermont population changes since the first U.S. Census are shown in Table 4.2 for 1790–1850, Table 8.1 for 1850–1960, and Table 13.2 for 1960–1980.

For greater fertility dearly they pay,
Who move from our excellent water away.
No land in the world is more favored than ours
By streams in their multiplied uses and powers;
They wind in our Vales, flowing down from our hills,
Many cattle to water, and move many mills.
Many streams in each township delightfully glide,
And each farm is with plenty of water supplied;
For washing and cleansing our water is best;
You may learn its high value by moving off west.
Fine factories rise where our currents go down,
Mechanics and farmers may thrive in each town.
In most of life's products of excellent kind
Our state equals others, or leaves them behind;
If we cannot raise wheat quite as much as we please,
We can produce sugar, and butter and cheese;
We have wool in great plenty, and with it the power
To turn it to cash, and the cash into flour.
Our ore is too plenty of iron refined.
We have minerals many of excellent kind;
If markets are distant they'll surely be near
As soon as the railroads projected are here.

from *The Vermont Watchman*, December 1849

5

Railroad Development

It is hard to imagine the influence railroads had on American civilization in the nineteenth century. A trip that was once a week's journey by oxcart, or two days by stage, came to be measured in hours. Areas that were self-sufficient no longer had to rely on their own production and could specialize in economic pursuits best suited to their location, their raw materials, and the skills of their people. Distance and isolation shrank in direct proportion to the growth of an iron network, and the country, heretofore fragmented, attained a unity never before dreamed of.

The traditional routes of western migration from Vermont were suddenly redundant; the Erie and other canals had served their purpose in transporting people, but now fulfilled another purpose in moving large tonnages of bulky freight at a low cost. Vermonters still went west in great numbers, but they took a far quicker and more convenient route. By 1848, they could almost reach Chicago by rail, but in that same year, nary an iron rail was on Vermont's soil. Northern New England had been forgotten in the push to the West; few railroad barons were interested in laying rails into a backwater area, and it was mostly local desperation that forced railways to penetrate the Green Mountain State in 1849 and 1950.

On a frigid December 18, 1849, bottles of murky water from Boston Harbor and crystal-clear water from Lake Champlain were ceremoniously mixed at the summit elevation of the newly completed Rutland and Burlington Railway in the town of Mount Holly (elevation 1,300 feet), some fifteen miles southeast of Rutland. The directors of the railroad, perhaps because of the many other bottles that accompanied the occasion, were in a state of euphoria over this

106

historic conquering of the Green Mountain range by twin bands of steel.

Had they but paused at the time, or even before the event, and looked northward, they would have seen another railroad racing to completion across the state. The Vermont Central, with former Governor Charles Paine (1841–1843) at the throttle, was focusing on the same terminus as the Rutland and Burlington, and though the rival rails did not enter Burlington until two weeks after the Rutland and Burlington arrived on December 18, 1849, it was abundantly clear that the small city (population 7,585 in 1850), growing on the shores of Lake Champlain, could hardly generate traffic enough to keep two almost parallel rail lines solvent.

And so the merrymaking at Mount Holly was some of the last rejoicing that directors or stockholders of the Rutland and Burlington would do for many years. The first major blow fell in 1852, when future Vermont Governor J. Gregory Smith (1863–1865) of St. Albans hitched his Vermont and Canada to the tracks of the Vermont Central at the place that was to become Essex Junction, then called Painesville. In a twinkling the Vermont Central–Vermont and Canada combination had connections with the growing Canadian areas to the north. Burlington remained at the end of a spur that amounted to a branch of the Vermont Central, a situation that prevails to this day (see Figure 5.1).

The fundamental problem faced by any railroad ever to operate in Vermont is that the state itself, because of low population and lack of major cities and industries, could not support railroads solely with local on-line traffic. The successful Vermont railroad had to rely on origin and destination traffic outside the state. Thus when, as early as 1852, the Vermont Central secured an outside source of traffic, its future was ensured, and it remains even today, under its present name, the Central Vermont, as the most prosperous Vermont railroad.

Yet early railway promoters can be forgiven for not knowing in advance that the population of Vermont would increase only by 85,899 or 29 percent between 1840 and 1850 (that's less than 4 percent per decade). Mirroring the national trend, the last half of the nineteenth century saw every community in Vermont clamoring for a railway. Already doomed when built, the lines served the local needs of their era only. Others managed to survive. Milk and rock and wood provided most of the on-line income. Passenger traffic, once

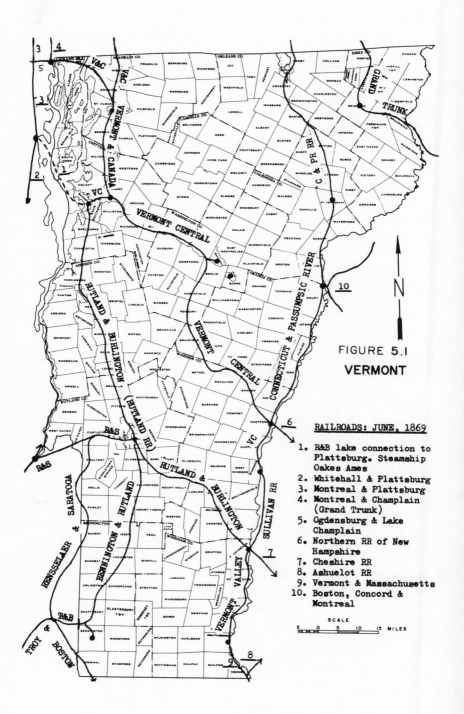

FIGURE 5.1

VERMONT

RAILROADS: JUNE, 1869

1. R&B lake connection to Plattsburg. Steamship Oakes Ames
2. Whitehall & Plattsburg
3. Montreal & Plattsburg
4. Montreal & Champlain (Grand Trunk)
5. Ogdensburg & Lake Champlain
6. Northern RR of New Hampshire
7. Cheshire RR
8. Ashuelot RR
9. Vermont & Massachusetts
10. Boston, Concord & Montreal

SCALE
5   5   10   15 MILES

important, declined with the fast-spreading automobile, competition that even the few electric lines in the state could not meet.

The rails as they pushed northward built an insatiable demand for low-cost laborers, and whether it was the "luck of the Irish," or not, they, as the earliest major ethnic group coming to the shores of the new land, were there at the right time. Besides the French Canadians, the Irish were, and probably are, the largest non-Yankee contingent in Vermont, although the Italians of the quarry towns remain a significant, though concentrated, group. The Irish settled in all parts of Vermont. They came with the rails, and as the rails penetrated every nook and cranny, so too did the people who built the iron highways.

It is easiest to look at Vermont's railway development in two major periods: the evolution of the basic network before 1870, and the filling-in that came after. The first period consisted of construction linking the north with the south, including routes joining Canada, southern New England, and the Atlantic coast; three major railways were involved (Figure 5.1). The second period involved creating east–west links, and filled in gaps in the network to meet local community demands. Nearly all railroads involved in the second stage of development have collapsed, or, failing that, are now owned by the state of Vermont.

The Early Years

The only railroad appearing on the 1869 map that had something of an east–west orientation was the 295-mile-long Grand Trunk through Island Pond, completed in July 1853, linking Montreal with Portland and the sea. Island Pond developed as a railroad town because it was halfway (147 miles) between its two terminating cities. Only a small portion of the route is in Vermont.

The clearest north–south railway pattern was made up of the various railroads that followed the Connecticut River Valley, providing together a direct route between Quebec City and Long Island Sound and its steamboats. North of Greenfield, Massachusetts, passengers had to endure travel, and often changes, on five railroads before they passed through Vermont. They rode the Vermont and Massachusetts as far as Brattleboro, and continued on the lines of the Vermont Valley Railroad (leased by the Rutland and Burlington

The railway yards and bridge at Island Pond in the 1940s and in the 1980s. Top photograph from Ardys Fisher.

in 1865) as far as Bellows Falls. There they could continue to Rutland and Burlington on the R&B, or continue northward in New Hampshire on the Sullivan Railroad (controlled by the Vermont Central) to Windsor and the tracks of the Vermont Central. Here was another route to Burlington, which generally paralleled the Rutland and Burlington tracks to the south, but after 1865, when the Vermont Valley was under lease to the Rutland and Burlington, the management scheduled trains to make interchange with the rival Vermont Central awkward and inconvenient.

The Vermont Central continued northward to White River Junction, where it swung northwest, following the White River toward Burlington and Montreal. North of White River, the Connecticut and Passumpsic River carried passengers over half the length of Vermont on one line.

This Connecticut Valley route was glowingly described in an advertisement in the *Travelers Official Railway Guide of the United States and Canada* for June 1869:

> This is the great Mail and Express Line from New York to all points in Central and Northern New England; is the direct route, and 60 miles shorter than any other, to the WHITE MOUNTAINS; and although long established and well known to the pleasure-seekers who frequent the many places of summer resort throughout the Valley of the Connecticut, has recently enlarged its connections, and . . . has now become a favorite route of travel from Washington, Baltimore, Philadelphia and New York to Montreal, Quebec and vicinity.
>
> This route, as the map will show, leads the traveler through the heart of New England. A constant succession of important cities, or thriving populous towns greets his eye at every stop, and nowhere else will he see the same perfection of variety in scenery peculiar to New England. There is room here barely to mention some few of the prominent objects of interest.

The Vermont Central, its rails pushing toward Burlington in 1849 from White River Junction, followed the White River Valley for much of its route. Its summit elevation at Roxbury (elevation 1,110 feet) crossed from the headwaters of the Third Branch of the White River into the valley of the Dog River, which it followed to the Winooski River. The maximum elevation was some 200 feet less than the Rutland at Mount Holly.

Although the route bypassed both Montpelier and Barre, it was selected for three major reasons. In the first place, the grade was much easier than the earlier-surveyed route up the Second Branch of the White River through Williamstown Gulf. Another reason was that it was considerably cheaper to build up the Third Branch. In 1845, Mr. T. J. Carter, engaged by the directors of the railroad, reported after an exhaustive survey that the Roxbury route, though five miles longer than a route through Barre, could be built for almost half the cost, $460,825 as opposed to $764,865.

But finally, Governor Charles Paine, a resident of Northfield, wanted *his* railroad to pass through *his* town. Although this desire may have influenced the decision, the costs and the grades certainly were equally important. For several years, however, Northfield served as the headquarters of the Vermont Central, until the shops were moved to St. Albans on the Vermont and Canada in 1860.

The Vermont Central Railroad

Ending at Burlington, the Vermont Central was at a dead end like that of the Rutland and Burlington. But to the north, J. Gregory Smith was building his Vermont and Canada southward, and the Vermont and Canada rails met those of the Vermont Central in 1852 at the place that was to become Essex Junction.

Financially ailing, the Vermont Central in 1852 passed to control by Smith and his Vermont and Canada. The new company subsequently became the Central Vermont Railroad in 1873.

North of Essex Junction and St. Albans, the Vermont and Canada had several optional routes to gather traffic from a large northern and western region. The earliest main line led due north of St. Albans, passed through Swanton, and, turning west, crossed Missisquoi Bay on a wood trestle. The route continued across Alburg and then used a bridge built in conjunction with the Northern Railroad (of New York) in 1852 to enter New York State. The Northern Railroad subsequently became the Ogdensburg and Lake Champlain, and provided the Vermont and Canada–Vermont Central combination an outlet to the Great Lakes. At Rouses Point, a connection was afforded to the north via the Montreal and Champlain Railroad, and some few miles down the track, with the Montreal and Plattsburg Railroad.

The summit of the Central Vermont Railroad at Roxbury is at an elevation of 1,110 feet, 200 feet less than the old Rutland maximum elevation in Mt. Holly. In front of the quaint station is a polished block of Verde Antique marble, long quarried in the town.

The once bustling Central Vermont Railroad yards in downtown St. Albans are now seeing some commercial development. The large station, now without its famous covered train shed, is in the background.

When the Victoria Bridge was built across the St. Lawrence at Montreal in 1861, the main route of the Vermont and Canada became a newly built (1864) stretch of track leading north from St. Albans through Highgate. This remained the main line of the Central Vermont until 1946, when the Canadian National trackage in East Alburg came to be used. Now abandoned, the old line can still be discerned where an old trestle crosses the mouth of the Rock River in Highgate.

With its northern and western connections well established by the early 1850s, the Vermont & Canada–Vermont Central needed a southern outlet. This end was achieved through arrangements with the Northern Railroad of New Hampshire, which crossed the Connecticut River at White River Junction and provided a direct route to Boston.

Although the Northern of New Hampshire provided a connection to Boston, the Vermont Central needed a route to New York and Long Island Sound. Even though it controlled the Sullivan Railroad in 1863, running south of Windsor as far as Bellows Falls, at the latter community the Vermont Central found itself on the unfriendly territory of the Rutland and Burlington, which had arrangements with both the Cheshire Railroad for connections to New London, and the Vermont Valley railroad south down the Connecticut Valley (leased by the Rutland in 1865). Thus, the Vermont Central, though it had considerable western and northern connections, found itself bottled up without good southern routes.

It was apparent that if the Vermont Central wanted access to the south it would have to effect agreements with the Rutland. That arrangement was not too likely, but in fact did come about in strange and mysterious ways.

The Rutland Railroad

The Rutland and Burlington Railroad, originally chartered as the Champlain and Connecticut River Railroad, was constructed between Bellows Falls and Burlington via Rutland from 1847 to 1849. With little traffic from Burlington because of competition with the Vermont Central, and minimal on-line traffic except for the Howe Scale Works in Rutland and marble from the West Rutland and

Proctor quarries, the road was hard put to generate much return for the shareholders who had so celebrated in Mount Holly in December 1849.

In 1867 the road was reorganized as the Rutland Railway Company under the able leadership of John Page, who was president of the Howe Scale Works, and destined to the another railroad governor (following both Paine and Smith).

The history of the Rutland tells of a railroad originally going from nowhere to nowhere, desperately trying to get somewhere. Finding that a northern connection was impossible because of the Vermont and Canada and the waters of Lake Champlain, the Rutland purchased the small steamer *Boston* in 1852 to connect newly built wharves in Burlington with Plattsburg across the Lake. With winter ice and minimal traffic, little business came along.

Although arrangements with the Cheshire Railroad and the Vermont Valley ensured traffic to the south to New London and the Connecticut Valley, with little traffic to generate on its own lines, the Rutland was not a particularly great benefactor to those two roads, and had not Page actually leased the Vermont Valley it might easily have become a part of the Vermont Central system.

Failing to secure traffic in the north, the management of the Rutland looked south toward Albany and Troy, New York. Until the Hoosac Tunnel was completed under the Berkshires in 1875 there was no direct route from the west to Boston, and though a route over the winding and poorly ballasted Rutland trackage might be a harrowing experience, at least it had a chance of securing some through traffic to keep the newly reorganized railroad solvent.

In 1867, the Rutland leased the Bennington and Rutland Railroad, running down the Vermont valley to North Bennington with a branch to Bennington itself. This railroad had been built to North Bennington and State Line in 1852 as the Western Vermont Railroad. In 1857, the Troy and Boston Railroad, which connected with the Western Vermont at State Line, some three miles west of North Bennington, acquired control of the route and was sending considerable tonnages from the west through the Western Vermont and the Rutland Burlington systems. No sooner had the Rutland leased the Bennington and Rutland, however, than the Troy and Boston pulled out of its interchange agreement, leaving the Rutland with a dangling leased line. The Bennington and Rutland was finally incorporated into the Rutland Railroad in 1900, but for a few years the Rutland lease brought nothing but increasingly rusted rails and little traffic.

Temporarily blocked at Bennington, the Rutland still had a chance for some western traffic. That possibility involved the Rensselaer and Saratoga lines, reaching west of Rutland toward Albany and Troy, with one line through Whitehall at the south end of Lake Champlain.

In March 1852, the Rutland and Washington Railroad had been built from Rutland westward to connections with the Troy and Rutland and the Troy and Boston. This road ran due west as far as Castleton, then followed a winding course southward along the state line through Poultney, Pawlet, and Rupert to Hoosac Falls, New York, where it met the main line of the Troy and Boston. This route provided a through connection to Troy, New York, and was viable until 1853, at which time the Troy and Boston pulled out of an interchange agreement to instead build to a connection with the Western Vermont Railroad at State Line.

Earlier (in 1850) the Rutland and Whitehall Railroad had been built from Whitehall, New York, to Castleton, and at its southern end, the Saratoga and Washington and other lines ran on to Albany. Both routes were acquired by the Rensselaer and Saratoga in 1860 and today are parts of the Delaware and Hudson system. The latter route, however, provided the Rutland with at least one outlet to New York City and western traffic. But stymied on the north, and with little on-line traffic to support itself, the railroad was in a sorry state. It desperately needed an infusion of capital and traffic.

Railroad Transition: 1869–1871

When John Page took over the reorganized Rutland Railroad in 1867, he was well aware of the geographic limitations of the area served as well as the paucity of off-line traffic. He was also astute enough to realize that salvation for the Rutland meant cooperation from the rival Vermont Central, which was in a position to interchange with his road. Although at the beginning he probably did not realize that his machinations would eventually lead to the Vermont Central's leasing the Rutland, he undoubtedly thought that he could force the rival road into cooperation. In that he was eminently successful.

Already the Rutland and Burlington, through Page's efforts, had leased the Vermont Valley Railroad running south of Bellows Falls, and had an arrangement with the Cheshire Railroad for access to the Boston area. Neither of these events had been received with much happiness at the Vermont Central headquarters in St. Albans. Also, through the arrangements made with the Rensselaer and Saratoga, the Rutland had access to the Hudson Valley, something that the Vermont Central did not have.

Then, in a series of moves between 1868 and 1871, Page and his Rutland put the screws on Mr. Smith and his Vermont Central.

The first blow fell in 1868, when the Rutland began operating the Steamship *Oakes Ames* from its dead-end terminus at Burlington across the lake to Plattsburg. This large and fast ship began to siphon off traffic from the Montreal and Plattsburg Railroad that up to then had been going to the Vermont Central. Also, as Burlington itself became an important lumber port, processing raw Canadian and Michigan lumber and shipping it by rail to the south, traffic began to increase rapidly.

Next, in late 1869 the Lebanon Springs Railroad, pushing north in New York State, had finally connected with the dangling Bennington and Rutland in Bennington (see number 15, Figure 5.2). On January 1, 1870, the Bennington and Rutland and the Lebanon Springs Railroad were merged as the Harlem Extension Railroad, which was finally incorporated into the Rutland in 1900. A direct link was now forged with New York City. The curves were sharp and the grades steep, so that the Lebanon Springs Railroad was later referred to as the "Corkscrew Division," but when it was a part of the Rutland, completion of this link was looked upon with uneasiness in St. Albans.

Two other events in 1870 disturbed the tranquility of the Central Vermont management. The first was the leasing by the Rutland, of the Vermont and Massachusetts Railroad from Brattleboro southward. This move, in combination with the previous lease of the Vermont Valley Railroad between Bellows Falls and Brattleboro, and with traffic arrangements with the New London and Northern Railroad, gave the Rutland access to Connecticut and Long Island Sound. The Rutland now had direct access to Albany, Troy, New York City, Connecticut, and the Sound. But only the *Oakes Ames* plying back and forth across Lake Champlain between Burlington and Plattsburg gave any access to the north and off-line traffic from that direction.

In the fourth move of the period, the Rutland set out to rectify that situation.

Railway construction along the western side of Lake Champlain in New York had lagged. Sparsely settled territory and formidable physical obstacles had discouraged any northward penetration of the railways from the Hudson Valley. Steamboats ran on both Lake George and Lake Champlain and, though passenger traffic was substantial, little freight was carried.

As the Adirondack iron mines developed in the mid–nineteenth century, and as greater amounts of lumber and milk were required by the growing southern markets, railroad entrepreneurs began considering lines to tap the area west of Lake Champlain.

In 1868 the Whitehall and Plattsburg Railroad had built a line from Plattsburg as far as Ausable, New York, only a year before the Golden Spike was struck in Utah. As its corporate name implied, it was eventually to forge a link between the Hudson Valley and the railroads and settlements of northern New York State.

Following this connection, in 1870, a stretch of the Whitehall and Plattsburg was built from near Ticonderoga, New York (later called Addison Junction), north to Port Henry and its nearby iron mines. Rails, ties, equipment, motor power, and even workers for this isolated section of track had to come by water.

Thus, by 1870, two fingers of a projected through route along the west side of Lake Champlain had been extended. Completion of the route would certainly take much northern and western traffic from the Vermont Central, because the route was direct to the south and New York City. Page leased the Whitehall and Plattsburg and Montreal and Plattsburg in 1870.

If anything, the managers of the Rutland were more aware of these events going on in New York than were the directors of the Vermont Central. They were also aware, perhaps because it was closer to home, of a small railroad being built across Addison County in Vermont. With much local pride and local backing, the Addison Railroad (Figure 5.2) was built in 1870 between Leicester Junction on the Rutland main line and Shoreham, where it came to a dead end on the shores of Lake Champlain. A dead end? The Rutland management did not think so, and with great rapidity in 1871, they leased the Addison Railroad and threw a floating bridge across Lake Champlain to effect a connection with the Whitehall and Plattsburg. Although the bridge had a propensity for frequently dumping trains into the waters of the lake and was a menace to navigation, it was a far greater threat to the Vermont Central Railroad.

The upstart road from nowhere to nowhere suddenly had rail and steamboat connections to the north and west, to the Hudson Valley and New York City on the southwest, and to Boston and Long Island Sound on the southeast. It also had its own marble-hauling business, and the growing lumber business from Burlington. In short, the Rutland had connections and was going places.

The directors of the Vermont Central were in shock. With completion of the railroad along the west side of Lake Champlain in the offing, with the *Oakes Ames* still churning back and forth, and with the connection to the south enjoyed by the Rutland, frustration, irritation, and consternation best St. Albans.

On December 31, 1870, the Vermont Central Railroad gave the Rutland Railroad its greatest Christmas present: a twenty-year lease of the Rutland Railroad Company, which involved a payment of $376,000 in the first year and a total payment over twenty years of $7.14 million. And more: a $10,000 yearly rental of the *Oakes Ames*, an 1,100-ton steamer than the Vermont Central no longer had any use for. For the next twenty years, the stockholders of the Rutland Railroad Company could look forward to receiving more income from their investment than if the line had remained independent.

After 1870, only one major railroad ran in Vermont, the Vermont Central, combining the rails of the old Rutland in its network. But the Rutland was not dead yet as a corporate entity, and many other events were to transpire before the present railway pattern evolved.

The Portland and Ogdensburg

By 1870, the primary railroad network was oriented mainly north and south. Figure 5.2 shows, however, that many railroads were built after this date, most only to serve local interests or provide access to local raw materials. But there was one attempt to forge a direct east–west route across northern New England.

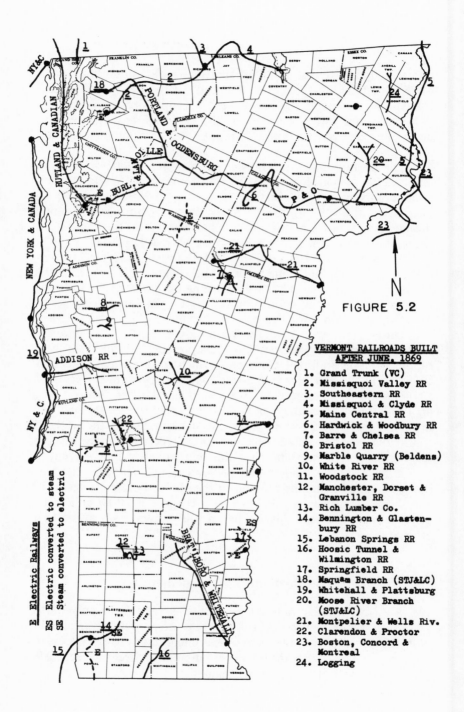

FIGURE 5.2

VERMONT RAILROADS BUILT
AFTER JUNE, 1869

1. Grand Trunk (VC)
2. Missisquoi Valley RR
3. Southeastern RR
4. Missisquoi & Clyde RR
5. Maine Central RR
6. Hardwick & Woodbury RR
7. Barre & Chelsea RR
8. Bristol RR
9. Marble Quarry (Beldens)
10. White River RR
11. Woodstock RR
12. Manchester, Dorset & Granville RR
13. Rich Lumber Co.
14. Bennington & Glastenbury RR
15. Lebanon Springs RR
16. Hoosic Tunnel & Wilmington RR
17. Springfield RR
18. Maquam Branch (STJ&LC)
19. Whitehall & Plattsburg
20. Moose River Branch (STJ&LC)
21. Montpelier & Wells Riv.
22. Clarendon & Proctor
23. Boston, Concord & Montreal
24. Logging

E Electric Railways

ES Electric converted to steam
SE Steam converted to electric

The Portland and Ogdensburg was part of a grand scheme assembled by Portland, Maine, interests to effect a direct route to the Great Lakes and thus divert traffic from Boston. The Vermont sections of the P&O consisted of the Essex County Railroad, the Montpelier and St. Johnsbury (never to get near Montpelier), and the Lamoille Valley Railroad. The route from the New Hampshire border to Swanton was built piecemeal, but finally completed in 1877.

Connecting with the Mountain Division of the Maine Central at the Connecticut River, the line had reasonably easy going as far as St. Johnsbury, but the section west of there over the hills of Danville and Walden was hard going. Grades were excessive, often requiring helper locomotives, and curves were sharp. The great curve at Greensboro Bend, where the line leaves the Lamoille Valley and rises into Walden, is reminiscent of the famous Horseshoe Curve of the Pennsylvania Railroad as it ascends the Allegheny Front at Altoona, Pennsylvania.

The summit elevation of 1,700 feet in Walden Heights is the highest of any present Vermont railroad, and winter conditions are severe. The ascent from Greenboro Bend in eight miles averages a grade of seventy feet per mile.

Irrespective of physical obstacles, the line was pushed to completion with the enthusiasm and backing of Governor Horace Fairbanks (1876–1878) of St. Johnsbury. Railroad ownership had become a key to political success in Vermont.

Following the Lamoille River as far as Cambridge Junction, the route swings away from the river and crosses into the Missisquoi Valley at a low elevation of 430 feet in East Fletcher and continues to Sheldon (and its famous Springs) before swinging west to Swanton.

There, in 1877, the railroad financially and physically came to an end. With no real connection to the west, and the Central Vermont unwilling to give the P&O traffic, the road was in receivership for the first of several times. In 1880 the old P&O was gone forever, and a reorganized company, the St. Johnsbury and Lake Champlain Railroad, took over operations of the poorly ballasted, rough, and rusty track. The "Slow, Jerky and Long Coming" was aptly named.

The new company, desperately seeking a western connection, in 1880 built the Maquam Branch to the shore of Lake Champlain, purchased a small steamer, and hoped that some freight and excursion traffic would materialize. Little did, and though the longest railroad covered bridge in Vermont still stands, spanning the Missisquoi River in Swanton, the branch was abandoned in 1917.

In 1877, the Burlington and Lamoille Valley Railroad had been completed from Burlington, through Essex Junction, to a connection with the Portland and Ogdensburg at Cambridge Junction. Burlington, already having the Rutland and the Central Vermont (which had been reorganized out of the old Vermont Central in 1873), could hardly be expected to provide much traffic for the new road, and the Burlington and Lamoille never amounted to much, finally being abandoned and torn up in the 1930s.

The B&L, however, originally chartered as the Northern Vermont & Lake Champlain Railroad, did contribute to the fame of Essex Junction as the most confusing railroad junction in Vermont. With the Central Vermont lines reaching north, west, and south, and now the B&L lines intersecting, five lines converged at the center of the village. Conductors, rather than calling out "Painesville," as the train slowed to a stop, would be calling out "Essex Junction." Stories are told of the confusion of travelers as they attempted to change trains. The following poem is said to have been written by Hon. Edward J. Phelps, who at one time was Comptroller of the Currency and Minister to England. The Hon. Mr. Phelps apparently left Burlington on the local to Essex Junction, where he was to change to the Boston train. As he waited for his main-line train to arrive, there was the normal switching and shuffling of trains. He then boarded what he thought was his Boston train, only to find that he was returning to Burlington on the same train that he had left only a few minutes before. In frustration he is said to have written:

With saddened face and battered hat
And eye that told of blank despair,
On wooden bench the traveler sat,
Cursing the fate that brought him there.
"Nine hours," he cried, "we've lingered here
With thoughts intent on distant homes,
Waiting for that delusive train
That, always coming, never comes,
Till weary, worn distressed, forlorn
And paralyzed in every function!
I hope in hell his soul may dwell
Who first invented Essex Junction!

"I've traveled east, I've traveled west
　Over mountain, valley, plain and river;
Midst whirlwind's wrath and tempest's blast,
　Through railroad's crash and steamboat's shiver
And faith and courage faltered not,
　Nor strength gave way nor hope was shaken,
Until I reached this dismal spot,
　Of man accursed, of God, forsaken!
Where strange, new forms of misery
　Assail men's souls without compunction,
　　And I hope in hell his soul may dwell
Who first invented Essex Junction!

"Here Boston waits for Ogdensburg
　And Ogdensburg for Montreal,
And late New York tarrieth
　And Saratoga hindereth all!
From far Atlantic's wave-swept bays
　To Mississippi's turbid tide
All accidents, mishaps, delays
　Are gathered here and multiplied!
Oh! fellow man, avoid this spot
　As you would plague or Peter Funk shun!
　　And I hope in hell his soul may dwell
Who first invented Essex Junction!

"And long and late conductors tell
　Of trains delayed or late or slow,
Till e'en the very engine's bell
　Takes up the cry, 'No go! No go!'
Oh! let me from this hole depart
　By any route, so't be a long one."
He cried, with madness in his heart,
　And jumped aboard a train—the wrong one.
And as he vanished in the smoke
　He shouted with redoubled unction,
　　"I hope in hell his soul may dwell
Who first invented Essex Junction."

　The St. Johnsbury and Lake Champlain next attempted to complete its line to Rouses Point, New York, where the long-awaited connection with the Ogdensburg and Lake Champlain would become a reality. In 1884, soon after tracks were laid and bridges built, the road was leased to the Boston and Lowell Railroad. Among the directors were men who also served on the Central Vermont. The Central Vermont could hardly condone tracks of a rival railroad paralleling their own. The tracks were torn up some six months after being laid, and this abortive attempt is not even shown in Figure 5.2.

In 1895 the St.J.&L.C. became part of the Boston and Maine (the successor to the Boston & Lowell), and with better connections some prosperity finally came to the struggling Vermont line. The B&M controlled the St.J.&L.C. until 1925, by which time the railroad owed the B&M some $5.5 million. The 1927 flood washed away most of the roadbed and also washed away any hopes that the management might have had of making the railroad a going concern. The St. Johnsbury and Lake Champlain received $195,000 from the State of Vermont to restore service, the first of many handouts the railroad was to receive in the coming years.

Finally, in 1944, the road was declared bankrupt, still owing the B&M several million dollars. Such was its poverty that upon reorganization the same lettering was used on the rolling stock and locomotives, except that now the "L.C." stood for "Lamoille County," rather than "Lake Champlain." Because the Maquam Branch had been abandoned in 1917, the new name was more appropriate anyway.

Two other branches had been built by the railroad during its checkered history, and both, in their time, provided some needed traffic. The Victory Branch, sometimes called the Moose River Branch, was built into the wilds of Essex County to tap the forest resource. Built in 1885, the logging railroads were abandoned in 1900, and the branch line was finally torn up in 1917. Today little remains of even the roadbed, although bridge abutments of Kirby granite can still be seen.

The Hardwick and Woodbury Railroad was constructed in 1896 to carry granite from the Woodbury quarries to the mills in Hardwick. Said to have had the steepest grades and some of the sharpest curves in the eastern United States, the rails were torn up in 1940 when the quarries were abandoned.

Meanwhile, the old St.J.&L.C. was struggling along. After the 1944 reorganization, the B&M still held the securities of the railroad. In 1947 the road was purchased by several on-line shippers, including the Eastern Magnesia Tac Company, with its mines and mill in Johnson, and in 1954 the Rubberoid Corporation, with its asbestos mine on Belvidere Mountain, took a stock interest. In 1957, the Maine Central Railroad attempted to buy the entire line, already having leased and eventually purchased the section from St. Johnsbury eastward in 1912. In 1959, however, the line was purchased by H. E. Salzburg Company, and deterioration continued. Having petitioned for abandonment in 1966, the road passed to Mr. Samuel Pinsley. During 1972 it had thirty-seven major derailments, and in November 1972 a turbine for a ship under construction at the Bath Ironworks in Maine was unceremoniously dumped into the Lamoille River. The line was embargoed—one would have thought this was the end, and a fitting one, too.

But the agony has been prolonged. In 1973 the State of Vermont persuaded Pinsley to keep going, and in that year finally purchased the property for $1,265,000. For a brief time in 1973 the railroad was again known as the Lamoille Valley Railroad, but the name never appeared on the equipment. In 1974, it again became the St.J.&L.C. when the state persuaded Morrison Knudsen Company of Boise, Idaho, to run the trouble-plagued line. Subsequently, local shippers have been operating the road, initially under the name Vermont Northern Railroad, and more recently as the Lamoille Valley Railroad once again! Nearly $3 million in state and federal funds have gone into upgrading the track and other improvements. Trains can now travel the whole line at twenty miles an hour, a considerable improvement over the ten miles an hour of the early 1970s.

In retrospect, one can look at the winding rails and consider the suitability of the right-of-way as a cross-Vermont snowmobile trail or bicycle route. But emotional arguments in 1973 depicted the old railroad as the economic lifeline of northern Vermont, and the state Legislature decided at that time to acquire the property, as it had already done with parts of the old Rutland system.

By some economic criteria, minimal justification might be found for the old right-of-way, but the railroad is still a part of the fabric of northern Vermont. Erastus Fairbanks's dream of a railroad connecting Portland to the Great Lakes died early, but perhaps the most poorly planned railroad in the United States is still chugging along after many other lines were fewer problems are nothing more than raised mounds of earth marking their former roadbeds.

Other Post-1870 Railroads

The old P&O, because it represented a dream, is a fascinating railroad. The rest of the lines on the map have less romance, but were in their time important to the local promoters who saw *their* railroad as bringing prosperity to *their* communities. Many have had little written about them, but because many of them represent visible testimony to much of Vermont's nineteenth-century geography, they deserve some mention.

All sorts of activity took place in northeast Vermont and adjoining ares of New Hampshire. The Maine Central built a line northward from its Mountain Division along the Connecticut River through Guildhall and Maidstone, Vermont. This branch continued through Beecher's Falls and on into Quebec, and for several years was a main line of the Maine Central, with through traffic from Quebec City to Portland. Competition with the parallel Grand Trunk through Island Pond eventually led to abandonment of much of the line. The stretch through Maidstone and Guildhall is now gone, and the line terminates at the Ethan Allen furniture plant in Beecher's Falls.

The remainder of the line, which runs from Groveton, New Hampshire north to Beecher's Falls, was severely damaged in 1973 floods, and was put up for final abandonment by the Maine Central. Shutting it down would have deeply affected the one Vermont customer of the line, the furniture plant, and the Northeast Kingdom was much alarmed. Subsequently the railroad repaired the damage, and the line was purchased by the state of New Hampshire, through which all but a mile of the track runs. Because the only important shipper is in Vermont, one wonders at such generosity. The answer is that the plant employs a large number of New Hampshire citizens and is the only large employer in the area. It is now the North Stratford Railroad.

A network of logging railroads was built along the East Branch of the Nulhegan River in Bloomfield, Lewis, and Averill. These were torn up in about 1920 but scattered remains can still be found. Now the area is laced with logging roads providing access for fishermen and hunters. Maps still show Camp 4, Camp 2, Camp 10, and others, a legacy of the old railroad days.

Woodsville, New Hampshire, became a prime railway junction, as did Wells River, when the Montpelier and Wells River Railroad was built in the early 1870s. Again, dreams of a successful east–west railroad across northern New England with the Montpelier and Wells River forging a final link, the road never amounted to much. Some freight and passenger service was interchanged with the Boston, Concord and Montreal across the river after a stupendous covered, double-deck railway bridge was built. Like many short lines that came of great dreams, most space in the timetables was taken up with advertising. The Montpelier and Wells River finally expired in the late 1950s. Its major on-line customer was at Rickers Mills, where at one time the oldest stationary sawmill in the United States turned out 150,000 board feet of softwood lumber annually. Rickers is now included in Groton State Forest, parts of the old roadbed are hiking tails, and the weathered grave of Joseph Ricker is in the Groton cemetery nearby.

Before leaving northern Vermont and the attempts at east–west rail connections, one link remains, not because of its on-line traffic, but because of its present ownership and its through traffic. In about 1880 the Southeastern Railroad built a line from Canada south to Richford, there effecting a connection with the Missisquoi and Clyde Railroad, which followed the Missisquoi valley from Richford to North Troy and Newport. The M&C, as it follows the river, is forced to bend northward into Quebec and shows as the loop on the map along the northern border of the state. Now part of the Canadian Pacific system, it remains an important freight route, for it connects with the CP line in Newport, and the old Connecticut and Passumpsic River road. The only important Vermont shipper is a grain mill in Richford.

This Missisquoi Valley Railroad was built from St. Albans to Richford and is now part of the Central Vermont. The Central Vermont now also controls this line that was originally built as a branch of the Grand Trunk to connect with the Vermont Central in East Alburg. That small line (number 1 in Figure 5.2) is now the main line of the Central Vermont to Montreal.

Another short Vermont railroad with business purely in raw materials was the Montpelier and Barre, formerly a part of the Barre and Chelsea. Even though the road never got to Chelsea, a branch at one time did extend to Williamstown (1888), and the steep roadbed can still be seen through Williamstown Gulf. One could pity Mr. Paine if he had tried to push his Vermont Central through that narrow gap back in 1849. The M&B served primarily the granite industry of Barre and, when judged vital to the economic well-being of the area, was purchased by the state of Vermont late in 1980. It is now the Washington County Railroad.

Other Vermont railroads were primarily built for accessibility to local raw materials before the automobile era. Or even if they had been built with greater aspirations, it was often raw materials or some specialized use that kept them going as long as they did.

In Middlebury and in Brandon, short lines were built from the Rutland to tap marble quarries. The two spurs in Brandon, less than a few hundred yards in length, are not shown on the map. In Manchester the Rich Lumber Company built a fantastic logging railroad with switchbacks directly up the side of the Green Mountains in 1912. The road was abandoned in 1919 when the mill burned, but the old roadbed can still be traced.

Similarly, in 1872 the Bennington and Glastenbury Railroad was built ten miles into the forests of that now unincorporated town. When the forests were depleted by 1895, the tracks were shortened, the road electrified for excursion traffic, and the line was renamed the Bennington and Woodford. The roadbed, wiped out by a flood in 1898, was never rebuilt.

The B&W was the only railroad in Vermont to start as a steam road, only to be electrified, but another started as an electric railway in 1897 and was converted to steam. The Springfield Railroad, now the Springfield Terminal Railroad, is owned and operated by the machine-tool companies in Springfield. The bridge across the Connecticut River to Charlestown, New Hampshire, now shared with a highway, is the only remaining toll bridge across the river between the two states. The "Rates of Toll" sign is a classic.

When the many independent marble companies in the West Rutland and Proctor area were combined into the Vermont Marble Company in 1892, the company in the following year built the Clarendon & Proctor Railroad, which remained as a wholly owned subsidiary of the company for many years. Its name was later changed to the Clarendon and Pittsford when branches extended into that town. Another raw-material road, much of the C&P trackage remains as part of the Vermont Railway, but it operates as an independent entity still hauling the little structural marble now produced. Most traffic today consists of ground marble.

Except for a pair of incline railroads powered by stationary steam engines reaching marble quarries on Dorset Mountain in Dor-

The imposing brick station is in back of this Historic Site sign.

The toll sign on the privately owned bridge across the Connecticut River in Springfield.

The rickety wooden trestle of the Mount Mansfield Electric Railway spans the valley of Bryant Brook in this 1920 photograph. The Waterbury Center School is in the background. One of several short electric lines in Vermont, this one was important for the development of Stowe as a major ski resort.

set, the only other raw-material-based railroad was the unique little Hoosac Tunnel and Wilmington. It was affectionately called the "Hoot, Toot and Whistle," or perhaps more objectively the "Hold Tight and Worry," as it navigated the cliffs along the twisting Deerfield River on its way to Readsboro and eventually Wilmington. It was built from a junction with the Troy and Greenfield Railroad at the east portal of the Hoosac Tunnel to Readsboro in 1885, and its duty was to transport pulp for the new mill built in Readsboro (1882). Holyoke, Massachusetts paper companies had invested considerable capital in acquiring the forests in the Readsboro area, and had also financed construction of the mill itself.

Initially chartered and built as the Deerfield River Railroad Company, its name was changed to the HT&W in the following year, and it was known by that name until its demise in 1970.

Like many other railroads, the last name of the corporate title reflected the optimism of the investors and directors. The HT&W *did* eventually get to Wilmington. In 1892 the first train ascended the Deerfield Valley from the Hoosac Tunnel base elevation of 770 feet to the newly constructed depot in Wilmington at 1,560 feet, some twenty-four miles away at an average grade of thirty-three feet per mile.

Wilmington developed a small base in forest-products industries as a result of the railroad, but did not see the prosperity that had been brought to Readsboro downstream; population of the latter increased from seven hundred to nine hundred in two years after arrival of the tracks.

Operations on the road were tough right from the start, with the ever-present derailments and runaway cars careening down the steep grades and around the too-numerous curves. But the extension to Wilmington, and eventually the entire line, was done in by water-power, when the Harriman Reservoir was built and flooded much of the right of way. Although in 1923 a new route was constructed bypassing the reservoir, little traffic developed, and the extension was finally abandoned in 1937. Little wonder: one section of the track rose 180 feet in just one-half mile! The stretch downstream from Readsboro was later demolished with the construction of the New England Power Company pumped storage plant at Bear Swamp.

Winding its way through the dissected plateau of southern Vermont, the HT&W was a scenic and easily accessible mountain railroad. For a while it enjoyed substantial tourist traffic.

The Deerfield Valley is now quiet except for the snarl of chain saws and the whir of turbines in the power plants. But at one time the hills echoed to the puffing and chuffing of the little HT&W locomotive. These lines were penned by E. A. Fitch of Wilmington in 1892:

> Did we ever hear a music
> > Sweeter than the one that thrills
> As it floats along the Deerfield
> > As it echoes o'er the hills?
> How we watch that little engine
> > As it stalks across the plain;
> Was there ever music sweeter,
> Was there ever sight completer
> > Than the coming of the train?

(From *Hoot, Toot and Whistle* by Bernard J. Carmen. Used with permission of the copyright owners, Stephen Green Press, Brattleboro, Vt., 1963.)

Another Vermont railroad with an optimistic title was the Brattleboro and Whitehall. Though it never got closer to Whitehall, New York, than sixty miles away in Londonderry, at least it had one end anchored in Brattleboro. Conceived as a through route across the Green Mountains of southern Vermont, it was initially built as a narrow-gauge line in 1880 along the banks of the West River. That was one of its major problems—sometimes the banks were too steep, the rails too low, the bends of the river too sharp. Every freshet was likely to wash out some section of the track.

Along with real problems in engineering, the "thirty-six miles of trouble" never really went anywhere. Londonderry was no Burlington or Rutland, and the only important on-line source of revenue was the granite quarry on Black Mountain in Dummerston, a few miles from Brattleboro.

The name was changed to the West River Railroad in 1905 when the road was taken over by the Central Vermont and was converted to standard gauge (4 feet 8½ inches). Horribly mangled by the 1927 flood, the CV turned the railroad back to local interest in the 1930s and after attempts to keep going—through local pride more than economic justification, the WRRR gave up the ghost for the last time in 1936. The only on-line traffic ended in 1942 when the quarry closed. The last remaining track was torn up in that year.

The shortest railroad in Vermont history appropriately carried the longest title. The Manchester, Dorset and Granville was built in 1903 for five miles west of Manchester along the Battenkill. Locally called the "Mud, Dirt and Gravel" because of its major traffic, it collapsed for all time in 1925. One wonders how it lasted that long.

The Bristol Railroad was built as a branch from the Rutland in 1892 and lasted until 1940. It was six miles long. Traffic was nearly all passengers and the railroad had little other excuse for existence.

Passenger traffic did, however, keep one Vermont road solvent for several years, mostly because of the famous Sanatoga Springs at its terminus. The Woodstock Railroad was constructed in 1874 in the declining years of the mineral spring era, and one must conclude that the high per capita income of the town of Woodstock kept the railroad going until 1933. One of the most expensive engineering works on any Vermont railroad was the $509,000 trestle across Queechee Gorge, which is used by the present highway.

The White River Railroad, twenty miles long, was built along the White River itself, rather than one of its branches. Promoted by local interests, it came much too late to become a real railroad. There was little on-line traffic except the talc mines at Talcville south of Rochester, but traffic from the mines delivered to the railroad by another incline railroad kept it going for a few additional years. A logging branch into Pittsfield also provided some traffic. Although it connected to the Central Vermont in Bethel, the CV never wanted any part of the line, and it existed, if that is the word, from 1902 to 1933, when, like so many marginal roads, it collapsed during the depression. The old depot in Rochester is now a private home, the old engine house houses a contracting firm, and the square, boxlike cheese factory is still there. Otherwise little remains.

The Rutland and Central Vermont Again

Over in western Vermont, the Rutland and the Central Vermont were still at it. Forced into leasing the Rutland in 1870 because of crafty John Page, the Central found itself with the *Oakes Ames*, a steamboat it no longer needed, and the Whitehall and Plattsburg and the Montreal and Plattsburg that it really didn't need either.

Then the depression of 1873 struck. The Vermont Central was reorganized into the Central Vermont, and soon disposed of all its

Rutland-acquired properties except the Addison Railroad and the primary railroad system. The eager buyer was the Delaware and Hudson Canal Company, which was interested in expanding its market for anthracite coal from the Wyoming Valley of Pennsylvania. The D&H had long been seeking connections to Canada, and with acquisition of the New York and Canada Railroad along the west side of Lake Champlain in 1875, and the scattered sections acquired from the Central Vermont, that goal became a reality. By this time, starting with the old *Oakes Ames*, the Delaware and Hudson also controlled most long-distance steamboat traffic on Lake Champlain. The Central Vermont lease arrangements with the Rutland remained in force.

Faced with growing D&H competition, in 1890 the Central Vermont renewed its lease of the Rutland for ninety-nine years. With the Delaware and Hudson in control of lines on the west side of Lake Champlain and with a direct route to New York and the Middle Atlantic states, the CV could only hope that its tenuous connection to the south on the former Lebanon Springs Railroad could be protected. Its routes to Boston and Connecticut remained ensured.

In 1898 the Central Vermont lease of the Ogdensburg and Lake Champlain was declared void because the Central had not made payments for two years. Assured of its northern connections to Montreal and the rest of Canada, the CV had to allow the D&H, through its New York and Canada tracks, to take all traffic destined for New York.

The loss of the O&LC was to hurt the CV because of the kind of traffic on the line. A Mr. Jonas Wilder, who had been the Central Vermont representative in Rouses Point, New York in 1851, had developed insulated boxcars for rapid shipment of perishable butter. The Central Vermont for years ran a weekly "butter train," from the Northern Railroad of New York, which was remarkably successful. Improvements on Wilder's invention were the refrigerated cars of the 1890s, which allowed rapid transportation of more-perishable fluid milk. The Central Vermont was to enjoy the butter trade, but could not take advantage of the later fluid-milk trade from northern New York. This commodity was to keep many northern New England railroads alive far beyond the time when they normally would have expired.

In 1894 came another severe depression. The Central Vermont, burdened with payments to both the Ogdensburg and Lake Champlain and the Rutland, defaulted. The Rutland was cast adrift in 1896 to fight for its own survival. Still, the Rutland would not have the necessary northern connections, and so the Central was not bothered by this treatment as it was about the loss of the Ogdensburg and Lake Champlain, and its butter traffic.

In 1896, when the Rutland had been presented with its forced and unwilling freedom, it had a desperate fight for survival. For two years the road had been nursed along by the Delaware and Hudson because that road feared a strong Central Vermont far more than it did a weak Rutland.

In 1898, Percival W. Clement acquired the Rutland shares held by the D&H. He assumed the presidency of the road, and, following tradition, became governor in 1919. Since 1870 the Rutland had not had any local control, first being a division of the Central Vermont for twenty-six years, and then a ward of the D&H for two more. Though it still had little money, the Rutland set out to improve itself.

The last main-line railroad built in Vermont was the Rutland and Canadian, thrown across long marble-block causeways from Burlington forty miles north through the Champlain islands. The Rutland literally went to sea, but it was the only way that the struggling railroad could secure a northern connection. The route swung westward in Alburg to effect a connection with the O&LC, and the road also continued due north into Canada, via the Rutland and Noyan Railroad. Built in only a year, the Rutland and Canadian was a spectacularly scenic railroad. Constructed mostly 1899, it officially became part of the Rutland in the following year. But the map shows its trackage as exactly paralleling that of the rival Central Vermont; it was doomed from the start.

This was a very expensive stretch of track to build. The causeways alone cost the Rutland in the vicinity of $1 million. But sitting in one of the directors was Dr. William Seward Webb, and some New York Central (Vanderbilt) money was involved.

While this expansion was going on, the Rutland also bought control of the O&LC, by this time referred to as the "Old and Late Coming" because of track deterioration brought on by several years of freedom from the Central Vermont. The price tag was high, more than $5 million in 1899. More than that, the Rutland also purchased the Ogdensburg Transportation Company (the Great Lakes ship division of the O&LC) for another $1,100,000. That immediately became the Rutland Transit Company. The little Rutland by 1900 had spent more than $8 million to get a northern and western connection. The small line could never recoup that amount of money.

The Rutland now controlled, owned, or leased a 392-mile line from the Great Lakes and Canada to New York, to Long Island Sound, and to Boston. The dream of fifty years had become a reality. But the Rutland was also destitute. The drive for non-Vermont traffic, the lifeblood of any major railroad ever to operate in Vermont, was to cause its eventual dissolution.

The system was now inflated, broke, and in desperate need of more money, and indeed, more traffic. William Seward Webb, son-in-law of Commodore Vanderbilt of the New York Central, ascended to the throne in 1902, and for a while the New York Central fertilized the Rutland. The Central routed many freight cars over the Rutland, and the on-line milk traffic contributed to many successful financial years under New York Central control. Express passenger trains flew over the Rutland tracks from Montreal to New York, although they had to slow considerably over the Corkscrew Division south of Bennington.

Unfortunately for the Rutland, the Webb era did not last long enough. Boxcars once proudly lettered "The New York System" soon found their logos dated. The romance of the Rutland with the New York Central came to an end in 1915, and on top of it, Dr. Webb never became governor of Vermont, a position he had coveted. The Webb legacy in Vermont can still be seen at the Shelburne Museum, even to the private cars and the station moved from Shelburne to the museum grounds.

During World War I, both the Rutland and the Central Vermont were taken over by the federal government. In 1919, broken-down boxcars and locomotive equipment that had seen much better days were returned to the railroads. The Panama Canal Act of 1915 divested the Rutland of its expensively bought Great Lakes connections, the Act requiring that no company could control both water and rail transport.

After 1915, the Rutland Railroad Company had a harder and harder time of it. The Central Vermont, acquired by the Canadian National in 1929, continued to have good origin and destination traffic. The Rutland, having to rely primarily on milk and stone from on-line shippers, continued to falter. Trucks began to carry fluid milk. The end came in 1950 when the road became bankrupt for the last time. It was then organized into the Rutland Railway (rather than Railroad), and struggled along for a few more years. The corporate ghost was not quite ready to expire.

Death finally came in September 1961, when the strikebound Rutland, its passenger and milk traffic only a fading memory, called it quits. No one could believe that the road was at last going to expire until then President William Ginsberg filed on December 4, 1961 with the Interstate Commerce Commission for permission to abandon the entire 331 miles of line from Ogdensburg to Bennington and to Bellows Falls.

Vermont could not let the old lady go peacefully. On-line shippers cried that they needed the line. Communities forecast economic ruination. In 1963 the state appropriated $2.7 million to acquire the Rutland tracks within Vermont.

The former Rutland management disposed of the Old and Late Coming for its salvage value and the tracks were removed across northern New York. The former Rutland and Canadian trackage through Grand Isle County was torn up. In 1964 the Vermont Resources Research Center at the University of Vermont urged that the beautiful right-of-way be retained for recreational use. This sensible step was not taken, and most of the old roadbed was sold to adjoining property owners or other buyers. The state retains ownership of limited sections. The striking marble causeways filled with rock from West Rutland and Proctor are favorite fishing spots, but some boat enthusiasts claim they are a menace to navigation. Others maintain that the causeways should be demolished, for they isolate the northeast part of Lake Champlain (the "Inland Sea" section) from the main body of the lake, contributing to accelerated eutrophication in that portion of the lake.

Without a connection to the north, the present Vermont Railway has only traffic that originates or terminates on the line. It has about 150 customers between Burlington and Bennington, and as in the past, considerably more traffic is terminated than originated. Major freight arriving in Vermont (about 360,000 tons annually) consists primarily of dairy feed and other agricultural products, road salt, lumber, coal, propane, gasoline, and fuel oil. Originating traffic, about 92,000 tons, is primarily raw materials: limestone chips, white pigment for paints, structural marble, paper, and other forest products. With greater hindsight than foresight, the northern connection is now missed. The Vermont Railway, no longer burdened with debt, is reasonably prosperous and could handle thru traffic once more. But the causeways will remain empty of track forever.

The old Bellows Falls subdivision of the Rutland was leased in 1963 to F. Nelson Blount, operator of the Monadnock, Steamtown, and Northern in New Hampshire, and owner and founding father of the Steamtown railroad museum, formerly in Bellows Falls. The Green Mountain Railroad now operates the trackage from the Rutland town line to Bellows Falls, all traffic within Rutland itself being handled by the Vermont Railway.

Total freight tonnage handled by the GMRR is about 130,000 tons annually through one daily round trip along the line. Fifteen customers account for this amount, of which about 80 percent is originating traffic, mainly from the talc mines in Ludlow and Gassetts, just north of Chester. Some bridge traffic comes from the Vermont Railway and D&H in Rutland. The ruling 1.8 percent grades still challenge the road, and freight trains of more than twelve cars normally require a helper locomotive.

Railroads in Retrospect

The railways of Vermont had an even greater influence on the state than the canals that preceded them.

The once arduous journey by stage to someplace outside of or within Vermont had become a comfortable, quick, and inexpensive journey for travelers. No longer did teams of oxen and horses have to struggle up steep grades with heavily loaded wagons full of goods that the state could not produce. No longer would wood have to be floated down the White River, with its shallow bottlenecks, to distant markets.

The railways brought Vermont and its people much closer to the rest of the United States. And they brought people from the rest of the United States into Vermont. The iron horse was directly responsible for the development and maturity of the state's recreation business, today a vital part of the Vermont economy.

The rails were influential in helping extract Vermont's raw-material wealth. Expansion of the granite, marble, slate, talc, and copper deposits was rapid after 1850. Lumber and pulp went out in significant quantities, and the railroads were directly involved in

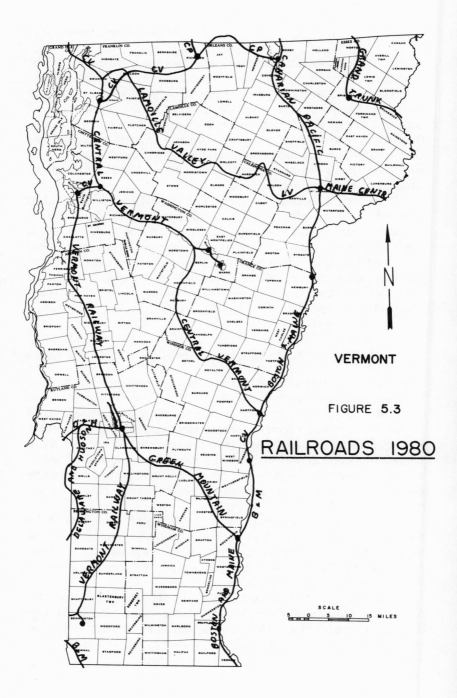

VERMONT

FIGURE 5.3

RAILROADS 1980

SCALE

5 0 5 10 15 MILES

N

Burlington's ascendancy as a leading sawmilling center in the 1870s.

The ease of transportation wrought by the often poorly laid tracks led to development of industry. Factories for the first time were not geared to supply only the local needs of a self-sufficient population, but looked to far wider markets. Vermont pine and hardwood furniture sold widely throughout the country, Vermont monuments began to stand in every cemetery in the northeast. Vermont wood was fashioned into axe and shovel handles, carpenter's squares were manufactured in Shaftsbury. Vermont even had its own automobile industry in Barre at the turn of the century.

As employment grew, the nineteenth-century tide of emigration slowed as jobs became available to Vermont farmers squeezed off their marginal farms. Laborers from many countries moved to Springfield and Windsor with the machine-tool industry, to Rutland with its stone and other industries. In Burlington, in Barre, in St. Albans, in Winooski, significant new elements in the population gave a different character to the old Yankee towns and villages.

No longer was it necessary for Vermont farmers to produce for the local market alone, or to produce a nonperishable product (wool). Mr. Wilder's invention made it possible for dairying to dominate agriculture. First cheese, then butter, then fluid milk rapidly shipped to urban markets became the lifeblood of Vermont farming. Cheese factories and creameries and later milk shipping plants were located along all rail lines, and provided employment for far more people than just the farmers supplying the raw material.

The Slow, Jerky and Long Coming, the Old and Late Coming, the Hold Tight and Worry, and the Thirty-Six Miles of Trouble, romantic and often curiosities to be sure, all managed to change the fabric of Vermont totally from what had gone before.

6

Nineteenth-Century Recreation

The railways made it easier for people to leave Vermont, but they also made it easier for people to come. And then, as now, most came to enjoy the delights of the land of the Green Mountains. Few settled permanently in the state, but many made annual trips to the many resorts catering to the pleasure seeker. Early visitors told of the beauty and Vermont's reputation as a recreation area of the northeast was ensured.

The two major attractions of the north country were the many mountain houses, perched atop nearly every elevation in the state, and the mineral springs that were developed to satisfy the needs of a population seeking not only improved health, but rest and relaxation as well.*

By 1840, eight families in Clarendon, Vermont, had produced one hundred and thirteen children, ninety-nine of whom attended the same school. Besides inordinate fertility, they had one thing in common—they drank the same water. Later, one man, perhaps seeking the fountain of youth, is reported to have consumed in one day one hundred and twenty-five tumblers of the same water "without injurious effects." Over in Middletown Springs, Vermont, another wrote that "in using less than a case of water procured from your company, my whole system has been benefited and my headache well nigh cured."

Whatever the cause or the circumstance, in an age of medical innocence, mineral springs throughout the United States promised

---

*Much of this chapter appeared as an article in *Vermont History* (Winter 1979), and my thanks to the Vermont Historical Society for allowing inclusion of the material here.

relief for every affliction in an atmosphere of relaxation and enjoyment. Thousands of resorts developed, almost overnight, to take advantage of those who desperately wished to be restored to health. Normally the worse the water tasted, the more beneficial it was thought to be.

One writer commented, "All Philadelphia was agog in the spring of 1773 with the news of the discovery of a mineral well on a vacant lot . . . just across from the State House." Subsequently it was determined that the "slight fetid smell" which had set the spring apart as a medicinal wonder was traced to a "neighboring necessary."

The same writer, however, makes the important point that the "North's first interest in the rural areas, other than for the staples of trade they produced and consumed, came in search for health in an era when the nature of disease was actually unknown." The railways for the first time made it possible for large numbers of people to do just that.

So it was with Vermont and the rest of northern New England. As knowledge of the wonderful healing qualities of the mineral waters spread, those seeking both the "cure" and relaxation began summer pilgrimages to the many spas developing to satisfy their needs. Perhaps the most affluent went to Saratoga, New York, or Poland Spring, Maine, but many came to Vermont as well. One exaggerated report was that Vermont's Clarendon Springs Hotel was a "mecca of the Rockefellers, Vanderbilts, Morgans and Astors who arrived in horse carriages." While the Rockefellers gravitated to Woodstock, the Clarendon Springs Hotel stood desolate and vacant for many years until recent partial restoration.

In the nineteenth century, two factors brought people to Vermont and northern New England. One impetus was escape form the city's heat by going *up* in elevation. As nearly everyone knows, simple going north in the summer means little relief from the heat, but going *up* does lower temperatures. Vermont had its share of mountain houses, yet the state could not compete with New Hampshire's White Mountains or the cool breezes playing along the coast of Maine.

At one time or another, accommodations were offered on Killington Mountain, Mount Mansfield, Camels Hump, Mount Ascutney, Breadloaf Mountain, Mount Equinox, Mount Anthony (Bennington), and even on Grandview Mountain (now Snake Moun-

The Clarendon Springs Hotel as it appeared in the 1880s (top). After many years of neglect, the structure has been partially repaired (bottom). Top photo by Alec Marshall, bottom by Austin Meeks.

tain) in Addison. There were probably many others as well, like the small shack erected on Mount Cushman above the village of Rochester. Most were small enterprises attached to larger hotels down in the valley towns, and a daily stage would connect the offspring with the parent. W. Storrs Lee, in his *Green Mountains of Vermont*, devotes much space to the old mountain houses, and though they were important in their day, they could not complete with the popularity of the many mineral springs that developed.

What is a mineral spring, really? Actually it is *any* spring. Fantastic claims were made for waters from Equinox, Middletown, Saratoga, Poland, Strafford, Clarendon, Highgate, and innumerable others. European resorts such as Baden-Baden, Harrogate, and Bath promised miraculous cures for their clienteles. In the United States, Warm Springs, Georgia, and White Sulphur Springs, Virginia, made the same promises.

Absolutely no medical evidence has been found that drinking the water from any spring will bring on the miraculous cures promised. At Middletown Springs, several openings were unearthed, and the springs were numbered appropriately. The Middletown Hotel Springs Company suggested that to effect a cure for asthma one should drink Number 3, followed by Number 2, and for relief from piles to drink and wish with Number 1. Perhaps dyspepsia was the horror illness of the age, because one was expected to drink Number 3 or 2, followed by Number 1. For curing diarrhea, it was suggested that the patient drink Number 1, but if chronic and feeble, to try Number 2.

Yet chemical analyses in abundance and statements from cured patients were proffered, always extolling the virtues of this or that establishment. Most analyses show about the same characteristics, except for those of more successful springs, which frequently were based on especially vile-smelling, tasting, or appearing water.

Number of Springs

In *Mineral Waters of the United States and American Spas* (1927), it was reported that at that time, Vermont possessed forty-seven spring localities with seventy-four individual springs, of which eleven were still being used as resorts. Some were listed with descriptive notes and chemical analyses. Many other sources refer to springs not mentioned here. In an attempt to develop as complete an inventory of Vermont Mineral Springs as possible, *Beers' County Atlases* of Vermont were examined. These atlases, available for all counties except Essex, show every structure, road, land ownership, and significant physical feature at the large scale of one and one-half inches to the mile. Although atlases were compiled by different individuals, some more interested in recording groves of maple trees and others more interested in recording mineral springs, nevertheless they remain the best inventory of Vermont land use of the period from 1860 to 1880. According to the atlases, there were 115 springs (mineral, sulphur, medicinal) in the middle to late 1880s. Sixteen others are mentioned in other sources, producing a total of 131 named mineral springs in Vermont in the late 1800s. Not counted are such springs as "Cold Springs" or "Boiling Springs."

At one time or another probably thirty-two spring locations supported hotels. Some, such as Clarendon, Sheldon, Guilford, Highgate, and Middletown, were large and diverse recreation spas with bowling alleys, croquet lawns, bottling works, and livery stables. Others, such as Wheelock, Plainfield, Waterville, Barre, and Hartland, were much smaller, although Wheelock did boast a short-lived bottling works. In North Wolcott, a mineral spring was developed along Wild Branch in 1868 by the Lamoille Spring and Hotel Company. A bridge across the stream was built, and apparently a spring house and hotel were constructed. The enterprise, however, was short-lived, the spring facilities being reported as "in decay" ten years later.

Location of the Springs

Each spring location is shown in Figure 6.1, as well as all offering hotel accommodations. Three factors account in large part for the pattern of locations shown: geology, accessibility to railways, and, for want of a better argument, regional awareness about the possibility of profit to be made from commercial development of a mineral spring. The classic case is Sheldon, with its seven spring-hotel complexes.

Notwithstanding abundant testimonials, the health seeker of the period often wanted visible expression of the water's medicinal

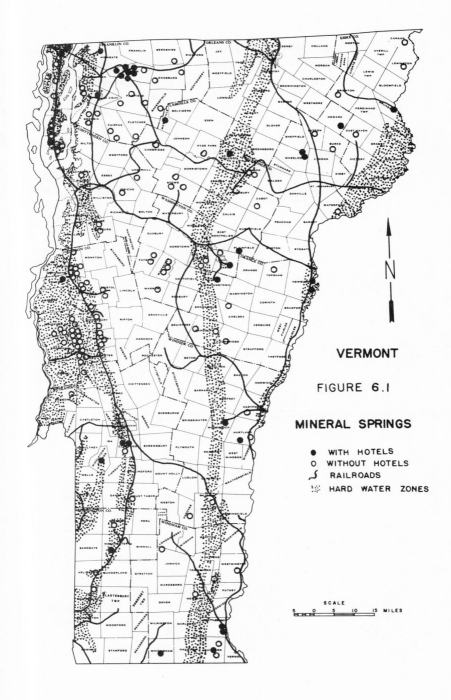

VERMONT

FIGURE 6.1

MINERAL SPRINGS

● WITH HOTELS
O WITHOUT HOTELS
∫ RAILROADS
∴ HARD WATER ZONES

SCALE

5 0   5   10   15 MILES

quality. Crystal-pure spring water, without a good public-relations effort, was not nearly as popular as water that gave off a sulphur odor or had a sulphur taste. Likewise, water issuing from a spring that stained the surrounding rocks with a yellowish or brown slime would be favored for this visible evidence of its mineral qualities.

In 1861, the State Geological Report separated Vermont's mineral springs into two categories: Magnesian springs, especially abundant in the Champlain Valley, were those which deposited calcareous tufa (or travertine), a light brown or yellowish white substance, mainly lime or magnesia. Sulphurous springs, on the other hand, were those with an odor that deposited an ochery substance resembling iron rust on the surrounding rocks. What such waters might to do one's insides is a matter of speculation.

We have no way of knowing which mineral springs were derived from surface runoff as opposed to those from deeper sources in the bedrock. Springs issuing from bedrock are likely to have a greater amount of dissolved solids than those from surface runoff and, all other things being equal, probably are therefore more "mineral." For example, the dissolved solids in the Clarendon Springs Water, issuing from a fissure in marble along the banks of the Clarendon river, have 374.04 parts per million, compared to the 31 parts per million of dissolved solids in the waters of Brunswick Springs, derived from a nearby lake. Those springs with smaller amounts of "mineral" matter probably had to have additional gimmicks to attract clientele; certainly that applied to Brunswick.

Mineral Springs and Bedrock

Like most of New England, the bedrock of Vermont is complex and varies remarkably within small areas. Most of the state is metamorphosed schist and phyllite, with scattered areas of slate and gneiss. Igneous intrusions (granitic rocks) are found in areas in eastern Vermont. Waters there tend to be lower in dissolved solids because the metamorphosed and igneous series are relatively insoluble.

In three roughly parallel north–south zones are Ordivician rocks, which are somewhat less metamorphosed. In the Champlain Valley of western Vermont they are sedimentary and metasedimentary limestones, shales, sandstones, and marbles. This area contains some of the "hardest" water in Vermont, often with the greatest amount of dissolved solids. In central and eastern Vermont the Ordivician strata are more metamorphosed, but nevertheless are often more soluble than the surrounding rocks. In Figure 6.1 these major zones are shown by a stippled pattern.

On the map, a correlation is evident between the mineral-spring locations and the geology. Of the 131 mineral springs, 80 are found within the hard-water zones, or about 60 percent of the springs. This variation is striking when we realize that the mapped Ordivician rocks comprise only about 20 percent of the state. The association is most evident in the central Champlain Valley, and in the marble belt south of Rutland.

Railroad Accessibility

In order to be a commercially successful venture, the mineral springs had to be located at a place that was easy for people to get to with minimal exertion. Many springs undoubtedly never saw a flourishing hotel because of location, but others prospered because of it.

Most mineral springs were known very early. Clarendon was probably the first, recognized as early as 1776. Newbury was known in 1782, Sheldon in 1783, Tunbridge in 1805, and at least Middletown, Equinox, Alburg, Highgate, Wheelock, Brattleboro, Hardwick, Woodstock, Brunswick, and Quechee were known before 1850.

The year 1850 is critical, because by then both the Rutland Railroad system's main-trunk line had been built (Rutland and Burlington Railroad), as well as the Vermont Central and connecting Vermont and Canada (which was to become the Vermont Central Railroad, and later the Central Vermont). Other lines were constructed up to the 1880s, one of the last being the Rutland Railroad extension across the Champlain Islands in 1899. The railroads provided the transportation needed to make passage to the mineral springs, rapid, safe, and convenient. Many springs close to the evolving railway networks became more important resorts after 1850.

Fully seventy-seven springs, or 61 percent, were within five miles of a railroad. More dramatically, twenty-five of the thirty-two springs that had hotels, or 85 percent, were located within that same distance.

At face value, the railroads appear to be mainly responsible for the springs that developed hotels. Although this connection generlly applies, many of the resorts were built before the coming of the railways, although often expansion took place when accessibility improved. Clarendon Springs had a log cabin for boarders as early as 1781, a hotel in 1798, and the Clarendon Springs Hotel was constructed in 1835 and still stands as one of the few remaining spring houses. In the 1850s, after the railway, the American House and Murray House were added to the Clarendon Springs complex.

In Manchester, Vanderlips Hotel dated from 1801, but the great expansion came in 1853 with the construction of the first Equinox House. Vanderlips and the Equinox House were combined in 1880 as the Equinox Inn, which had its final season in 1973.

Alburg Springs saw the Mansion House built in 1834, but the larger and more prestigious Missisquoi House was built in 1854, again after the railway. Other springs resorts saw their hotels constructed early, such as the Franklin House in Highgate Springs in 1840 (later expanded) and the hotel in Wheelock in 1830, renovated in the 1860s by Royal Winter. The hotel complex in Sheldon is an interesting example. At least seven hotels with their associated springs were in existence at one time or another. One source even lists ten hotels in 1860, but several were not associated with any particular spring.

The east–west railroad through Sheldon, originally the Portland and Ogdensburg, was not built until 1872, and the intersecting railroad between St. Albans and Richford, the Missisquoi Valley Railroad, dates from the late 1870s. Yet in 1866 bottling works were in operation at the Missisquoi Spring, and in 1867 construction was begun on the Missisquoi Springs Hotel, which was to be the largest hotel in the United States. When half completed, this hotel burned to the ground in July 1870, and was never rebuilt, all this happening two years before the construction of any railroad. It is reported that "people suffering with diseases . . . came from all parts of Franklin County, lower Canada, and northern New York to be healed by this wonderful spring. Many of them drove over a hundred miles to get to this spring, and upon reaching it, put up tents to live in or obtained temporary lodgings in homes nearby." Furthermore, "The visitors came by rail as far as St. Albans, and from here were obliged to drive twenty miles by the old plank road . . . in order to reach the spring."

The great boom in Sheldon occurred between 1865 and 1870, as other miracle springs were quickly discovered and hotels erected. But

The Equinox House in Manchester, a survivor of the mineral spring era, gets finishing touches before its grand reopening in 1985.

The Montvert Hotel in Middletown Springs as it looked in the 1870s. It was demolished in 1906 and its site is now a grove of pines. Photo courtesy of Alec Marshall.

the boom was over by 1871, with the burning of the greatest and most famous, the Missisquoi Springs Hotel. Over the years, other hotels burned or disintegrated until by 1890 only two were left, the last structure finally disappearing in 1978. The railroad may have prolonged the business, but the great period of development came earlier.

Thus the railways certainly helped the early Vermont spring industry, but, depending upon the time of construction of hotels and the construction of the railroad, the close relationship suggested by the map may not be as positive as one might immediately think.

Naturally, some mineral spring areas *did* develop in direct response to the railroad. Wheelock was one, and the Montvert Hotel at Middletown Springs was built in 1870 and 1871, only to be torn down in 1906. The Wesselhoeft Water Cure in Brattleboro flourished after 1840, and was even mentioned in an advertisement of the Connecticut Valley Railroad in 1869 (Chapter 5).

The Old Sanderson Spring in Woodstock, dating from 1830, later renamed the Dearborn Spring, was cleverly resurrected as the Sanatoga Spring in 1890 after completion of the railroad connection between Woodstock and White River Junction.

The Elgin Spring of Vergennes (actually in Panton) was developed in the 1850s, and the Brunswick Springs Hotel dates from 1869, after the coming the Grand Trunk Railroad. The latter, after burning three times, was destroyed for all time in 1930. Even the old primitive hotel in Newbury, first built in 1793, was enlarged, with a library added in 1869. It burned to the ground in 1879.

The geographic distribution of the Vermont mineral springs certainly owes much to the geology of the state. The railroads to some extent acted as localizing forces on the pattern, either in contributing to the expansion of certain mineral-spring resorts, or possibly in the naming of various issuances of water from the ground as "mineral springs."

But for many places the pattern cannot be easily explained. Whether the water was truly "mineral" or not, or whether there was railroad accessibility, some sites and areas developed commercially and others did not. Some Vermonters had a regional awareness of the money to be made from commercial exploitation of mineral water, and individual entrepreneurs played a significant part in the location of the mineral-spring resorts.

Commercialization of the Springs

The citizens of the village of Wheelock in Caledonia County for years were aware of three springs in the community. Not much attention was paid to these springs, except the third one near the center of town, which gained the reputation of being a "stinking spring." On the main street in front of this spring (and hiding it from view) was the Brick Hotel, built by Samuel Ayer in 1830. The hotel, rather grand for these parts, had three stories, including a dance hall on the third floor. It was so important, in fact, that it was said to have changed the stage road between Boston and Montreal so that it passed through the village.

When, in the early 1860s, news filtered into the village of various mineral springs in the state making a good business, residents of Wheelock thought twice about their "stinking spring." Seeing the possibility of using the spring to enhance the growth and development of their town, the spring's "healthful properties were remembered, rehearsed, and enlarged until there were few known ailments that the healing waters could not cure." Word-of-mouth advertising was, however, not enough to bring the desired horde of pleasure seekers. Instead, it brought a Boston promoter by the name of Royal Winter in the late 1860s. Winter bought the old Brick Hotel and renovated it, putting a French roof and a two-story verandah on it, brought the water flowing into the building, and renamed it the Caledonia Mineral Springs Hotel.

Winter published a fourteen-page pamphlet with testimonials and chemical analyses by Dr. S. Dana Hayes and waited for the people to flock in. Apparently they did for a couple of years. Winter erected a bottling works and had 1,400 bottles made with the name of the spring on the glass. Most of the glass bottles were never used and are now collector's items. The problem with Winter's water was that it did have a sulphur taste when bottled, but the gas soon leaked out and customer found themselves drinking tasteless water. Furthermore, people came, but not in sufficient numbers to support the hotel. The French roof was too heavy and was taken down. As a final blow, the copper pipe directing water into the hotel was dissolved by the water it was carrying. Royal Winter lost about $15,000, no mean sum in the 1860s, and the boom, if there ever had been one, was over.

Highgate Springs developed with the Franklin House after

1840, but as Hitchcock says in his 1861 *Geology of Vermont*, the springs "were not known or resorted to until several years after Alburg Springs had become a place of public resort." Highgate and Alburg are separated by only two miles of Missisquoi Bay on Lake Champlain.

C. Bainbridge Smith, a wealthy New York lawyer, was advised by his doctor to travel to Canada, where the cooler weather might alleviate his tongue cancer. Stopping at Sheldon along the way, he was cured in a very short time by drinking the Missisquoi Spring water. He subsequently built the Missisquoi Springs Hotel and the bottling works, and was indirectly responsible for the other medicinal springs that were discovered overnight in Sheldon.

A. J. Congden of Lancaster, New Hampshire, may have been the champion promoter of all time. Purchasing the property containing the Brunswick Mineral Springs in 1869, he was aware that "the efficacy of the water in curing cutaneous diseases is . . . well established." He soon erected a hotel, and "being so near the great line of thoroughfare between Montreal and Portland," expected that, "with judicious management, [it would] doubtless become a favorite resort for those in quest of health or pleasure."

What Congden purchased was a unique site that included the Brunswick Springs, a small lake, and more than twenty acres of land. The springs themselves issue from a high bank of the Connecticut River, and in the 1860s apparently six springs were there. Earlier there were "one or two," and today seven separate springs are active.

With more imagination that scientific fact, Congden identified his six springs as Number 1, Iron Spring; Number 2, Calcium Spring; Number 3, Magnesium Spring; Number 4, White Sulphur Spring; Number 5, Bromine Spring; and Number 6, Arsenic Spring. By judicious recipes combining quantities from each spring, nearly every human ailment could be cured. People flocked to such a promised land and the business flourished.

The fact is that the water in all the springs is practically identical and derives from the neighboring lake, whose bottom is clay and whose water moves along the top of the clay layer until it intersects the Connecticut River bank, where the water emerges in several fissures. The water, soaking through the decaying vegetative matter at the bottom of the lake, assumes characteristics that impart a stain to the rocks and silts where the spring issues. In any case, the Brunswick Mineral Springs were successful for many years, although no bottling works were ever constructed. Today one can stroll the once nicely landscaped grounds and descend to the springs, still issuing beneath their concrete slab.

And so it went. Springs of every sort and description promised miracle cures, and entrepreneurs were only too eager to provide for the needs and desires of the Victorian vacationer. Often without regard to location, springs in Vermont and elsewhere assumed almost mystical qualities overnight. They did not necessarily have to be high in dissolved mineral content, nor did they have to be located along a railroad, although that helped. Much of the locational pattern defies rational explanation: there was water, there were individuals, there were testimonials, there was suitable promotion, and there was a mineral spring.

The Mineral-Spring Resort

The mineral-spring resort, in Vermont and elsewhere, was very much a social event. Families and even succeeding generations would return to a resort summer after summer. The mineral spring in its appearance and role became very familiar to the patrons and was considered a home away from home, but rather more elegant, for most. Lasting friendships were formed, and even marriages.

Initially the most obvious reason for which people frequented the mineral springs was for health remedies. Without sanitation systems, preventive medicines, and modern drugs, few people in the late 1800s reached adulthood in sound health. No wonder they were so preoccupied with their health and well-being. People tended to overeat. The health spa, though open for only a few months a year, prescribed that people eat less and drink plenty of water. This diet gave the digestive system a rest, and for that alone the individual felt better. The cure for dyspepsia was to eat less. Bilious attacks were caused by overstimulation of the gall bladder. Diabetes (insular) was dealt with through one's diet. Fewer people now get these ailments because our diet has changed. It was not the mineral water as such that cured ailments and diseases, but rather a change in the diet pattern. A recent study of the old Brunswick Springs contains this information:

> It is very doubtful if the waters . . . where used internally have any medicinal value as a result of their high mineral content,

except perhaps a slight cathartic effect from dissolved sulphates. It seems, rather, that the admitted health benefits derived from many of the world's famous watering places are the result of other factors such as: (1) the thorough elimination of waste products from the body by the drinking of large quantities of clean fresh water; (2) the external application of water in the form of hot water baths; (3) long periods of mental rest and relaxation; and (4) the psychological effect of knowing that others have been helped by following the same procedures.

Thus the mineral springs lured the first tourists to Vermont. Primarily of the middle class, these people were often unhealthy specimens, calling for the mineral waters to cure their ailments and diseases. The residents and owners of hotels wouldn't understand why you would come to Vermont unless you were somewhat of an invalid and wanted to be cured. Consequently, unless an enterprise had a mineral spring with healing qualities that could be advertised as essential and attractive to the public, investors would be apprehensive about sinking money into any new recreational establishment. The upper class or very rich frequented Saratoga or applied the European grand tour to the United States and, in place of Rome, Paris, and Vienna, visited seaside "watering places" such as Bar Harbor and Newport.

As late as 1913, four commercial springs in Vermont were still bottling their water, together processing 17,725 gallons with a value of $7,068. At an average price of 40 cents a gallon, this was the most expensive spring water in the United States after Indiana's. Yet, by then, the era of medicinal water had well nigh passed as better sanitation came to the cities along with improved medicine and diet. Of the total value of the water bottled and shipped from the Vermont springs, only $168 was for "medicinal water." the balance was for "table water."

The demise of the mineral-spring resorts is sometimes blamed solely on the Civil War and the loss of patronage from the southern states. Although these difficulties certainly affected the Clarendon, which had a large clientele from Virginia and the Carolinas, the explanation is not that simple.

After 1850, the mineral-spring hotels had to compete with the city hotels, which were gaining popularity, and it has also been remarked that the sublime landscape of Vermont was not perceived by the visitor as superior to that of New York, New Hampshire, or

Maine. State agencies interested in promoting tourism attempted to reassure visitors that there was a difference. This passage is from a 1913 publicity release:

> The Vermont mountains are friendly mountains, with few exceptions, being clothed with verdure from base to highest peaks, mountains that invite the visitor to close acquaintance. Their summits are not capped with eternal snows, they are not stark, jagged masses of barren rock. the tourist does not court death by attempting to scale their highest elevations. They induce admiration and affection rather than awe and terror.

But to many, Vermont was too agricultural, too rural, too familiar for the visitors, many of whom had just stepped off the farm a generation past or even less.

Vermont's landscape was dotted with white farmhouses (white being easily obtained from a lacquer base; later the mixture of white paint and iron oxide introduced the color red, so familiar on old barn structures today). White, being out of fashion to the Victorian in the latter half of the nineteenth century, was hardly considered picturesque in the landscape.

Finally, the hotels in Vermont charged only about one dollar less a week than those in New York, New Hampshire, or Maine. For the same price one could have more spectacular scenery, often greater amenities, and, all things being equal, the same waters, if one still sought the "healing" springs.

Often smelly, and sometimes from stagnant ponds, the water flowed into the health seeker and vacationer of another era. The mineral springs, partly because of the geology, partly also because of the accessibility of the railroad, were the first commercial resorts of the north county. John Godfrey Saxe, in the last stanza of "The song of Saratoga," written in 1868 at Highgate Springs, sums it all up:

> In short—as it goes in the world—
> They eat, and they drink and they sleep;
> They talk, and they walk, and they woo;
> They sigh, and they ride, and they dance-
> (with other unspeakable things);
> They pray, and they play, and they pay—
> And that's what they do at the Springs.

The railroads, then, were in part responsible for the mineral springs. And they introduced thousands of urban people to the Green Mountains. Their children were to come later.

7

Butter and Cheese

In 1850 the railroad brought Vermont into the mainstream of New England economic development. Distant places were but an overnight or a day's journey for people, and only a little longer than that for goods. Quick transportation, at least for people, led to development of Vermont's early recreation-oriented economy. It also led to a change in agriculture from nonperishable to perishable products. For manufactured products, the change was important not so much for the element of time, but for the overcoming of distance. Vermont stayed up in the northwest corner of New England, but its relative location changed. The interstate highways of the 1960s had a similar influence in bringing the state even closer to large populations and consumer markets lying to the south.

From Sheep to Cows

In 1840, the federal government attempted to take a farm census, but the enumeration was as bad as it had been with manufacturers (Chapter 4). Even with its limitations, that census provides a base for knowing the status of Vermont agriculture at the time. In that year, Vermont was reported to have 379,392 "cattle," whatever that term meant. Later, the census clearly differentiated cattle from milk cows. In 1860, there were 174,667 milk cows out of a cattle population of 370,450; or 47 percent. In 1880, the proportion of milk cows was 54 percent. Rather arbitrarily calculated, perhaps 40 percent of the number of cattle in 1840 were milkers, which would give a total of

157

151,757. Probably this is a little high, as are the numbers of cattle for that year, but it is the figure used in Table 7.1. Like any tabulation using the U.S. Bureau of the Census, or any other statistical source, the numbers often change more because of a change in definition than a change in what is counted. Over the years, for example, many changes have been made in the definition of improved land, but the judgments of individual enumerators cannot be estimated in adjusting the data. After 1920, the improved-land category was dropped from the Census, and in 1930 and subsequent years the figures include the total of what is reported as cropland plus pasture that is "plowable." After 1960, the figures apply only to the category "cropland." The same problems arise in determining what is and what is not a milking cow. In 1900, this number relates to the number on June 1, in 1910 to April 15, and in 1920 to the total as of January 1. Milking cows on farms are usually fewer in the middle of the winter than the middle of summer. Thus, although the figures show a change of more than 20,000 cows from 1900 to 1920, the number of milk cows may not have changed at all! To add to the confusion, in 1920 the enumerators were told to record only "cows kept mainly for milk production," but in 1910 any bovine milked for three months or more during the year was considered a cow.

Table 7.1 clearly shows that Vermont never had more cows than people. Even allowing for inaccuracies, the table also shows the decline in sheep farming, along with the increase in dairying. The figures show stability in the number of farms through the nineteenth century, and in the number of acres per farm. Even the proportion of the average farm that is improved shows little change through the period to 1900, most of the changes simply reflecting changing definitions and enumerators. In other words, into the early 1900s change in Vermont agriculture was not too great, except for increasing emphasis on dairying. Little land was added to the "farm land" category of the Census; no land was left that even with the greatest imagination and enthusiasm could be farmed. Specialized dairy breeds began to replace the multiple-purpose animals in about 1880, but that change, though enormously important in milk production, is not reflected in the number of animals called cows. For about fifty years, the use of land for agriculture in Vermont changed little.

Although the amount of land farmed changed little and farm sizes and numbers remained about the same, land use changed dra-

TABLE 7.1

Population, Cows, Sheep, and Farms, 1840–1982

Year	Population	Cows	Sheep	No. Farms	Percentage of farmland improved	Average farm size, acres
1840	291,948	151,757	1,681,819	—	—	139
1850	314,120	146,128	1,014,122	29,763	63.1	136
1860	315,098	174,667	752,201	31,556	66.0	134
1870	330,551	180,285	580,347	33,827	67.7	137
1880	332,286	217,033	429,870	35,522	67.3	135
1890	332,422	231,419	333,947	32,573	60.4	143
1900	343,641	270,194	296,576	32,890	45.0	143
1910	355,956	265,483	118,551	32,709	35.1[a]	143
1920	352,428	290,122[b]	62,756	29,075	40.0	146
1930	359,611	264,000	51,175	24,898	36.0	157
1940	359,231	279,141	35,946	23,582	40.1	156
1950	377,747	261,370	—	19,043	41.2	185
1960	389,881	240,928	—	12,099	41.5	243
1970	444,732	195,828	6,715	6,874	43.6[c]	279
1978	511,456[d]	184,860[e]	9,073[e]	5,852	49.1	279
1982	520,000[f]	191,098	12,840	6,315	49.0	249

[a] In 1910, pasture land was excluded from "Improved land" unless it was used in alternate years for crops.
[b] Cows "kept mainly for milk production," U.S. Census Bureau.
[c] After 1970, "Improved land" is "Cropland," using U.S. Census of Agriculture definition.
[d] Population, 1980.
[e] After 1978, U.S. Census of Agriculture. The last year in which Vermont Town Listers were required to report livestock numbers was 1977.
[f] Population estimate from Vermont Department of Health.

Note: Unless otherwise specified, all animal numbers are from Vermont Town Listers. Other material from appropriate U.S. Census.

matically, from sheep grazing to cows. In 1868, the Vermont State Board of Agriculture, trying to help the sheep farmer grazing a hundred animals on upland bedrock, showed that converting to milk farming has its merits: Sell off the sheep, use the cows, and make a better profit. This rationale was expressed in the following estimates for the profits in keeping five cows or forty sheep; it was assumed that in the feed, acreage, and housing required for each animal, the two were about equal.* Also,

Gross Annual Income—Sheep vs. Dairy (1868)

Sale of calves	$ 40.00	Sale of lambs	$120.00
Cheese manufacturing	$250.00	Wool production	$ 90.00
Butter manufacturing	$ 67.50		$210.00
	$357.50		

Source: Vermont Board of Agriculture, Annual Report, 1868

because automatic milking machines, silos, and even primitive barn stanchions were generally unknown, little capital investment was needed to change the operation. Furthermore, most farmers in Vermont were general farmers in the truest sense of the word, always having a few cows for home milk production, along with a variety of other animals. One James Spaulding of Weston, whose farm was possibly the largest in the whole town in 1860, is listed in the original census enumeration:

Total land owned	230 acres
Improved land	130 acres
Value of farm	$2,500
Value of machinery and implements	$ 160
Number of horses	1
Number of milk cows	12
Number of oxen	2
Number of swine	2
Value of livestock	$ 705

*A better ratio would probably have been eight cows to forty sheep, which would have made dairying an even more attractive proposition.

Production:

wheat	45 bushels
Indian corn	28 bushels
oats	130 bushels
peas and beans	3 bushels
potatoes	190 bushels
value of orchard products	$10
hay	55 tons
maple syrup	400 pounds
butter	1390 pounds
cheese	210 pounds
value of animals slaughtered	$67

Mr. Spaulding apparently was one farmer who had gotten out of sheep before 1860. Just down the road was the smaller farm of John Bigart, who was operating 105 acres and had eleven cows and eight sheep on a farm valued at $800. Bigart also had one horse and two swine but grew rye, buckwheat, and barley. His eight sheep gave him an income of $40 from wool. His neighbor, William Lenny, had a small thirty-five-acre farm, on which the only animals were fifty-seven sheep, which produced 242 pounds of wool.

In the era of sheep farming, the quality of the land made little difference; even the poorest land could grow sheep, though not at the density of the better Champlain Valley acres. Dairy cows, however, required better land both for pasture and for growing the grain crops that would support them through the long winter months. The change to dairying meant, over a long period, retreat from the marginal farms that simply could not support a commercial dairy herd as well as the flatter, better, and warmer lands of the valleys. That the change to dairying did not immediately signal a decrease in the poor upland farms is a measure of late nineteenth and early twentieth-century self-sufficient farming. Even as late as 1940, 62 percent of Vermont was still classed as "farmland" by the U.S. Census Bureau, a figure not too different from the high point of the 1880s, when 72 percent of the state was in that category. In 1940, there were some 12,000 fewer farms than sixty years before, but the average farm was almost twenty acres larger. In other words, the marginal uplands were kept in production far longer than they probably should have been, contributing to a large number of poverty-level farmers with a

TABLE 7.2

Density of Cows per Square Mile, 1860–1982

County	Square miles	1860	1880	1890	1913	1930	1950	1959	1969	1978	1982
Addison	785	17	26	24	26	31	37	39	40	44	45
Bennington	672	10	13	14	10	10	9	9	6	4	5
Caledonia	614	19	23	25	27	35	31	27	17	17	18
Chittenden	532	35	43	45	41	46	47	47	31	27	25
Essex	663	4	5	6	7	8	6	5	5	4	4
Franklin	659	39	45	49	49	54	58	64	55	56	61
Grand Isle	77	20	28	31	49	53	64	68	57	52	51
Lamoille	475	20	23	23	26	30	25	25	15	16	16
Orange	690	17	19	22	25	27	25	25	18	18	19
Orleans	715	16	26	30	32	43	43	43	32	36	38
Rutland	929	19	26	27	24	24	22	22	15	15	15
Washington	708	25	29	30	27	28	23	20	13	10	10
Windham	793	15	14	14	12	12	10	10	8	7	7
Windsor	965	15	19	20	18	19	17	17	9	7	8
State	9,267[a]	19	23	25	29	28	27	27	20	20	21

[a]This is *land* area only. Total area of Vermont, 9,609 square miles. Cows do not graze on water.

Source: U.S. Bureau of the Census, except for 1913, when reported by the Vermont Board of Agriculture. The last year in which Town Listers reported a complete cow count by towns was 1977. The U.S. Census of Agriculture no longer reports data for individual towns.

few cows trying to eke out an existence from meager land resources.

As commercial dairy farming began to develop, it was unevenly distributed. Certain areas persisted in growing sheep and wool long after other parts of the state became oriented toward dairying. In an 1897 inventory of all animals in Vermont, the state Board of Agriculture reported (Annual Report, 1898) that more than eighty towns still had more sheep than cows, but the only region of good land being used for sheep was Addison County.

Table 7.2 charts the rise and fall of dairying in Vermont's fourteen counties. Calculating the number of cows per square mile is the best method for showing the importance of the activity because the unequal size of counties does not bias the result. Tiny Grand Isle County had fewer cows than any other county in Vermont, with the possible exception of Essex. Yet considering cow density, it is probably the most agricultural county in the state, and in 1982 ranked second only to Franklin.

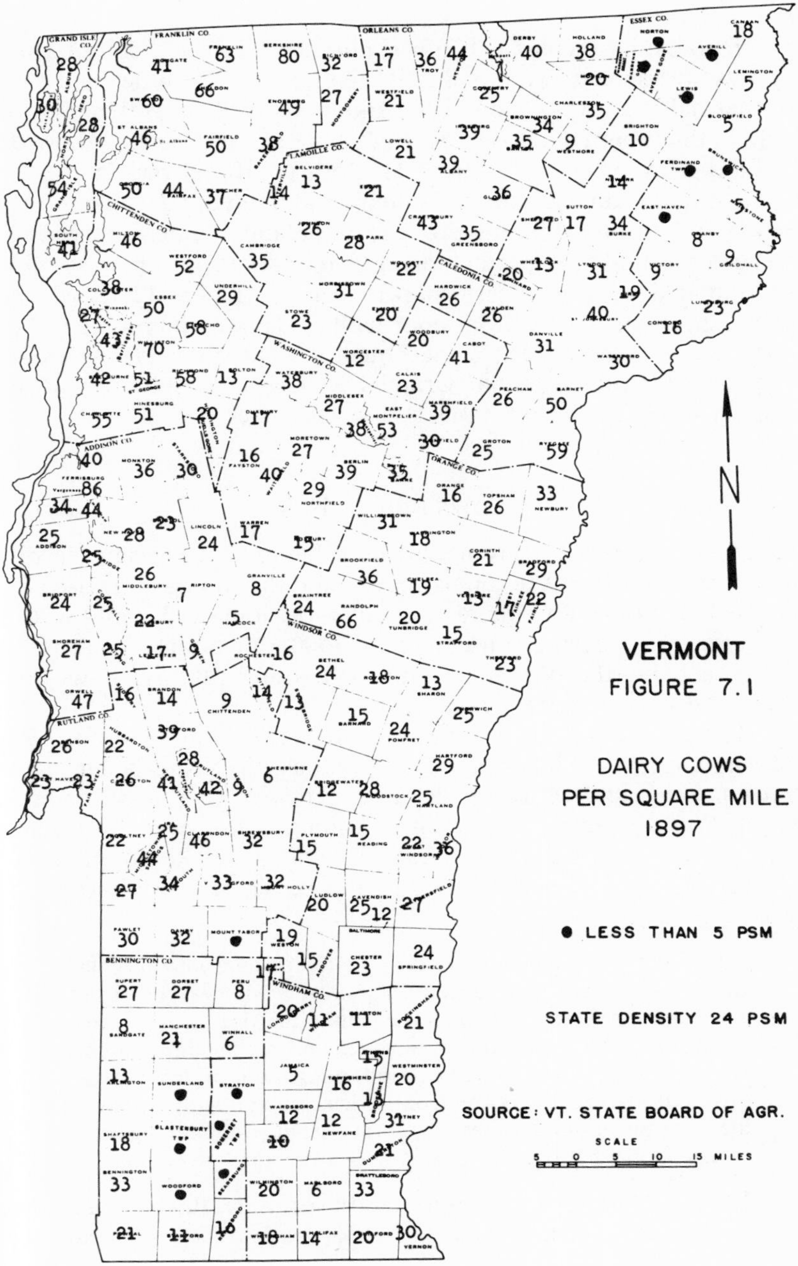

VERMONT
FIGURE 7.1

DAIRY COWS
PER SQUARE MILE
1897

● LESS THAN 5 PSM

STATE DENSITY 24 PSM

SOURCE: VT. STATE BOARD OF AGR.

SCALE

5   0   5   10   15 MILES

N

Throughout the last half of the nineteenth century, dairy farming was widespread. The quality of the land meant little, and the premier dairy counties and towns had not yet evolved as they began to do in the twentieth century. In 1897, little rational pattern showed in the density of cows (Figure 7.1). Both good and bad land was supporting the same number of animals and if anything, some of the higher densities were found closer to population centers, reflecting the need for fluid-milk production close to market. This map should be compared with a modern map of density (Figure 12.1), which clearly shows the retreat from poor land as dairying has come to be associated with land of the highest quality in the state. The development of Addison, Franklin, Grand Isle, Orleans, and Chittenden counties as major dairy regions is discussed later.

Cows and Milk

After 1880, technology was making itself felt in Vermont dairy farming. Specialized breeds began to appear, and the silo was first used in about 1882. Originally square or angular, the improved round wood silo came into widespread use in about 1900. Often tacked on to the end of a barn, the silo led to improved winter rations. Cows got larger and began to produce more milk.

The average production per cow in Vermont in 1890 was 396 gallons, but in 1900 it was up to 525 gallons, thanks to better care, better feeding, and better breeds. This increasing output per animal was to characterize American dairy farming in the years ahead.

As the hill farmers rushed into dairying, a Mr. Rollin Smith of Pittsford, a member of the state Board of Agriculture, was moved to comment in 1890:

> It is proverbial among ourselves, that for rushing into business where a few men have made a profit, Vermont will beat the world; and Vermont literally made a rush into the dairy. Cows were picked up with very little knowledge, and much less thought; bought wherever they could be found, bought out of droves being driven to Massachusetts and Connecticut, bought without knowing anything about whether they sprang from good milking stock or not, bought if they were only cows and would give milk.

In truth, Vermont cows were pretty sorry creatures. Most were of dubious ancestry and were raised for both milk and meat. As early as 1865, an enterprising New England dairyman had advertised that he would be willing to pay a hundred dollars for any cow that would produce fifty pounds of milk or more per day for three consecutive days on his farm. No takers appeared at a time when dairy cattle were selling at about forty dollars. In 1899, the U.S. Department of Agriculture flatly stated that any cow producing less than 4,500 pounds of milk annually was not economical and not worth the feed supporting the beast.

In retrospect, the Department of Agriculture was being optimistic. In Vermont the average herd production of milk reached 5,100 pounds only in 1940, and it was not until the late 1970s that the average reached 11,000 pounds; only those farmers in the Dairy Herd Improvement Program were reporting production of 13,000 pounds or more. In 1970, a good benchmark year, Vermont's production per cow was just under 10,000 pounds. A comparison with other states at that time shows that local farming had come a long way from poor beginnings, but by this measure of dairy-farm efficiency still fell far short of many areas in the country. In that year, Vermont ranked eighteenth. By 1977, production per cow was 10,984 pounds, but other states had gained as well, and Vermont's national ranking had fallen to twenty-sixth. California was the leader.

The reason for the higher production per cow and per herd mainly reflects the increasing popularity of high–milk-producing Holsteins at the expense of other dairy breeds. Holsteins first came to western Vermont when Vermont farmers began to ship fluid milk to the southern markets. When milk-marketing districts were organized by the U.S. Department of Agriculture in 1915, most of the western part of the state was designated as a supply area for New York City, and it happened to be a market area with lower butterfat requirements. Holsteins are large producers, but their milk averages only about 3.5 percent fat, low among dairy breeds, but suitable for the market at the time. Much of eastern Vermont came under the Boston milkshed, a higher butterfat market, and as a result the changeover to lower-butterfat Holsteins was much slower in Orange, Orleans, and Caledonia counties. Even today, far more herds of tan and brown Jerseys, Guernseys, Brown Swiss, and Ayrshires are found in the northern and eastern parts of the state, whereas Addison and Franklin counties have become the domain of the black and white. Also, as long as butter production was important, farmers had strong economic reasons to maintain high-butterfat cows; but when

Vermont began to be a fluid-milk supplier, farmers had to switch to higher-producing breeds.

The Era of Cheese

As the sheep left, farmers began to look at their cows as a money-making proposition. Heretofore the cow or two had provided milk, cheese, and butter for the family and perhaps the local town; without refrigeration, neither butter nor fresh milk could be transported any distance. Butter could last six days before becoming rancid, but cheese, properly waxed, could last almost indefinitely. For years, farm families had been making butter and cheese for their own use, and even during the maximum period of sheep farming, cheese and butter production was an important Vermont farm industry. In 1849, 8.7 million pounds of hard cheese were farm-produced, and 12.1 million pounds of butter.

Until recently, cheese made in Vermont, both on the farm and later in the many cheese factories, tended to be cheddar, Colby cheddar, bakers, and cottage. Only after 1940 did "ethnic" cheeses begin to become important. Most Vermonters, springing from other New England stock, were familiar with only the English varieties. Settlers in other parts of the country, such as the Dutch in the Hudson Valley, were making Edam and Gouda, as were Germans to the south. Local cheddar cheeses like "Narragansett" cheese and "Braintree" cheese had established themselves very early in southern New England, although the true cheese capital of the early nineteenth century was probably Goshen, high in the Litchfield Hills of western Connecticut.

In 1801, Goshen, apparently with all the farm wives feverishly making cheese, produced 270,000 pounds of "Goshen Cheese," which was nothing but good American (or English) cheddar with some additional coloring. So many of Vermont's early settlers came from western Connecticut that it is no accident that cheesemaking came with them and cheesemaking in Vermont was a natural pursuit from the first settlements onward.

All this early cheese industry was a home occupation. In 1818, Lewis Norton of Goshen began to make pineapple cheese (so called because of the shape), for which he was subsequently granted a patent. As the business boomed, he kept enlarging his dairy herd until he had fifty cows producing milk; but these were still not enough. In 1843 he began buying from neighbors and perhaps established the first official cheese factory in the United States. That claim is challenged by Rome, New York, which recalls a cheese operation in 1851 by one Jesse Williams. Whoever was first, by the turn of the century, the idea of a centralized factory for producing cheese was well established, and the technology was available. Farm wives who had laboriously produced good (and sometimes very bad) cheese since the colonial period could breathe a sigh of relief. Large amounts of cheese, delivered to one customer, of guaranteed quality, had come to New England. The first cheese factory in Vermont, at Wells in 1854, soon followed, and the factories in Poultney and Pawlet were not far behind.

In any area, the progression from cheese to butter to fluid milk as the primary dairy product was a familiar one in days of limited transport. Close to the consuming market had to be fluid-milk production, simply because the product would spoil quickly. As the cities of southern New England began to develop, fluid-milk dairying had to be just beyond the last house in town, for otherwise workers would get sour milk each day. Butter, lasting a few days more, would be produced just outside the fluid-milk zone, and beyond that, cheese, least perishable of the three. In 1800, Goshen, Connecticut was at the outer fringe. In the 1840s, Vermont was in the same position, as more southern New England farms became butter or fluid-milk producers. And as population grew, so too did the widening ripples of dairying tied to these growing markets. By 1915, Vermont was included in "milksheds," and for the first time became an area of fresh-milk production and shipment, butter and cheese having gone their economic ways.

After 1850, though fluid milk continued to be the major product of Connecticut and Massachusetts, Vermont farmers had something of a choice, because of the nearness of the rails, market demands, and even what their neighbors were doing and where the early butter creameries and cheese factories were. Some parts of the state began to make cheese; other places became butter areas.

An unexpected fact revealed by the map (Figure 7.2) is that most cheese manufacturing was concentrated in south-central Vermont, closer to southern markets, and the more-perishable butter production was in the northern two-thirds of the state. It should have been the other way around, and would have been had it not been for the

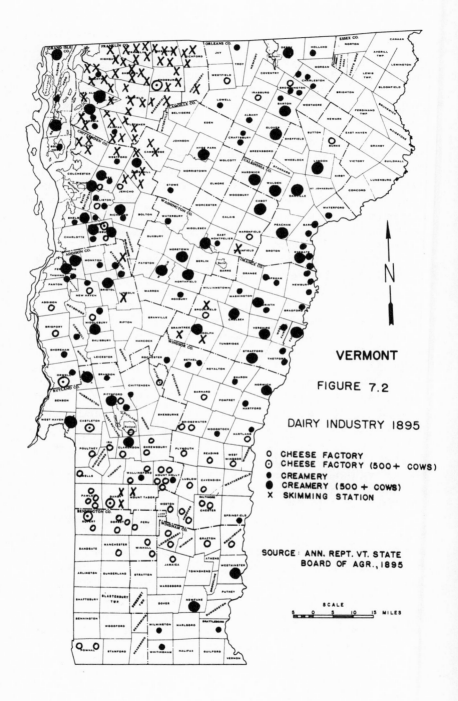

VERMONT

FIGURE 7.2

DAIRY INDUSTRY 1895

○ CHEESE FACTORY
◉ CHEESE FACTORY (500+ COWS)
● CREAMERY
⬤ CREAMERY (500 + COWS)
✕ SKIMMING STATION

SOURCE: ANN. REPT. VT. STATE
BOARD OF AGR., 1895

SCALE

5 0   5   10   15 MILES

railways, and the choice of individual entrepreneurs and farmers.

By 1900, only five years after the date covered by Figure 7.2, Vermont could boast 66 cheese factories. But at the same time we find 1,227 already in Wisconsin, 1,150 in New York, 221 in Ohio, and far more than the Vermont numbers in both Pennsylvania and Michigan. The cheese era, if there ever had been one, was already over. The 66 factories of 1900 are the maximum number in Vermont's history, although the period of maximum cheese production was considerably earlier, even before the first factories in the 1850s, and modern production far exceeds anything in the past.

The statistical record of cheese production begins in 1849, as reported in the 1850 census. In that year, 8.7 million pounds of cheddar cheese was produced, all coming from farm kitchens, and factories or no factories, that production was not exceeded until 1954, more than a hundred years later. Hard-cheese production in the nineteenth century followed a downward trend as butter became the most important dairy product, and increasingly, most Vermont cheese came from the factory rather than the home.

Vermont Whole-Milk Cheese Production,
1849–1919, in millions of pounds

1849	8.7
1859	8.2
1869	4.8
1879	6.0
1889	6.1
1899	5.1
1909	3.0
1919	5.0

Source: H.F. Wilson, *The Hill Country of Northern New England*

Until 1879, no information was available on how much cheese was produced by factory and farm, but in that year, 75 percent of cheese output came from scattered factories. In 1889, it was 92 percent, by 1919, about 98 percent.

The change to a factory system provided escape from the drudgery of home manufacturing and also guaranteed a market for the milk and a dependable source of income. The transition, how-

Butter making — the old way.

Butter making — the new way.

Photographs from the 1899 *Yearbook*, U.S. Department of Agriculture.

ever, was not particularly easy; the reports of the Vermont State Board of Agriculture and the Vermont Dairyman's Association through the 1860s and 1870s abound in debate on the merits of home versus factory production.

In 1898 a movement was set off to increase the overseas export market for Vermont-made cheese, and colorful pamphlets and other literature were prepared and sent to England to encourage consumption of the local product. As early as the 1870s, cheese had been sent to England, but because manufacturing standards were lacking, much of the cheese had been diluted with skim milk and the attempts at market penetration met with failure.

In 1860 and earlier, Vermont was briefly a major United States cheese-producing state. In that year, the 8.2 million pounds of Vermont cheese compared with only 1.1 million pounds from Wisconsin, today acknowledged as America's premier cheese state (although California produces more). Even as late as 1890, Vermont was making more cheese than Wisconsin, but New York was far and away the national leader, with Ohio a close second.

As production continued to decline, eventually dropping below a million pounds in 1927, repeated efforts were made to revive the industry, most with little success. Besides trying to increase an export market, Vermont cheesemakers attempted to establish a state brand like New York State Cheddar or Iowa's State Brand Butter. Vermont's product, much of it homemade, was of dubious quality, but military demands during World War I gave a temporary boost. More important perhaps, butter began to dominate the dairy industry, and it was more profitable for farmers to divert their milk to the creameries rather than the cheese factories. Later, as fluid-milk markets evolved, interest in the continuing manufacture of cheese was minimal. In Vermont, the popularity of Colby (Colby cheddar) reflects the changing market conditions. This cheese, along with traditional cheddar, always dominated Vermont's hard whole-milk cheese production. Colby is a washed-cured cheddar: before the curd is pressed, it is washed with cool water. The curd absorbs some moisture, so that the resulting cheese is moister and heavier than cheddar; the milk goes further and the cheese is therefore popular in areas where milk prices are higher—a given amount of whole milk will make more cheese. Usually, depending upon the quality, Colby has more body than true cheddar, but sometimes it does not have the distinctive taste.

This added-on-to structure in Wells began its life as Vermont's first cheese factory in 1854. It is now a private home.

Creameries and Butter

Like cheese, butter was long a homemade product on Vermont farms, and, also like cheese, creameries evolved to manufacture a standardized product, and to relieve the farmer of this additional chore. Unlike cheese, however, butter production was always more important and in 1849, 12.1 million pounds of farm butter were churned out, compared to 8.7 million pounds of cheese.

The great growth of butter production accompanied the introduction of iced butter cars on both the Rutland and the Central Vermont, making it possible to transport the product throughout the year. The first creamery in the state appeared in 1871, the year in which Carl DeLaval invented the cream separator, but Vermont farmers were as unwilling to change over to creameries as to cheese

**Vermont Butter Production,
1849–1919, in millions of pounds**

1849	12.1
1859	15.9
1869	17.8
1879	25.7
1889	29.1
1899	40.9
1909	35.4
1919	16.8

Source: H. F. Wilson, *The Hill Country of Northern New England*

factories. By 1879, only 5,000 pounds of butter were churned in creameries, although conversion took place rapidly after that, as more plants were located close to the farms. In 1899, 55 percent of production came from creameries, and by 1919 the figure was 77 percent, although production then was down from the high years of the late nineteenth century because of the low cost of transporting western butter into eastern markets in steam-cooled refrigerator cars.

The number of creameries in Vermont peaked at 180 in 1900, at which time Vermont led the nation in production. The map (Figure 7.2) shows a concentration of creameries in northern Vermont, in contrast to the pattern of cheese factories in Rutland, Bennington, Windham, and Windsor counties. St. Albans boasted the world's largest creamery, and the Franklin County Creamery alone produced two million pounds of butter (5 percent of Vermont production) from the cream collected from 15,000 cows. That creamery also had sixty "skimming" or "separator" stations, to which farmers would bring their whole milk to have the cream skimmed, a saving on work that was usually done on the farm. From the milk brought daily to the creameries and skimming stations, about a third of the extracted cream was sent to market as sweet cream, for which the farmer was paid $1.10 a gallon. The remainder of the cream went into butter, for which 90 cents a gallon was received. With this price differential, it was already more profitable to export the fluid rather than the solid product, a harbinger of both the future change to fluid-milk production and the two-tiered pricing system of Class I and Class II milk.

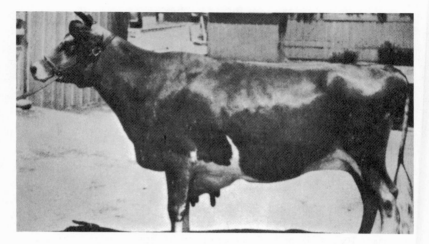

While nineteenth-century Vermont cows were generally regarded as sorry creatures, this one has more than normal problems.

Today, all milk produced in Vermont is held in bulk tanks to be picked up periodically by tank trucks. The conversion to bulk tanks from milk cans was rapid during the 1950s and 1960s.

Farmers producing for a creamery wanted cows that would provide the largest amount of butterfat, and those producing for a cheese factory wanted the largest amount of milk. More than anything else in the nineteenth century, these factors led to the need for improved herds. They also led to regionalization of different breeds in different parts of Vermont, a trend that was intensified when the Boston and New York fluid-milk networks developed.

Grain and Other Crops

Some writers have talked of a grain stage in Vermont agriculture, mostly in the period up to the 1820s and the opening of the Erie Canal (Chapter 4). If such an emphasis really existed, it probably was in the period between 1850 and 1900, as dairy cows multiplied and farmers sought to feed hungry cows for the milk that was the lifeblood of the economy. The developing and somewhat nebulous "West" was not yet growing grain for export to Vermont, as it began to do early in the 1900s.

In 1849, when the record of crop production begins, the production of wheat, corn, barley, oats, and buckwheat amounted to 5,125,054 bushels, with oats accounting for 45 percent of the production and corn another 40 percent. The trend in grain production is given in Table 7.3.

TABLE 7.3

	Vermont Grain Production, 1849–1929					
Year	Total production[a]	% wheat	% corn	% oats	% barley	% buck-wheat
1849	5,124,054	10.5	39.7	45.0	.8	4.0
1859	5,897,331	7.4	25.9	61.6	1.3	3.8
1869	6,289,444	7.2	27.0	57.3	1.9	6.6
1879	6,723,051	5.0	30.0	55.7	4.0	5.3
1889	5,873,536	2.8	29.0	56.6	7.2	4.5
1899	4,636,190	.7	28.5	59.1	8.2	3.5
1909	4,315,906	.3	39.7	49.6	6.6	3.8
1919	3,787,888	4.6	24.7	63.3	5.2	2.2
1929	1,390,405	1.0	20.1	72.7	6.0	.2

[a]in bushels

Source: Harold F. Wilson, *The Hill Country of Northern New England*, and U.S. Bureau of the Census, appropriate years.

Since 1930, grain production has consistently been below two million bushels annually. Corn has been grown for silage rather than grain, and oats, once the staple grain for horses and cattle, have well nigh disappeared from Vermont fields. In 1982, 1,321,432 bushels of all grain crops in the preceding table were harvested; the relative percentages were: corn, 88.8 percent; wheat 0.8 percent; oats 5.3 percent; barley, 5.0 percent; and rye only 1,600 bushels. Certainly Vermont has the potential for growing considerably more grain, and with the high cost of prepared feeds shipped from distant suppliers, the future may show some increase in production.

In the nineteenth century and early in the twentieth century, some grains found their way into locally made flour, and some into a few local distilleries. Though not grain crops, other products generated by Vermont agriculture were potatoes and apples, both commodities that have seen a precipitous decline over the last century. In 1895, Vermont produced 5,134,052 bushels of potatoes, enough to achieve a national ranking of thirteenth among forty-seven states. In that year, Idaho, now the largest producer, produced 480,000 bushels. In 1982 Vermont grew only 107,000 bushels on ninety-five farms. The state's largest producer is in Guildhall in Essex County.

Years ago, every small farm had a few apple trees, and sometimes the only present evidence of past farming are the wild apple trees that we are surprised to come upon throughout the forests. In 1899, nearly 1.7 million apple trees were cultivated in Vermont, with the largest number in Windsor County. By 1960, 146,000 were left, and the number in Windsor County had declined from 260,622 to only 9,580. Today, Addison County leads the state in apple orchards and in apple production, but the totals are far below what they were at the turn of the century.

8

Nineteenth-Century Industry

The unknown author of these words: "If markets are distant they'll surely be near,/As soon as the railroads projected are here" was generally correct. The change to perishable dairy products was one result of the rails' arrival, and the beginnings of a recreation industry was another. The third major effect was an industrial structure geared to more-distant markets, providing some employment but still based primarily on native raw materials.

TABLE 8.1

		Vermont Population Change, 1850–1960[a]		
Year	Population	Net change	% change	U.S. % change
1850	315,120			
1860	315,098	+ 978	+ .3	35.6
1870	330,551	+ 15,453	+ 4.9	26.6
1880	332,286	+ 1,731	+ .5	26.0
1890	332,422	+ 136	+ .1	25.5
1900	343,641	+ 11,219	+ 3.4	20.7
1910	355,956	+ 12,312	+ 3.6	21.0
1920	352,428	− 3,528	− 1.0	14.9
1930	359,611	+ 7,183	+ 2.0	16.1
1940	359,231	− 380	− .1	7.2
1950	377,747	+ 18,516	+ 5.2	14.5
1960	389,881	+ 12,134	+ 3.2	18.5
	Total:	1790–1850 + 228,645	(60 years)	
	Total:	1850–1960 + 75,761	(110 years)	

[a]See also Table 4.2.

Source: U.S. Census.

Population changes and shifts accompanied the expanding railroad network. For one thing, emigration continued, because the rails made it even easier to move away. (By 1860, 43 percent of native-born Vermonters were living outside the state.) As a result, population growth was minimal as natural increase and immigration balanced the number seeking greener pastures. Table 8.1, which continues Table 4.2 in Chapter 4, traces population changes from 1850 to 1960, when Vermont increased by only 24 percent, many of whom were immigrant groups coming to work in developing industries. Probably the French Canadians were the most numerous newcomers.

Ethnic Groups

As the most isolated of the New England states, Vermont did not attract as many immigrant groups as the more coastal states. Also, as the least industrial state in the region, its demands for labor were proportionately less.

The railroads attracted the Irish to Vermont; the stone industries brought Italians and other groups from southern and eastern Europe, as did the machine-tool industries growing in the Windsor and Springfield areas. In 1850, only 10.5 percent of the population was foreign born, and half had been born in Ireland. They were followed by French Canadians and Scots, many of whom came even at this early date to work in the granite industry of Washington County.

The Irish spread widely throughout the state. On the other hand, many Italians were drawn to the quarry towns, with the greatest influx between 1900 and 1906. By 1910, more than 14 percent of Barre's population was Italian born, and 2.6 percent of the population of Rutland County (including the marble works in West Rutland and Proctor) were of Italian nativity. But the group who over the years have been numerically the greatest have been French-speaking immigrants from Quebec. They not only supplied industrial labor when it was needed, but have also become Vermont's major farming group.

In 1970 the U.S. Census Bureau reported that the French Canadian population of Vermont was 39,284, or 8.8 percent of the population. This figure is based on the census definition of "foreign stock" as "foreign born, or one or both parents foreign born." In 1900, 45,000 were reported, then amounting to 13.5 percent of the population, and even in 1860 the 16,984 had comprised 5.4 percent of the people in Vermont.

The French migration came in three periods. The first, before 1830, was primarily an urban movement. Quebec, even at this early date, was running out of good land, or at least land that was available to the French. No longer could the father pass on or subdivide land for his growing family. Forced off the land, the earliest French Canadian migration was in the early nineteenth century; poor harvests were an added impetus. The earliest U.S. Census (1790) reported 153 French Canadians in Vermont. In 1815 there were 100 "Canadian Catholics" in Burlington alone, and by 1832 the city had a French Canadian population of more than 500. The early French arrivals worked in industries: the Champlain Glass Company, the iron foundry in Brandon, and the quarries of Rutland County. It was an urban migration, confined mostly to the growing population centers of the Champlain Valley.

A second migration occurred after 1840, when English–French tensions culminated in an armed rebellion in Montreal. Vermont served as a haven for French political agitators, and a place of asylum when the Papineau Rebellion was put down in 1837. Most migration was toward Burlington, but St. Albans had more than 700, and French Canadians were reported in Milton, Newport, Colchester, Shelburne, Williston, Essex, Hinesburg, and Charlotte. It was still an urban migration, supplying labor for growing industries, but the people were agricultural in their background and many longed for land and rural isolation in which they could more easily retain their cultural identity.

The acquisition of farmland by a growing French population has not been studied, but it was continual long before 1880, when another period of immigration began. The best example of this is the French Canadian population of Grand Isle County, where in 1860 nearly a quarter of the population was from Quebec, and few opportunities other than farming were available. It is entirely probable that many, if not most, "farm laborers" listed in the census were French, and that many of them were able to acquire the farms on which they worked as higher-paying industrial jobs attracted the

FIGURE 8.I

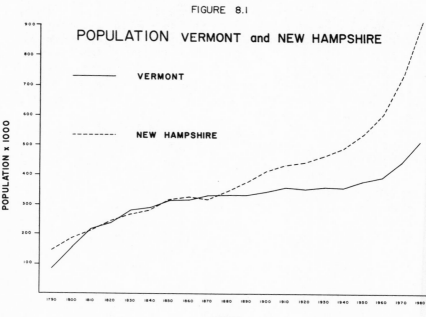

original Yankee owners.* By 1930, Vermont was 11 percent foreign born (compared with Connecticut's 22 percent), but two thirds of foreign-born Vermonters in rural areas were of French-Canadian heritage.

The last major migration occurred after 1880, as rapidly growing New England mill towns provided employment opportunities. Figure 8.1 compares population growth in Vermont and New Hampshire. Until 1880 both states developed similarly as New England frontier areas. But after 1880, New Hampshire's population was increased dramatically by foreign labor in mill towns like Manches-

---

*In 1860, Grand Isle County was 23.3 percent "French." Grand Isle was followed by Franklin (17.2 percent), Chittenden (15.3 percent), and Addison (10.3 percent). In 1860 the Champlain Valley was the dominant area for French-Canadian settlement. Orleans County followed. Source of this information, unpublished Ph.D. dissertation by Ralph Vicero.

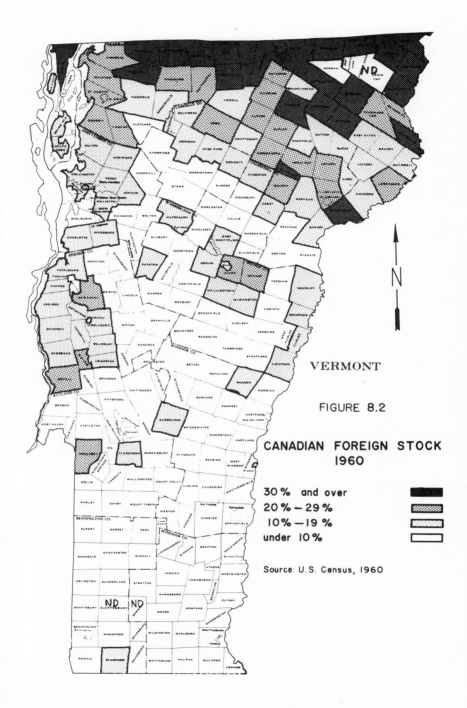

N

VERMONT

FIGURE 8.2

CANADIAN FOREIGN STOCK
1960

30% and over
20% — 29%
10% — 19%
under 10%

Source: U.S. Census, 1960

ter, Nashua, and Concord. Vermont was too far from southern New England's centers of growth, industrial development was more moderate, but nonetheless significant numbers of French Canadians once again headed toward the Green Mountain state.

Those who came to Vermont concentrated in the mill towns, especially Winooski (at that time included in Colchester). Most wanted land, but it was harder to come by in 1900 than fifty years earlier. Vermont was changing over to profitable fluid milk, and good land was at a premium. Although the earlier arrivals had been able to carve out a piece of farmland, the mill workers of later years were unable and often unwilling to take up farming, but as Vermont mills gradually closed, or as the French made enough money, many did migrate to rural areas to replace Yankees lost through long years of emigration. A modern map of French Americans (Figure 8.2) shows them as the dominant ethnic group still farming in much of Vermont. Aucoin became O'Callaghan, Ouellette turned into Willett, Pontbriand suddenly was Pomeroy, and Boucher became Bushey. Mailloux quickly became Mayo, but after another generation one is hard pressed to fathom McGee. To save trouble, some of the French translated their names into the English equivalent, as Dubois became Wood and Beauchamp changed to Fairfield.

Population Changes

Although the French and other ethnic groups were perhaps responsible for preventing an absolute decline in the state's population, certainly Vermont did not grow. Instead, along with emigration, the remaining population was rearranging itself. In 1850, 154 towns had more than 1,000 people, but by 1930, only 102 towns were in that category, and in 1960, before recent growth, only 94 towns and cities in the state had populations of more than 1,000. Vermont, after 1850, was becoming more urban; people were clustering where the employment opportunities were, and most clusters were related to railroad transportation.

The population map of 1840 (Figure 8.3) can be compared with the map of 1880 (Figure 8.4). The 1880 map has only 400 more dots (40,000 more people), but the pattern is very different. Small population nodes had grown, nearly all along rail lines, as people sought

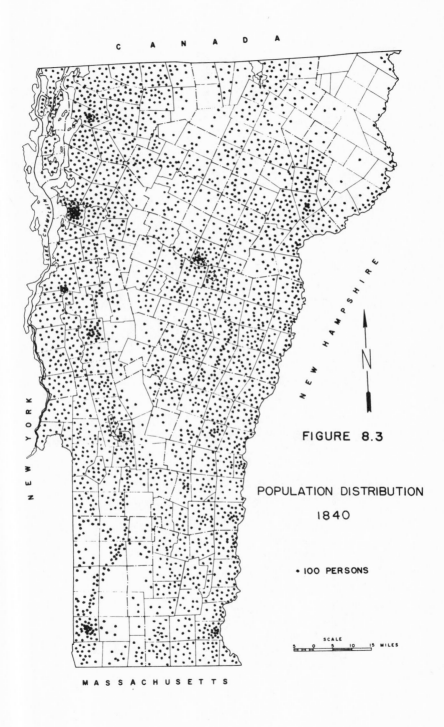

FIGURE 8.3

POPULATION DISTRIBUTION

1840

• 100 PERSONS

SCALE
5 0 5 10 15 MILES

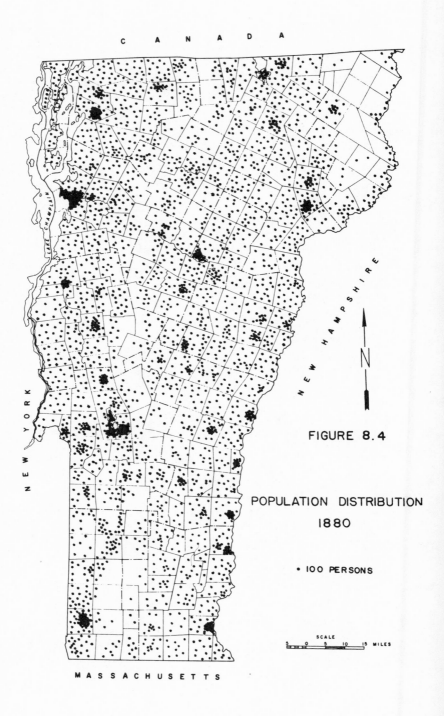

CANADA

NEW YORK

LAKE CHAMPLAIN

MASSACHUSETTS

NEW HAMPSHIRE

N

FIGURE 8.4

POPULATION DISTRIBUTION
1880

• 100 PERSONS

SCALE
5 0 5 10 15 MILES

greater economic opportunity in the small industries responding to improved transportation.

Fully eighteen towns in Vermont went through population explosions as they were touched by the rails. Surprisingly, at least in population, neither Montpelier nor Randolph grew rapidly, but other communities more than made up for them. Readsboro, way down south on the HT&W, went from a population of 767 in the 1840 prerailroad era to 1,107 in 1870 thanks to the expanding paper industry. St. Johnsbury went from 1,887 to 4,665 during the same period, mostly because of the railroad junction the town had become, and the scale works described later in this chapter. Burlington increased from 4,271 to 14,387 in thirty years, to become by 1870 Vermont's largest city by a considerable margin. St. Albans, thanks to the railroad shops, grew from 2,702 in 1840 to 3,567 in 1870. The same happened in Northfield, early headquarters of the Vermont Central before relocation to St. Albans. There the 1840 population of 2,031 had increased to 4,329 in only twenty years. After that, decline set in, and in 1870 the number of people had shrunk to 3,410, graphic evidence of how much railroad employment matters in a small community. Newport, another railway junction, went from 591 to 2,050 between 1840 and 1870, and Brighton (Island Pond) exploded from 157 to 2,050 during the same period.

The larger stoneworking towns grew rapidly, but much of their growth came later with the immigrant groups who made up a major part of the workforce in the quarries and shops. Hardwick had a population of 1,216 in 1840, but saw little growth until the 1890s, so that its maximum nineteenth-century population was 2,466 at the turn of the century. Barre had 2,126 people in 1840, and by 1870 had 244 *fewer*! In 1888 the railroad linked Barre with Millstone Hill (Quarry Hill), the Italians were arriving, and by 1900 Barre's population reached 11,790. Rutland was not only the home of the Rutland and Burlington Railroad, but also was Vermont's great marble center. Neither West Rutland nor Proctor had been formed as political entities at the time, and so Rutland's growth from 2,708 to 9,834 between 1840 and 1870 reflects the influence of those industries. When the Howe Scale Works were erected in the 1870s they ensured continued employment and population growth, and the community continued to prosper.

Brattleboro, Waterbury, and Wallingford all saw growth during the early railroad era. Springfield grew from 2,625 in 1840 to 2,937 thirty years later, but competing Windsor decreased, with relocation of the Machine Tool Industry. The textile towns of Bennington, Ludlow, and Cavendish all showed growth as transportation improved. After a long period with stable population, Rockingham (Bellows Falls) increased, as did Hartford with its White River Junction railroad community.

Machine-Tool Industry

The earliest industry to export manufactured products from Vermont was the small machine-tool company, of which many were forming in the Windsor and Springfield areas. That unique industry owes its origin not to raw materials, transportation, or availability of power, but to the vision of several ingenious men who with an inventive turn of mind began the industry in small machine shops early in the 1820s.

In 1827, John Cooper of Guildhall patented a device that he called a "rotative pump," in other words, a pump that went around and around rather than up and down. Cooper, believing that his invention would have application in pumping bilges of Connecticut River steamboats, hurried to Windsor, where everyone was excited about the prospects of navigation on the dew of the upper Connecticut. He secured backing and produced pumps, but most of them did not work and the firm went bankrupt. That might have been the end had not Asahel Hubbard become interested. Hubbard, working out of a small shop in the place that is now West Windsor, expanded on the pump idea and built an improved model after finding capital in the form of Jabez Proctor of Proctorsville. Jabez, father of Redfield, later governor of Vermont, sank enough money into the venture that he and Asahel incorporated the National Hydraulic Company with a capitalization of $50,000. Rotary pumps began to be produced in Windsor in the early 1830s by prison labor at the state prison, where Jabez, with his influence, had installed a stationary steam engine and had Hubbard installed as warden.

The principle behind production of the successful pump was interchangeability of parts. Up to this time each manufactured machine was unique, no identical parts being available if one failed. Hubbard spent more time producing parts for his pump than he did producing pumps, and for the first time the customer could be assured of an identical part to replace the one that had expired. Skill was needed, and in the early years machines that could produce identical parts were nonexistent. Hubbard built them in the prison where he was warden. Later in 1835 his son-in-law, Nicanor Kendall, came to work for the Hydraulic Company and invented an improved underhammer, a rifle-firing mechanism. Production of guns—an improved version of the Kentucky rifle—commenced in, of all places, the state prison. Trigger and firing mechanisms were produced in Windsor, and the barrels were forged, bored, and rifled by Eliphalet Remington of Ilion, New York. From Remington's small shop grew the great Remington industry, originally based on Remington Arms. Kendall rifles were sold through the agents of the pump company and earned a fine reputation throughout the country.

In the 1840s the firm moved out of the prison and occupied facilities on Mill Brook. There it became Robbins and Lawrence, and did a booming business providing arms to the forty-niners on their way West. Robbins and Lawrence also began to manufacture machine tools, and exhibited their rifles at the Crystal Palace in London. The English were impressed, and in a couple of years the small Windsor, Vermont company was given a contract to produce the Enfield Armory rifle, as well as replacement parts for that famous gun. Unfortunately, the Crimean War (1854–1856) came to a close just as Robbins and Lawrence were gearing up for full production. The company had been unable to meet the contract specifications, and the end of hostilities was a severe blow to the gun makers in Windsor. What had become known as the Windsor Armory collapsed in the middle 1850s. The bankrupt firm became Jones and Lamson, an outstanding name in Vermont machine tools to the present.

With no capital in Windsor, a group of Springfield businessmen bought the firm for $20,000 and moved it to that community. They secured the services of twenty-seven-year-old James Harkness of Torrington, Connecticut to manage the enterprise, and Jones and Lamson prospered after Harkness became superintendent. Springfield gradually assumed a place in the national machine-tool industry. Windsor meanwhile diversified further, but continued to grow even after losing the J&L firm.

Banding together, many of the fine machinists of Windsor who had not followed the relocation to Springfield bought the machine shop on the north bank of Mill Brook. They formed the Windsor

Machine Company and the operation tottered along, though severely hurt by the depression of 1893. In 1895 Frank L. Cone went to work for the company and soon became superintendent, a position he held for eleven years. Business still was not too good, and in 1915, the Windsor Machine Company was bought by the National Acme Manufacturing Company of Cleveland, and much of the operation moved to that growing city in the Midwest. Cone resigned from Windsor Machine, and in 1916 bought five acres next to the railroad tracks; the Cone Automatic Machine Company was born. Today Cone-Blanchard and Goodyear Tire and Rubber are the two largest employers in Windsor.

Over in Springfield, Harkness had perfected the turret lathe, and between 1891 and 1904 the only source for that important machine was in a small backwoods Vermont town, just recently connected to the outside world by an electric railway (1896) running on power generated for the machine shops growing along the south side of the Black River. Inventiveness breeds inventiveness and like industries attract like industries. There is no other reason for the intensification of machine-tool production in Vermont's Precision Valley. Twenty-four-year-old Edwin Fellows came to Springfield and worked for Harkness, and between 1889 and 1896 developed a new method of cutting gears. Leaving Jones and Lamson, Fellows in 1896 founded his own firm, the Fellows Gear Shaper Company. William Bryant succeeded Fellows as chief tool designer at Jones and Lamson. A graduate of the University of Vermont, Bryant in 1909 resigned and formed his own company, the Bryant Chucking Grinder Company. Finally, Fred P. Lovejoy came along and took over Bryant's job at J&L. While there he invented an improved cutting tool, and, encouraged by Harkness, started his own company in the original Jones and Lamson structure in Springfield. The Lovejoy Tool Company and Foundry was, strictly speaking, not a machine-tool producer, but their entire output was consumed by the three machine-tool-company neighbors.

By 1915, Springfield was perhaps Vermont's major manufacturing center. With a population of 7,202 in 1920, the town ranked fifth in the state, exceeded only by Bennington, Brattleboro, St. Albans, and Burlington. The three machine-tool companies and the Lovejoy concern were employing more than a thousand people, many of them recently arrived immigrants from Europe, quickly trained in the Springfield shops. Measured by the value of the product being made, the Springfield-Windsor combination was probably the most important industrial area in the state, and although Bennington, Burlington, and Winooski (Colchester) all employed more people, the cottons and woolens had much lower value, and much of the product was being consumed within the state. Not so in Springfield, where finely machined tools contributed to America's effort in World War I and served a national market.

During World War II, more than 13,000 people were working in machine tools, and though Vermont was producing only about 5 percent of the nation's supply of machines that build other machines, the four major companies were humming briskly. The industry had come a long way from its beginnings, and the war years contributed to the state's reputation as a producer of high-quality precision equipment, a fact not lost on more recent company moves to the Green Mountain state, like Simmons Precision in Vergennes, International Business Machines in Essex, and the several General Electric plants.

Yankee ingenuity was not confined to the machinists of Springfield. William Davenport invented the electric motor in Brandon, and both John Deere and John Glidden were Vermonters who did their work far to the west. Deere's steel plow made it possible to turn the tough prairie sod of Iowa, and Glidden's perfected barbed wire made it possible to fence the land.

Platform Scales

Some inventive Vermonters stayed behind. Seventy miles north of Springfield another industrial empire was building. In St. Johnsbury, brothers Erastus and Thaddeus Fairbanks in 1834 incorporated the E. & T. Fairbanks Company to manufacture platform scales, the first company to do so in the United States. The Fairbanks Company came to dominate the life of sleepy St. Johnsbury as the machine-tool industry did in more vibrant, ethnic Springfield. St. Johnsbury Academy, the Athenaeum, the Music Hall, and the Museum of Natural Science were built with Fairbanks money, and even the forever-troubled St. Johnsbury and Lake Champlain Railroad (Chapter 5) was directly related to the goings-on at the scale works. Erastus ran for governor in 1852 and was elected with considerable help from the good citizens of St. Johnsbury, who endorsed him with a plurality of

As waterpower sites and railroads developed in valleys, whole upland settlements moved downhill. This is what remains of the Church at Corinth Corners, at an elevation of 1,500 feet.

Behind this historic site sign outside of St. Johnsbury is the modern Fairbanks Weighing Division of Colt Industries.

The beautiful old woolen mill in Ludlow provided a home for General Electric until that company relocated to Rutland in the late 1970s.

70 percent. Vermonters apparently approved of the Fairbanks paternalism, in sharp contrast to later paternalistic empires that came crashing down in the 1880s and 1890s with the growth of the American labor movement. That St. Johnsbury never received many immigrants to staff the factory may have had something to do with this acceptance. For its entire life, the Fairbanks Scale Works in St. Johnsbury was run by Vermonters and employed mainly Vermonters. Now as a subsidiary of Colt Industries, the old factory has been razed, but the empire is still alive and well outside of St. Johnsbury.

The production of weighing scales must have been an obsession in Vermont. Local farmers throughout the state always had large bundles of bulky, heavy, and usually poorly tied raw material to convert to something more useful. The story is that raw hemp led to the Fairbanks scale, but a hundred miles to the southwest another Vermonter was working on a scale, similar to the Fairbanks but mounted on ball bearings. Credit for the 1865 invention goes to Frank Strong of Vergennes; it was manufactured in Brandon at the Howe Scale Company, owned and operated by John Howe. When the Howe Scale Company burned to the ground in 1873 the plant was resurrected in Rutland four years later and for many years was, along with the railroad and the marble industry, the major employer in the vicinity. Just after World War II, more than eight hundred people were working at Howe Scale.*

For many years the scales made in out-of-the-way Vermont dominated the United States market. As late as 1950, Fairbanks and Howe scales accounted for about three quarters of national production, and the industries were vital parts of their communities. Producing a commodity that was heavy and bulky, with most materials shipped in and the finished product shipped out, was not particularly logical, defying the laws of industrial location. The industries were there solely because of the inventive genius and business acumen of individuals. Like the machine tools of Springfield and Windsor, the scale works reflected manufacturing in a uniquely Vermont style for a non-Vermont market. Like the production of textiles, they were the backbone of Vermont nonlocal industry late in the nineteenth and early in the twentieth century. Along with them went development of

---

*The scale works are now closed, and in 1985 the buildings were vacant, the owners seeking a new use for them.

Barre granite cutting and continued growth of wood industries of various kinds.

Textiles

Given a temporary boost by demand created during the Civil War, the fledging Vermont textile industry floundered briefly during the depression of 1873, but not enough to obliterate it and prevent the industry from achieving record production levels after 1920. Having been a small industry geared to local raw materials and markets (Chapter 4), the wool and cotton mills after 1850 had to import their raw material and export from the state most of their finished product. On the fringe of New England textile manufacturing, the Vermont businesses were in an even worse location than the larger southern New England factories, which felt Carolina competition later than the local industry did.

From 1850 to 1860 the number of Vermont textile firms shrank almost in proportion to the number of sheep. Even the railroad didn't help, and had it not been for the Civil War the industry might quietly have passed from the scene. As it was, demand for wool skyrocketed with hostilities, and during the 1860s new factories were started in Chester, Derby, Franklin, Bristol, Northfield, Springfield, Richmond, Montpelier, and Fair Haven. The number of wool firms alone reached a high of sixty-nine during the war. Their locations are shown on the map of textile operations from 1860 to 1869 (Figure 8.5). Cotton textiles went into decline because there was no cotton, and though some ceased operations entirely, others turned to wool.

After 1850, cotton factories and wool operations were interdependent. Wool, a weak fiber, was often woven with cotton warp (threads running lengthwise in the loom) to increase the strength of the cloth. Most cotton mills were producing cotton warp for local consumption in the woolen mills, and whenever the wool industry went into decline so too did the cotton industry. The cotton and wool mills that weathered the bad years of the early 1870s expanded greatly in the last three decades of the nineteenth century. Railways were reliable, freight rates were relatively low, demand for products was growing, and the backwater Vermont industry grew significantly, though in fewer places. The number of textile operations shrank from sixty in 1870 to forty-six in 1900 as the smaller mills disap-

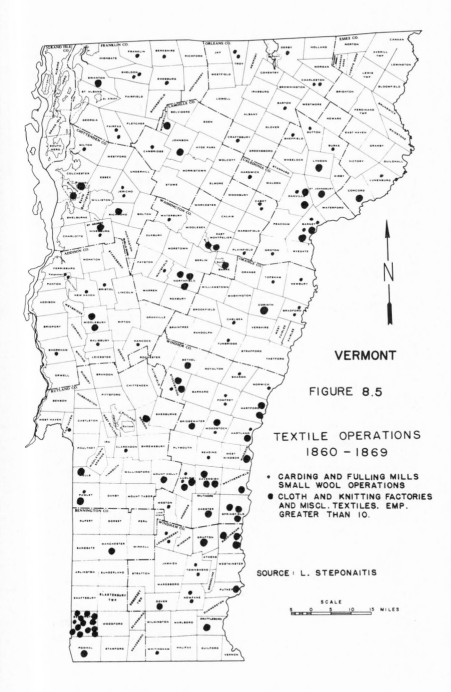

VERMONT

FIGURE 8.5

TEXTILE OPERATIONS
1860 – 1869

• CARDING AND FULLING MILLS
  SMALL WOOL OPERATIONS
● CLOTH AND KNITTING FACTORIES
  AND MISCL. TEXTILES. EMP.
  GREATER THAN 10.

SOURCE: L. STEPONAITIS

SCALE
5   0   5   10   15 MILES

peared. The loss was greatest in northern Vermont, farthest from the southern New England and Middle Atlantic markets. In Franklin, Orleans, Caledonia, and Lamoille counties, the thirty mills of the 1860s had become the eighteen operations of the 1890s.

The larger mills grew. During the decades after 1870, mills (or factories) employing more than a hundred increased rapidly. In 1885 the Hartford Woolen Company, the Aegean Mill in Ludlow, the Proctorsville Mill in Cavendish, and the Colchester Mill (1880) in the section that was later to become Winooski, all reached an employment of more than a hundred. The Colchester Mill was largest, with 850 workers and more than 10,300 spindles. Even with these large mills, however, the production could not make up for the drop in the smaller operations, and the output of woolen cloth fell during the period. In 1890 the production of wool cloth in Vermont was below that in 1860.

Employment in the industry is difficult to estimate, but from around 2,000 in the 1840s (Chapter 4), and with several ups and downs, probably a few more than 6,000 people were working in the mills in 1900. The high point came in 1920, when 7,600 textile workers were concentrated in thirty-nine larger, more efficient operations. After 1920 the industry began to decline rapidly. Only twenty-five factories were working in 1940, seven in Bennington alone, but the American Woolen Company in Winooski was employing 2,500, or 43 percent of the textile employment of 5,800. In the early 1980s, the entire textile and apparel industry had fewer than 2,000 employees.

From the large number of plants shown in Figure 8.5, the industry gradually contracted. In 1900, twenty-six towns or cities had at least one textile operation. By 1920 the number was twenty-one, and in 1940, before World War II broke out, the mills were concentrated in only twelve locations: Bennington (7), Brattleboro (1), Bridgewater (1), Cavendish (1), East Montpelier (1), Fair Haven (1), Hartford (3), Johnson (1), Ludlow (4), Northfield (3), Springfield (1), and Winooski (1).

Mill Towns

Because the technology for producing wool and cotton cloth are almost the same, and the same equipment can be used, with modifications, over the years many Vermont and New England manufacturing plants shifted back and forth depending on the market and availability of raw materials. That happened in Winooski, which was to become *the* textile center of Vermont before the American Woolen Company ceased operation in 1956. There, the Colchester Merino Mill was completed in 1880, the first of several Winooski mills. On occasion the mill produced cotton yarn when the market demanded it, though it was primarily a woolen-cloth operation. The old Colchester Mill is downstream from the bridge over the Winooski. In the 1927 flood, water flowed through the second floor of the structure, and later a concrete floodwall was built, still to be seen around the base of the old building. In its heyday, the Colchester Mill employed more than eight hundred people; after serving long as a discount department store, it now houses apartments.

Just downstream of the Colchester Mill was a structure built later, originally the home of the Winooski Worsted Company. Smaller than the Colchester Mill, it was constructed in the 1890s along with another mill that burned in 1961. The three buildings were acquired in 1902 by the American Woolen Company, and all production then became wool cloth. The old Colchester Mill became Building 3, and was converted at that time from the production of cotton to the manufacture of woolens. The American Woolen Company also constructed, in 1912, the Champlain Mill (Building 4), which lies just upstream of the bridge between Burlington and Winooski. In 1981 the Champlain Mill became an attractive indoor shopping center.

In Winooski the wounds of nineteenth-century industrial growth and later decline have been slow to heal, but in the other major Vermont textile community, Bennington, the transition was easier simply because other users of the old textile buildings were waiting to utilize the properties as they became available. Unlike the recently vacant old mills along the Winooski, the red-brick factories of Bennington have tenants, are producing, and are employing many Bennington people.

In number of plants, Bennington was by far Vermont's most significant early textile center. In the list that follows, employment figures are estimates based on the installed capacity of the factory, number of spindles, and other information on the physical plant, where available. In a general way the employment figures mirror the rise and fall of the Vermont textile industry. Also, the operations were fascinating because of their products. In 1910, Bennington mills churned out balbriggan and worsted underwear, children's knit wrists, union suits, cotton underwear, cotton and worsted hose, cotton-ribbed anklets, sweater coats, hosiery, cassimere hose, fancy woolen and worsted dress goods, and yards and yards of lisle. Other years give similarly diverse products, most made in small and medium-size shops never approaching the gigantic Winooski mills, or the large Queen City Cotton Company in Burlington, which closed in 1939.

		Bennington Textile Plants, 1770–1970	
Year	*No. of operations*	*Production*	*Employment (estimated)*
1770	1	wool?	
1780	3	wool cotton / fulling	
1790	3	wool cotton / fulling	
1800	4	cotton / wool / fulling	
1810	6	cotton / wool / fulling	20 est.
1820	11	cotton / wool / fulling	75 est.
1830	14	cotton / linen / wool / fulling / carding	125 est.
1840	20	cotton / wool / fulling / carding	240 est.
1850	11	cotton / wool / knitting	200 est.
1860	15	cotton / linen / knitting	350 est.
1870	16	cotton / wool / linen / knitting	
1880	15	cotton / knitting / clothing	900 est.
1890	12	cotton / wool / knitting / silk	1,300 est.
1900	12	knitting / wool	2,000 est.
1910	16	knitting / wool	2,300 est.
1920	10	knitting / wool	2,300 est.
1930	9	knitting / wool	2,000 est.
1940	7	knitting / wool	825 est.
1950	8	knitting / wool	200 est.
1960	7	knitting / wool / clothing	250 est.
1970	5	wool / clothing	150

Source: Derived from Louis Steponaitis, *The Textile Industry in Vermont, 1790–1973: Its Development, Diffusion and Decline*. Master of Arts Thesis. Dept. of Geography, University of Vermont, October 1975.

Bennington was unique in Vermont in that its industrial growth was based not on the local wool resource, but on imported cotton and the manufacture of knit goods. By 1854 the last of the woolen mills had been converted to production of knitwear, and the knitting industry, using both fabrics, prospered until the early years of the twentieth century. Names like "Cooper" and "Allen A." are parts of

Bennington's textile history and when in the 1880s the old mills began to show signs of being obsolete, these companies built modern mills and enabled the community to retain its role as an industrial textile town. But the handwriting was on the wall. In 1907 the Bennington Waxed Paper Company took over one of the old mills, the first of many alternate industries. The biggest blow was the closing in 1938 of the then Holding and Leonard Co. "Big Mill," which wiped out eight hundred jobs overnight, one fourth of the employment in Bennington. Other large employer mills like Bottum and Torance and the Bennington Hosiery Company ceased operations in the late 1930s and early 1940s. From an employment of about two thousand in 1930, the work force had shrunk to eight hundred or fewer in 1940 and to two hundred by 1950.

In Bennington, Union Carbide moved into old textile plants, as did the Bijur Corporation and Bennington Display. Benmont Papers uses an old mill. Globe Union (batteries) has built a large new plant on the outskirts. In the 1970s at least four small knitting operations were carrying on a once-proud tradition and the town finally had some economic stability after thirty years of flux. Bennington has managed to survive as a viable town despite the disasters of textile closings; the community is fortunate compared to several other old Vermont cloth towns.

When the Queen City Cotton Company closed in 1939, Burlington lost seven hundred jobs but the effect on Vermont's largest city was less than the loss of eight hundred jobs in Bennington a year before. Fortunately for Burlington, World War II came along, and Bell Aircraft took over the old plant to manufacture airplane components. General Electric inherited the structure, and in the early 1980s GE Burlington employment was about two thousand, manufacturing armaments on Defense Department contracts.

All over Vermont, the often-empty mill buildings stand as testimony to a vanished industry. In the late 1970s the Little Mill in East Montpelier was razed after manufacturing textiles for more than 140 years. The modern mill of the Nantanna Worsted Company in Northfield, built about 1920, recently stood vacant. In Burlington, the Chace Mill, just across the Winooski River from the old wool town, is occupied partially by wholesale distributors. The site may become important for a hydroelectric plant. Probably the best-preserved old textile mill in the state is in Proctorsville. There the old stone building of the former Black Bear Woolen Company, built about 1830, lacks a tenant. Proctorsville itself shows probably better than any other place in Vermont the architectural styles of nineteenth-century mills. Most are unused, and there is the problem. What company would utilize picturesque ancient buildings, removed from markets, in the cold north, when at the same time new buildings are available in warmer southern areas? Not too many, it seems.

As Vermont developed an industrial base during the nineteenth century, the two most important manufacturing industries were machine tools and textiles. Vermont had a virtual New England monopoly on the former, but was in competition with its own region and the South in the latter. By 1920, which was perhaps the greatest period for Vermont textiles, the state's factories were contributing only about 5 percent of the New England output of fabrics and knit goods. That the American Woolen Company in Winooski kept going as long as it did is nothing short of a miracle; the secret was tradition plus the terribly low wages paid to the workers. In 1890, it was calculated that Vermont had the lowest labor costs in New England.

Labor Cost per Spindle, 1890

Vermont	$2.90
Massachusetts	4.45
Connecticut	4.65
New England average	4.50
U.S. average	4.75
South average	4.50

The low cost of labor kept Vermont industries from migrating South long after they had fled much of southern New England.

The industries that made Vermont a manufacturing state are still around. Together the machine tools and the successors to the scale industries employ about 15 percent of the manufacturing labor force, although the significance of Springfield has markedly declined. All that is left of the old textile industry now employs about 1,800 in the textile and apparel industries, which generate about 9 percent of the manufacturing payroll in Vermont. Although the industry is now relatively unimportant, there has been some recent growth in the manufacture of sportswear, especially in Newport, Bennington, and Middlebury.

Many other industries with non-Vermont markets began during the 1800s, but except for stone and wood industries, were less important than scales, machine tools, and textiles. Bottles of liniment and curealls from Enosburg had their day, to be sure. By 1910 more than 80 percent of industrially employed Vermonters were working in wood, stone, machine tools, scales, or textiles. Many more probably wanted to get off the farm, but the opportunities simply were not multiplying as rapidly as were the sons and daughters.

II

Modern Vermont

For me at least, writing (and reading) about what is going on now is much less fun than dealing with the past. Yet since 1960, Vermont has seen unprecedented growth and change, which need to be appreciated and understood before we can end this story. Two decades and more in the life of a topsy-turvy state are hard to generalize about, but in this section I'll do my best to tell what has been going on.

Just about every facet of Vermont culture and ways of life has changed. Burlington, largest city in the state, elected a socialist mayor; state agencies—admittedly with the support of the population—began to tell Vermonters what they could do and not do with their land. Through federal legislation, "poverty" no longer was the responsibility of local communities, but became a national program—the old Poor Farm disappeared. Dairy inspectors began to tell farmers how many feet away from the barn their water supply had to be. The state got into the business of building access roads to expanding ski resorts. National right-to-know laws often made it difficult for elected officials to function efficiently, having to conduct business in a fishbowl-like atmosphere. No longer could firms erect advertising signs away from their place of business. Vermonters were given a say when railroads wanted to spray herbicides along their rights-of-way. Although some of the rapid changes owe their origin to federal policies, in many areas of regulation Vermont was in the forefront of rapid change.

What has triggered all this change, at least in a Vermont context? More than anything else the reason has been an exploding population. But whether population growth has caused change, or whether change has caused population growth, is a moot question.

Most likely both are catalysts. Population increases result in economic and social changes, which in turn lead to further growth, which in turn often leads to more change. A snowball effect is set in motion, the ultimate result of which will significantly alter Vermont's geography from anything that has gone before.

The immediate cause of the initial surge in Vermont's population after 1960 appears to be quicker and more convenient accessibility brought by construction of the Interstate Highway network. It seems appropriate to refer to the state's recent development as the Interstate Era, with changes comparable to those in the Railroad Era of the late nineteenth century.

We will deal with recent population growth and the changes related to more people. These include the maturity of a recreation industry, significant changes in farming, development of new types of industry, and even changes in what people are thinking about their state.

9

Changes in Population

Vermont's population increased by about 150 percent between 1790 and 1810, as the young people from the rocky farms of southern New England moved northward. At the beginning it took only twenty years for the state's population to increase by 133,000. But it took between 1810 and 1950 (140 years) for the population to increase by an additional 160,000. The initial tide of settlement swept over Vermont in a few years. Afterward came virtual stagnation, as natural increase was absorbed through emigration. Vermont did grow, but its growth was among the slowest of all the states, and in two decades it even lost population. Tables 4.2 and 8.1 summarized population change from the first census of 1790 through 1950. Geographically, the growth that did occur was concentrated in a few towns. The shifts of population were subtle, but usually reflected migration from poor farm areas to better ones, and the growth of industrial communities in the valleys served by railroads and water power.

Recent Changes in Population

After World War II, the automobile became a symbol of necessity rather than luxury. Suburban growth made it necessary to have an automobile to get to work, or even to shop in the glamorous new shopping centers. The weekend excursion on the electric trolley of 1910, or the hazardous rigors of a motorcar tour in the 1920s and 1930s became twenty-minute or one-day Sunday drives for a growing number of Americans.

The effects of the new mobility were first felt in Vermont's recreation industry; these influences later translated into more new residents. During the 1950s the population grew by only a little more than 3 percent. The next ten years showed a growth of 14.1 percent, and between 1970 and 1980 it was 15 percent. The most direct cause of this increase was the approaching completion of the National Defense Highways, a system begun under the Eisenhower administration in 1956. In 1960 the population was 389,881; by 1970 it had reached 444,732, and in 1980 it was 511,456. Vermont, in twenty years, gained about 121,000 people, representing an increase in population density of some thirteen people per square mile.

Provide a mobile American population, already having the means to move over large distances, with a limited-access highway system. Mix in the desirable perceptions that places like Vermont enjoy. Add the work that Vermont has done in promoting its image for many years. Figure that because of civil rights decisions in the early 1960s nearly anyone can claim public-assistance benefits anywhere, irrespective of residency in a particular place. The American population began to move, and without constraints, to move to those areas considered most "desirable."

Accessibility provided by fast and well-engineered highways directly affected growth in population and recreation. These same corridors for rapid communication also made it possible for industries, once more closely tied to railways or to markets, to branch out into areas of lower-cost labor, specialized labor, environmental amenities, and the like. In 1980, a truck could get from White River Junction to New York City in the same time that it would have taken that same vehicle to negotiate the route between Hartford, Connecticut and New York City before completion of the Interstate. Mileage was unimportant, but *time* did count! The railroads, rapid for their era, could not always compete, but innovations such as trailer trains and guaranteed overnight deliveries were devised as a response to the competition offered by the trucking industry.

In Vermont, population exploded, but along with more people, jobs and economic opportunity grew, and the state began to develop industrially, a change that the hill farmer as late as the 1940s could not have dreamed of. And as the economy continues to develop, so too does the attractiveness of living in Vermont and even, at the same time, of making a living there.

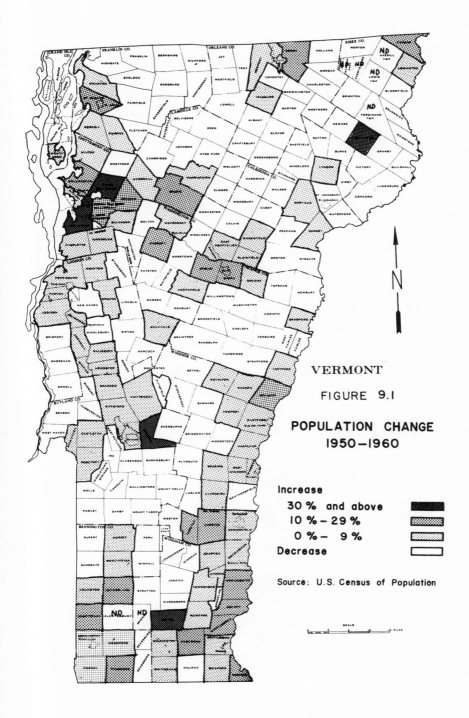

VERMONT

FIGURE 9.1

POPULATION CHANGE
1950–1960

Increase
30 % and above
10 % – 29 %
0 % – 9 %
Decrease

Source: U.S. Census of Population

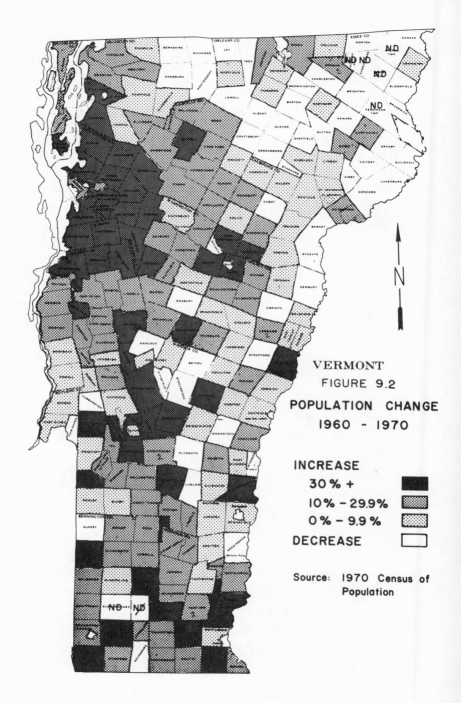

VERMONT
FIGURE 9.2

POPULATION CHANGE
1960 - 1970

INCREASE
30 % +
10 % - 29.9 %
0 % - 9.9 %
DECREASE

Source: 1970 Census of
Population

Any change in the number of people living in a place combines two factors. One is natural increase, or the excess of births over deaths. The other is migration, the number of people moving into or out of a place. Between 1930 and 1940, Vermont had a natural increase of 17,628, but an emigration of 18,008, giving a net change in the population of *minus* 380. For the years 1940 to 1950, the natural increase was 37,123 and the emigration 18,607, and so the population actually grew by 18,516 during the decade. During the 1950s the natural increase was 49,776, but this growth was matched by a significant increase in emigration, to 37,642. Thus the population increased by only 12,134 between 1950 and 1960.

But then came the highways and jobs and affluence. In the 1960s, the turnaround in trends was abrupt and surprising. The population increased by 38,976 through natural increase, but to that figure has to be added an astounding 15,571 immigrants, for a total increase of 54,547. Another way of expressing this difference is that 28.5 percent of the state's growth in population was due to new Vermonters.

Census returns for 1980 show the trend continuing. In keeping with a national phenomenon, natural increase is slowing; during the 1970s it was 29,027, but the population increased by 66,724, and so 37,697 people were added by immigration. About 56 percent of the most recent growth, then, has been accomplished by people moving into Vermont. These changes are shown in Table 9.1, which continues Tables 4.2 and 8.1.

TABLE 9.1

		Vermont Population Change, 1960–1980		
Year	Population	Net change	Percentage change	U.S. % change
1850	314,120			
1960	389,881	+ 75,761 (from 1850)	24.1 (from 1850)	
1970	444,732	+ 54,851	14.1	13.2
1980	511,456	+ 66,724	15.0	12.0

For comparison, we see how, during the 1970s, the other New England states changed: Connecticut, + 2.1 percent (64,734); Rhode Island, − 0.4 percent (− 3,971); Massachusetts, + 0.7 percent (39,118); Maine, + 13.1 percent (129,838); and New Hampshire, rapidly becoming a Boston suburb: + 24.6 percent (181,433). The

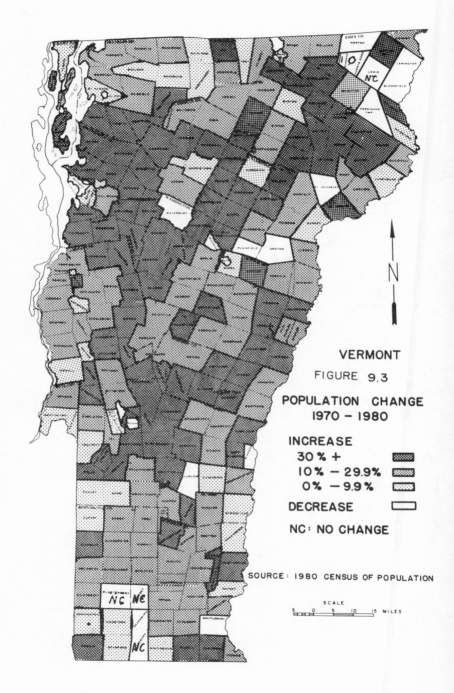

VERMONT

FIGURE 9.3

POPULATION CHANGE
1970 - 1980

INCREASE
30 % +
10 % - 29.9%
0 % - 9.9%
DECREASE

NC: NO CHANGE

SOURCE: 1980 CENSUS OF POPULATION

SCALE
5   0   5   10   15 MILES

N

three southern New England states had a net gain of 99,181, and the
northern states grew by 377,838!

Patterns of Population

In three maps (Figures 9.1, 9.2, and 9.3) we see how population has
grown since 1950. Each map uses the same categories.

During the 1950s any growth that appears is almost entirely
suburban and southern. Vermont was still losing population. During
the 1960s the suburban trends intensified; ski areas continued to see
an influx of new people, and growth patterns are more difficult to
generalize about. Between 1970 and 1980, little pattern appears in
the increase in population; it was growing everywhere except in a few
scattered rural towns and in the larger urban places. Comparing the
three maps illustrates a changing state, with a flood of growth between 1960 and 1980. One focuses on those areas which lost population, not those which gained.

TABLE 9.2

Vermont County Population

County	1900	1950	1960	1970	1980	Percentage of change 1960–1980
Addison	21,912	19,442	20,076	24,266	29,406	15.6
Bennington	21,705	24,115	25,088	29,282	33,345	32.8
Caledonia	24,381	24,049	22,786	22,789	25,808	13.3
Chittenden	39,600	62,570	74,425	99,131	115,534	55.3
Essex	8,048	6,257	6,083	5,417	6,313	3.6
Franklin	30,198	29,894	29,474	31,282	34,788	17.4
Grand Isle	4,462	3,406	2,927	3,574	4,613	56.9
Lamoille	12,289	11,388	11,027	13,309	16,767	52.1
Orange	19,313	17,027	16,014	17,676	22,739	42.1
Orleans	22,024	21,190	20,143	20,153	23,440	16.4
Rutland	44,209	45,905	46,719	52,637	58,347	24.9
Washington	36,607	42,870	42,860	47,659	52,393	22.2
Windham	26,660	28,749	29,776	33,476	36,933	23.9
Windsor	32,225	40,885	42,483	44,082	51,030	19.8
State	342,633	377,747	389,881	444,732	511,456	31.2

210   *Modern Vermont*

Major Population Centers					
	1900	*1950*	*1960*	*1970*	*1980*
Burlington	18,640	33,155	35,531	38,633	37,712
(S. Burlington, Essex,					
Colchester, Winooski)[a]	8,526	17,841	26,131	37,068	44,018
	27,166	50,996	61,662	75,701	81,730[b]
Rutland City	11,499	17,659	18,325	19,293	18,436
(Rutland Town, Proctor,					
West Rutland)	6,159	5,820	5,946	6,724	7,649
	17,658	23,479	24,271	26,017	26,085
Barre City	8,448	10,922	10,387	10,209	9,824
(Barre Town)	3,346	4,145	4,580	6,509	7,090
	11,794	15,067	14,967	16,718	16,914
Bennington Town & Village	8,033	12,411	13,002	14,586	15,815
Brattleboro Town & Village	6,640	11,522	11,734	12,239	11,886
St. Albans City & Town	7,954	10,460	11,109	11,352	10,863
Montpelier City	6,266	8,599	8,782	8,609	8,241
Springfield Town & Village	3,432	9,190	9.924	10,063	10,190
St. Johnsbury Town & Village	7,010	9,292	8,869	8,409	7,938
Milton Town	1,805	1,874	2,022	4,495	6,829
Newport City	1,874	5,212	5,019	4,664	4,756
Rockingham Town & Bellows					
Falls Village	5,809	5,499	5,704	5,501	5,538

[a]Essex Town and Essex Junction Village, 14,392; Colchester, 12,629; South Burlington, 10,679; Winooski, 6,318. All 1980 population.
[b]Burlington Metropolitan Statistical Area (MSA), 115,308.
Source: U.S. Bureau of the Census, Census of Population, appropriate years.

Something is happening: Vermont is showing all the signs of suburban development typical of New York and Boston. One can see this trend in towns peripheral to Montpelier, Barre, Rutland, and Burlington. The thought that Montpelier, with a population in 1980 of 8,241, has suburbs is somewhat ludicrous, but the trend is going on all the time.

Table 9.2 summarizes the patterns on the maps, showing Vermont county totals and changes that have been going on in the larger places. The agricultural counties of Orleans, Franklin, and Addison show slower growth, but Grand Isle, with its proximity to Chittenden County, has shown a remarkable increase in population.

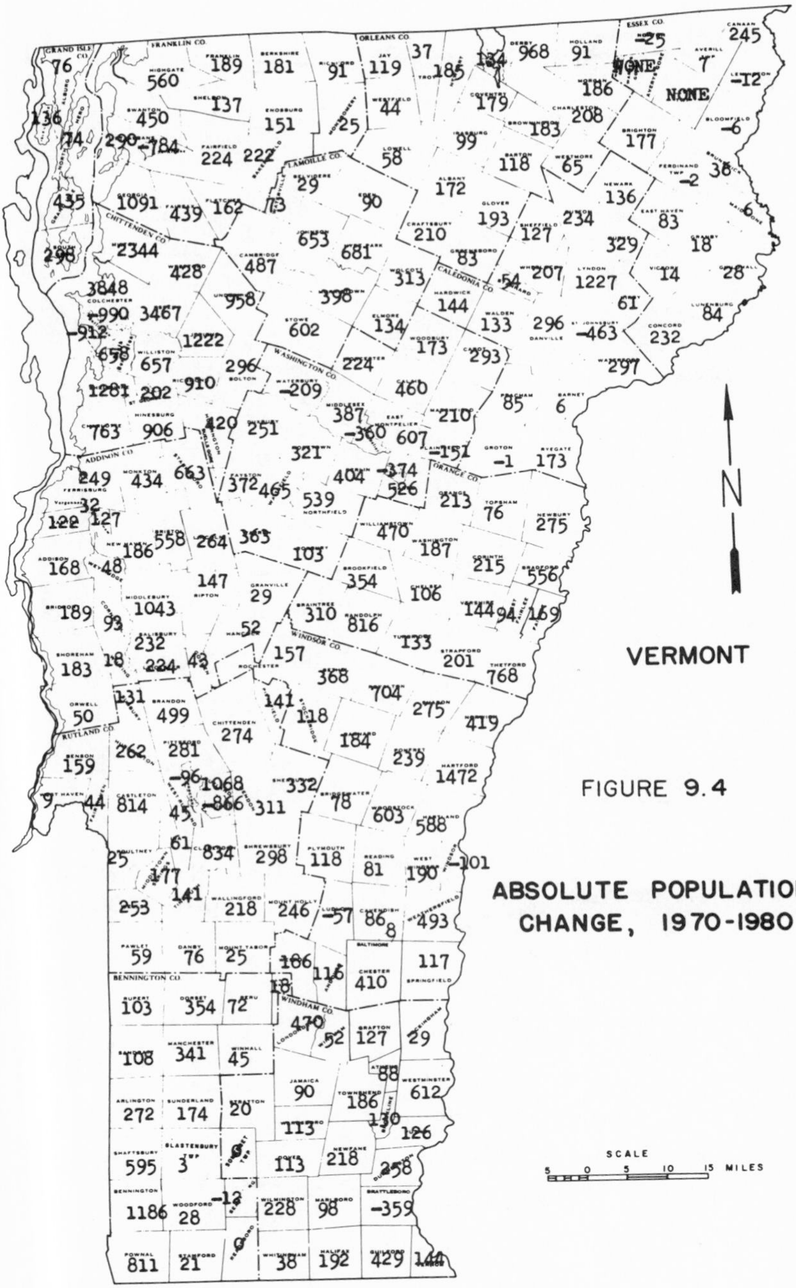

VERMONT

FIGURE 9.4

ABSOLUTE POPULATION
CHANGE, 1970-1980

SCALE
5 0 5 10 15 MILES

N

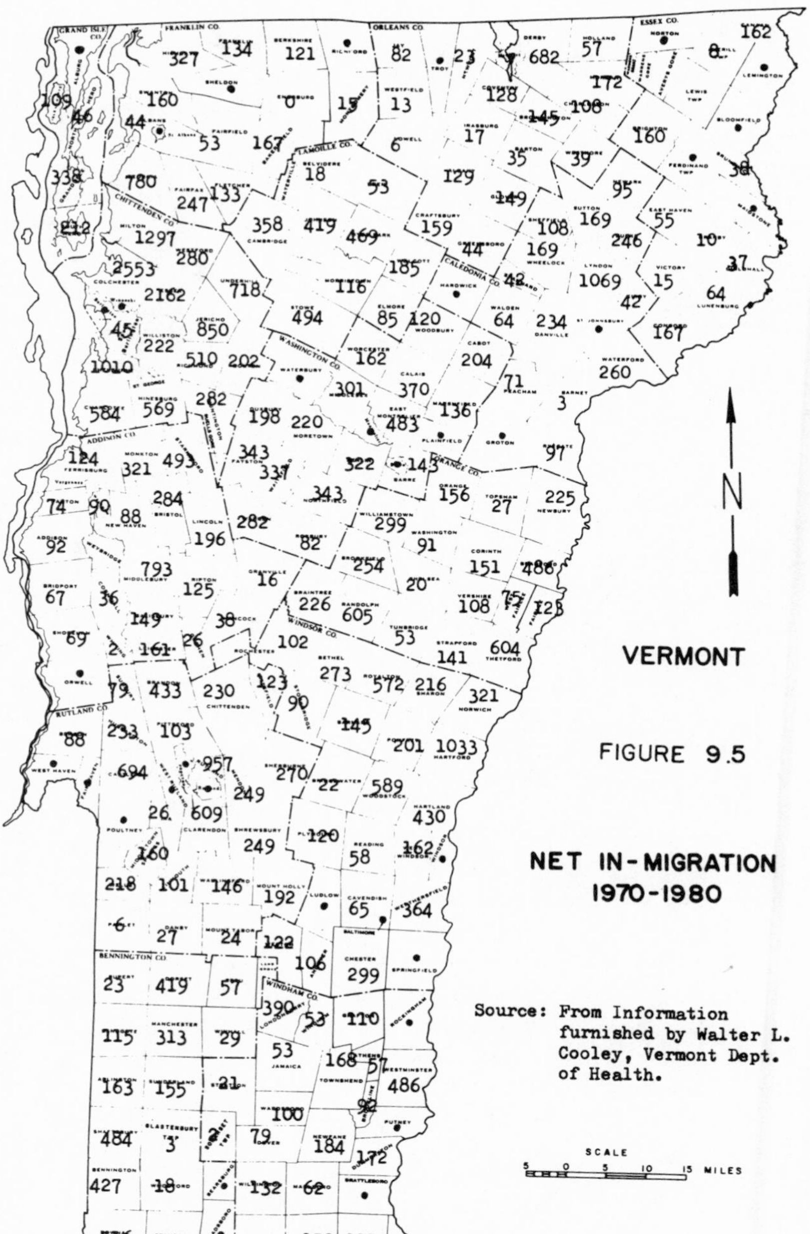

VERMONT

FIGURE 9.5

NET IN-MIGRATION
1970-1980

Source: From Information
furnished by Walter L.
Cooley, Vermont Dept.
of Health.

SCALE
5 0 5 10 15 MILES

Percentage changes (shown on the maps) can often be misleading because of the few people involved. The best illustration of this effect is Fayston in Washington County. Fayston increased by an incredible 127.4 percent between 1970 and 1980 (the greatest increase of any town). This figure, however, translates into a gain of only 372 people. Hubbardton in Rutland County was similar; its increase of 114.9 percent amounted to only 262 new residents. On the other hand, Colchester, just outside of Burlington, increased by a small 43 percent, but that amounted to 3,848 individuals—the largest numerical growth in any town in the state!

Figure 9.4 shows the *actual* number of people involved in 1970 to 1980 changes in population. In contrast to maps based on percentages, it shows the growth surrounding Burlington and Montpelier—Barre, as well as around Rutland. Places like Lyndon, Johnson, Castleton, and perhaps Middlebury are influenced by larger enrolments, for college students are counted as residents (at least by the Bureau of the Census) of the communities in which they attend school. Growth in student population at the University of Vermont was not sufficient, however, to offset the decline in Burlington's population. Partial closing of part of the Vermont State Hospital in Waterbury resulted in a loss of 209 people in that town. Canaan increased because of its furniture plant, and most of the gain came from immigration from New Hampshire.

More than half of Vermont's growth in population from 1970 to 1980 was the result of new residents moving into the state. Figure 9.5 displays migration; communities that showed emigration are indicated by a small dot. Only 39 places had more people moving out than moving in. Nearly all towns in Vermont showed significant immigration of new residents. Many were complete newcomers; others were native-born citizens, but the number of new residents in many smaller communities is striking. If we compare this map to Figure 9.4, the amount of growth in population in every city and town resulting from immigration or natural increase can be discovered. Canaan increased by 242 persons, of which 162 (67 percent) was due to immigration. Randolph had 816 more people than ten years previously, of which 605 were new residents (74 percent).

Each place is a story in itself. In most of them, people still want their acre or more in the rural countryside. But in places like Richford, Hardwick, Ludlow, Readsboro, and Bellows Falls in Rockingham, the continual emigration reflects the serious loss of economic

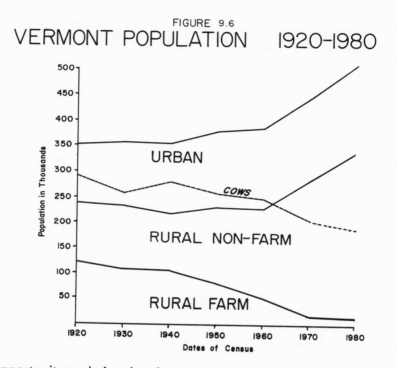

FIGURE 9.6
VERMONT POPULATION   1920-1980

opportunity as industries close or relocate and jobs are fewer. To some degree the same holds true for Windsor and Springfield.

The migration trends also show more new residents. One cannot account for the reversal of movements in the Northeast as resulting from greater economic opportunity, nor has Woodstock expanded industrially. Many of the newcomers in Vermont towns are from distant pastures; some are retirees, and some are trying to eke out some sort of existence on rundown farms. Others have turned to various arts and crafts; some write. All treasure the Vermont image. It used to be that movements of people could usually be explained by economic opportunity. That is no longer true, and the migration trends in Vermont defy easy explanation.

Rural and Urban People

Vermont is considered to be the most rural state in the United States, according to standard U.S. Bureau of the Census definitions. As

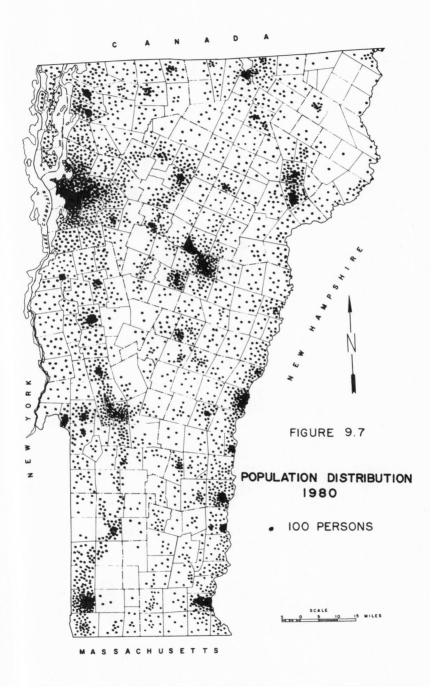

FIGURE 9.7

POPULATION DISTRIBUTION
1980

• 100 PERSONS

SCALE

5 0 5 10 15 MILES

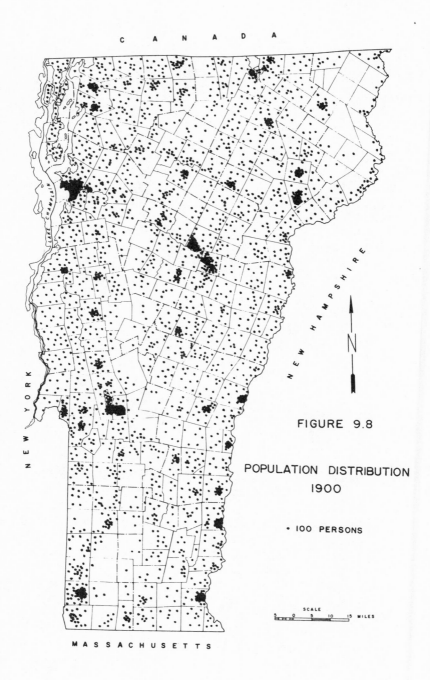

FIGURE 9.8

POPULATION DISTRIBUTION
1900

• 100 PERSONS

such, many federal programs targeted for rural areas are tried out in a demonstration program in the state before they are widely applied. One recent illustration has been federal funding for rural transit ystems. As a result, Vermont has done well in getting funds for many programs, and far fewer dollars go to Washington than the state receives from that source. In 1979, the state received $1.17 from the federal government for every dollar sent. In 1980, every man, woman, and child in Vermont received $689 from Uncle Sam. In 1978, on a per capita basis, Vermont ranked fifth in the nation in federal monies received. With respect to federal rural water and waste-disposal grants, Vermont received $82 million. California was a distant second with $17 million.

Population is segregated by the census into an urban and a rural component. Urban population includes those people who: (1) live in an incorporated village or city of 2,500 or more; or, (2) in unincorporated places of 2,500 or more; or, (3) people living on land, incorporated or unincorporated, in a designated "urbanized area." Anyone not included in this definition is automatically part of the rural population.

Through 1979, Vermont had no "urbanized area" and, were it not for the Census Bureau's changing its rules for 1980, the state still would not have such a place. The Burlington Metropolitan Statistical Area (MSA) was created with a population of 115,308, which gains it a national ranking of 254 out of 365 MSAs in the United States.

From a purely geographic point of view, the end result of this change has been to artificially create a greater urban population, so that making comparisons between rural and urban Vermont people between 1970 and 1980 is hard. Figure 9.6 traces the changes in the state's total population and its rural and urban parts since 1920. I couldn't resist the temptation to add cows. Table 9.3 gives the population statistically.

The rural population has two very different parts: those living on farms, as opposed to most rural people who have other occupations. The U.S. Bureau of the Census began separating two categories of rural people in 1920 when, for the first time, the automobile was making it possible for people to commute some distance to work. In Vermont as elsewhere in the urbanized Northeast, the rural nonfarm population is far greater than the farm population, and if it were not for another census definition of what is or is not a farm (Chapter 11), the actual rural farm population in 1980 would be smaller than that listed.

TABLE 9.3

Rural and Urban Population, 1920–1980

	1920	*1930*	*1940*	*1950*	*1960*	*1970*	*1980*
Total	352,428	359,611	359,231	377,747	389,881	444,732	511,456
Urban	109,976	118,766	123,239	137,612	149,921	142,889[a]	172,735
Rural	242,452	240,845	235,992	240,135	239,960	301,441	338,721
Rural nonfarm	118,007	128,947	130,477	159,003	191,085	275,855	320,642
Rural farm[b]	124,445	111,898	105,515	81,132	48,875	25,586	18,079

[a]The urban population was probably undercounted by 5.5 percent by the U.S. Bureau of the Census.
[b]There have been several changes in the definition of a "farm," some changes in numbers result from changes in definition.

Vermont, the most "rural" state in the United States, earns much of that designation only because of U.S. Bureau of the Census definitions. Vermont's rural nonfarm people, 60 percent of the population in 1980, are often not very "rural" at all. The thing most rural about them is that they live in the "country." Otherwise they shop and work in urban places, get their medical, dental, and legal services in urban places, send their children to a union school district, and go to concerts, movies, restaurants, and bars in more urban areas. The only thing that makes most modern Vermonters "rural" is the land they live on.

Figure 9.7 shows the distribution of population in 1980. It demonstrates how most people, regardless of census labels, have an urban orientation. Greatest clusters are in or close to larger cities, towns, and villages. The automobile has made Underhill a suburb of Burlington, just as it has made Northfield a suburb of Barre-Montpelier, Dummerston a suburb of Brattleboro, and Clarendon a suburb of Rutland. Yet in a general way, the population in its distribution today is not too different than it was eighty years ago. Except for more black dots because people are more numerous (511,000 now, compared to 343,000 in 1900), a population map of 1900 (Figure 9.8) looks much like the modern map. The hill farms lost numbers during the twentieth century, only to find a rebirth as restored farmhouses. The population first contracted into the cities, then expanded into the countryside. The population of many rural towns is now what it was at the turn of the century. Count some of the dots. Modern ski-area towns like Stowe, Waitsfield, Mendon, and Sherburne have more people today than at any time in their history, but otherwise, the population of Vermont is now distributed much as it was in 1900, but for very different reasons and with very different people involved.

10

The Recreation Industry

The most direct cause of Vermont's recent population growth has been better accessibility by means of an improved highway network. But if the state had an undesirable image, or was located in the Great Plains, no amount of improved transportation would have created a surge in population.

Thus, most recent immigration has causes rooted in both the location of the state relative to large numbers of people, as well as the desirable image of rural living among the Green Mountains. The recreation industry for a long time has done much to promote Vermont living, and the newcomer is certainly becoming a greater percentage of the population. According to the U.S. Bureau of the Census, in 1960, Vermont was approximately 72 percent native born; in 1970 that figure had shrunk to 66 percent. Returns from 1980 indicate that the native-born population, including the young sons and daughters of the newcomers, were about 60 percent of the state's population.

Outside of Rutland, heading east toward the Killington ski area, is a real estate sign urging the traveler to "Buy a Piece of Vermont." Until a few years ago, another in Bethel proclaimed "Gas and Vermont Acres for Sale." Many real estate brochures promise utopia, and visitors are assured that they can experience vivid, exciting night life, an opportunity to see real Vermonters, and even a chance to attend a symphony orchestra concert. Vermont has everything, from rundown farms whose owners eagerly await a buyer far more profitable than cow farming, to small condominiums stacked one above

220

the other as in Stratton, Warren, Stowe, and other ski-resort communities.

Recreation has always been important to Vermont's economy because the state has always been close to large numbers of people in search of the recreational opportunities provided by open space, water, and mountains. In the early years, railroads brought people to the mountain houses and mineral springs (Chapter 6). Later, as the tin lizzy began to replace the horse and roads were improved, the visitor became more mobile, no longer chained to public transportation. Back roads were sought out, small country inns blossomed, small cottages began to appear around lakeshores, a marble exhibit was opened in Proctor and a granite one in Barre. As more cars, more people, and better roads appeared, Vermont became a popular touring place both as a destination and for through traffic. The Ideal Tour of 1920 routed the adventurer north to the Equinox House in Manchester, exactly two days' drive from the Hotel Biltmore in New York City. Explicit directions were given for navigating the harrowing curves on the Peru Turnpike, which was to become Route 11.

> Manchester is a quaint and attractive village, practically unchanged since the days of the Revolution. As one promenades the famous marble walks in the cool of the evening, the modern motor car running silently along seems out of place, and one almost expects instead to hear the tread of martial feet and to see Ethan Allen at the head of his Green Mountain Boys go marching past.
>
> Peru Mountain Pass, much improved as to grade, is negotiated soon after leaving Manchester. Between the prosperous and pleasing villages lies, perhaps, the most primitive section of the entire tour, and one feels the old New England atmosphere of granite hills and stony farms which have sent many famous men into the world's affairs.

The Ideal Tour kept the tourist to a predetermined path; to venture far was inviting danger. What Vermonter could be expected to understand the inner workings of the new motorcar in case of a breakdown? Garages were carefully described and checked as to their reliability, but the touring party was expected to have a long list of implements and spare parts to take care of the inevitable emergency. Three spare tires were standard.

The more daring motorist of the period had recourse to the *Official Automobile Blue Book*, a massive volume of 1,300 pages (price $3). Here in one volume were all the road maps of New England, detailed descriptions of all routes, places to stay, places to have the car repaired, hints in case of breakdown, a recommended survival kit, and, thoughtfully, which places provided accommodation for the chauffeur.

After World War I the first courageous drivers headed northward. Many had first visited Vermont by rail after reading Secretary of State Guy Bailey's colorful, romantic, inaccurate *Land of Green Mountains*, published in 1913. As far as we know, this is the first official state-sponsored volume designed to attract tourists. Each town is listed with a capsule description of history and scenic wonders. In the Introduction, the prose reaches poetic heights:

> . . the wisdom of unnumbered centuries . . . 'I will lift up mine eyes unto the hills from whence cometh my help.' The help of the hills is recognized everywhere . . . health of body and soul, for sturdy virtues of character, for independence of tyranny and hatred of sham, for the qualities of mind and heart that keep a nation clean and strong and true. The help of the hills may be obtained in an abundant measure in the Green Mountains of Vermont.

Who could resist the temptation to refresh one's spirit in such a pleasant way?

The 1920s were an era of discovery, or perhaps rediscovery, on four rubber tires. During the late 1920s the National Survey in Chester began to publish their "Bookform Maps," forerunner of the official state highway maps that would appear later. Advertisements continued the traditions established in the Ideal Tour and *Blue Book* era.

MAPLE MANOR, Townshend, Vt., Four miles north of Newfane. Tea and Antiques, Hardy Perennials and Bulbs.

THE ADNABROWN is one of the best known hotels in the state with distinctive features that appeal to a discriminating public. Its lobby is original in design, all visitors admiring its richly paneled walls, and the frieze portraying the English coaching scenes of other days. . . .

SEVEN GABLES, Pawlet, Vermont. A quiet, restful summer resort. Fifteen miles north of Manchester. Good home cooking. Fresh vegetables, eggs, poultry and dairy products. Tourists accommodated. Rates Reasonable. . . .

THE GREEN MOUNTAIN SERVICE STATION. At the junction of the Ideal Tour and the Long Trail. Manchester, Vermont. Home cooked lunches served from 7 A.M. until 9 P.M. Good trout fishing in season.

In Figure 10.1, all the advertisers in the 1926 *National Survey Bookform Map* have been located with small dots. Similarly, all the places buying space in the 1920 *Blue Book* are indicated by an X. A few represent the same establishment, but in general the pattern on the map shows the major touring areas and destinations of the period. Orange County was pretty much a recreational wasteland, as was anything north of a line between Burlington and St. Johnsbury. In Essex County, visitors, if they went there at all, went to the Averill Lake Camps, owned and operated by Mrs. Quimby. "The Only Maine Camps in Vermont" were advertised.

In the 1920s, no one had thought of downhill skiing, but Stowe was already established as the village nestling beneath Vermont's highest mountain, and the tourist of the time certainly had to negotiate the highway to the summit and spend a night at the highest lodging in the state. It was only natural that Stowe, with its name and its familiarity, would evolve into Vermont's first major ski resort. Few ventured into the Mad River Valley where Sugarbush and Mad River Glen now are. Stratton was unknown, as were the future ski areas north of Wilmington, advertised in the 1920 *Blue Book* as having a good garage for servicing motorcars. Bromley Mountain, on the road across the Green Mountains from Manchester, followed Stowe; again it was an early area familiar to many people.

In modern Vermont, Woodstock and Manchester are often regarded as unique towns with high per capita incomes. Many summer residents and permanent new Vermonters live there. Aside from the old mineral springs in both places, their importance is reflected in the tour books of the 1920s. They were familiar, they had fine accommodations, and they were logical first destinations for those wanting to break away from the crowded conditions farther south. Both towns were very acceptable socially, and though Manchester and Woodstock have never rivaled Newport in Rhode Island and its stately

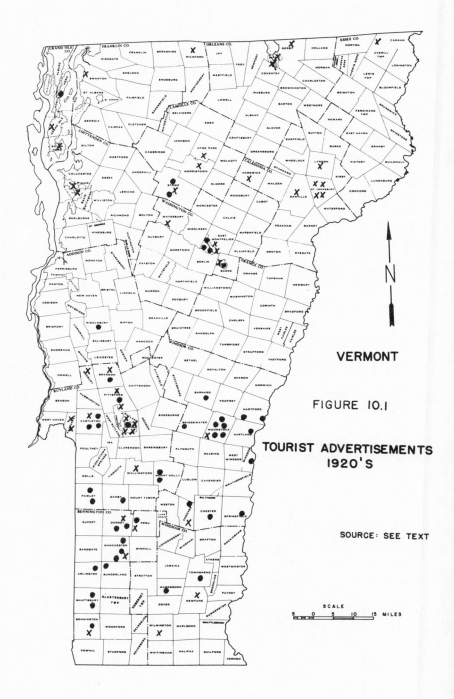

VERMONT

FIGURE 10.1

TOURIST ADVERTISEMENTS
1920'S

SOURCE: SEE TEXT

SCALE
5 0 5 10 15 MILES

mansions, the small summer place in Woodstock was a viable alternative and was closer to the growing idea of roughing it a bit in the north country.

Aside from commercial establishments, catering more often than not to overnight guests, the stay-awhile tourist was generally attracted to the southern part of the state. The area was closer, more roads were improved, places had been recommended by others, and by the 1930s southern Vermont had become a distinct tourist region. The Middlebury Inn in Middlebury catered to those who would brave the "Addisonian Wastes of Clay." Few, however, would stop in the flatlands of Addison. Hills and mountains were what people demanded, and Vermont had plenty to offer.

Getting off the beaten path was a continual desire, but it was not without problems. Many Vermont highways were a sea of mud after a heavy rain, and in April and May no one but the foolish would venture forth on an expedition. The 1920 *Blue Book* advised the motorist that

> Some sort of emergency tire chains should always be carried, whether your tires are anti-skid or not. For heavy deep mud heavy single chains or mud hooks fastened over the tire and around one spoke of the wheel will insure a prompt getaway from the worst mud hole.

One farmer in southern Vermont had the great fortune to have a nearly permanent mud hole on the highway in front of his house. It was a lucrative source of income, to be gained by pulling out mired motor vehicles. Every evening during the middle of the summer, as the story goes, this enterprising Vermonter would apply more water to the low spot so that the following day an unsuspecting tourist would get stuck. Gravel might eventually have been poured into the hole, but not before some marginal farmer earned more money off stuck travelers than from five cows.

After 1930 the Great Depression struck. Fewer Vermont farmers left their hills because there was no place to go. Fewer people visited the state because they could not afford to travel. Academics turned to federally supported writing endeavors, and a mass of literature poured out about Vermont's farms, its economy, its green hills, its people and its future and its past. The prestigious American Geographical Society sponsored a volume entitled *New England's Prospect.* Many Vermonters got together and produced *Rural Vermont:*

A Program for the Future. Vermont: a Guide to the Green Mountain State was published in 1937 as part of the Federal Writers Project to produce good guidebooks for all the states. The Federal Writers Guides were excellent; the Vermont volume, recently updated and revised, is again available. *Let Me Show You Vermont* was written by Charles Edward Crane in 1937 and is still a classic of sorts. All this activity meant plentiful information about Vermont was readily available and more people were becoming curious about this verdant land with conservative farmers and lots of cows just a few hours' drive from home. Hollywood discovered the hill farmer and the movies began to advertise the state. *Vermont Life* magazine began publication in 1946, just after World War II, with the intention of doing what the state government could to attract people (and *money*) to a traditionally poor state with heavy losses of young people and limited economic opportunities.

The first issue of *Vermont Life*, "The Vermont State Magazine," appeared in the fall 1946 at twenty-five cents a copy. Published by the Vermont Developmental Department, its purpose was clearly stated in a paragraph in a covering letter from Governor Mortimer R. Proctor:

> If you are one of those who has not yet had an opportunity to know at first hand our beautiful countryside, the friendliness of our people, and the "Vermont Way of Life," this magazine will be a preview of what you may expect.

Where the idea of the "Vermont Way of Life" came from is debatable, but on the eve of the post-World War II deluge of tourists the state was doing all it could to promote the image. Even before official state support of the image, it was there, it was popular, and it certainly meant people and cash.

In 1937, Charles Crane mused on the Vermont image problem while writing his popular guidebook. "It is natural for the native Vermonter to experience a certain sentimentality about his state; it remains strange that so many non-Vermonters also seem to experience a similar feeling about Vermont." Crane speculates that the many outsiders "approach Vermont not always with the same degree of reverence but usually with some sense of a spiritual change such, perhaps, as they feel upon crossing the threshold of a church." People living in Vermont probably never equated their landscape and culture with religion, but maybe it is not too far from the truth to say that people from outside, then as now, had a reverence for the state and its beauty that the natives took for granted. This is probably one of the reasons why today the newcomers are most active in environmental and preservation affairs, and why they prefer cross-country skiing to the busy roar of snow machines.

The 1930s

Thanks to the mineral-springs era, Guy Bailey's colorful publicity, the automobile following the Ideal Tour or the *Blue Book*, and word-of-mouth promotion by the scattered sons and daughters of Vermont across the American landscape, people came. They came in search of a Vermont Way of Life, a nebulous image that they wanted to become a part of.

And all spent money and most were welcome. In 1930 it was estimated that the value of property aimed toward the recreation business was worth more than $26 million. The state had 250 hotels for summer visitors; 27 boys' and girls' camps; 485 tourist homes (of the bed-and-breakfast variety); 110 cabin developments (forerunners of the modern motel); and countless summer homes, ranging from hunting and fishing shacks to refurbished hill farms. In *Rural Vermont* (1931), the Vermont Commission on Country Life emphasizes the economic contribution that tourism could make. Assuming that 250,000 cows brought an income of $22 million a year to the state, imagine what 250,000 tourists would do! Further assuming that each one left $100 behind, why, people were worth more than cows! But a note of caution lay hidden in all this enthusiastic selling, and strangely enough it was focused on the social problems that tourism might bring to smaller communities:

> In considering the attitude of Vermonters toward summer visitors, two extremes should be avoided. There should be no fawning or servility in their relations toward their guests. On the other hand, a narrow intolerant, suspicious attitude should be avoided. The traditional dignity and independence of Vermonters should be maintained in a friendly way.

Tourists were divided into three groups: the transient, the brief vacationers who spent a week or two, and the property owner who became a permanent member and taxpayer in the town. The first two did not cause any particular problems in the view of the Commission, but the last might be something else again.

> While the development of this time remains small so that the
> summer population is only a small part of the resident population
> and is not displacing them from their farms, the effects are simple
> and economic in nature. When they expand as in Fairlee or Man-
> chester, other factors come in. Where the summer people out-
> number the native population, the whole town is occupied in
> direct contact with them in all capacities from laundress, caddy or
> waitress to local merchant.

Other problems mentioned (remember that the year is 1930),
were inflation of agricultural land values, making it difficult for
natives to continue farming, and the cyclic limits on employment
that was so dependent upon recreation.

> In Manchester, particularly, almost all the farms have been turned
> into summer properties. Some opportunity is presented to the
> truck farmer, but the small grower is too dependent on weather to
> be reliable enough to suit the better hotels. The wage scale is
> raised to a point where it is practically impossible to get farm help
> during the summer and at other seasons the working men try to
> get summer pay.

The problems of a recreation-based economy were recognized long
ago, just as they are today, yet Vermont, poorest state in New England, could not possibly turn its back on a lucrative source of
income.

The study of tourism and recreation conducted by the Vermont
Commission on Country Life arrived at one far-reaching conclusion:
The industry must be strengthened, more publicity must be developed, and everything possible should be done to attract visitors. One
recommendation urged the state to acquire all the highest mountain
summits and then lease the land to visitors so that vacation homes
could be built on the top of Camel's Hump, Mt. Mansfield, and
Lincoln Peak, among others. Looking further ahead:

> Valuable as is the rapidly growing tourist traffic in this state, the
> most promising feature of recreational development in Vermont
> probably lies in the extension of the summer homes movement.
> Everything possible should be done to call the attention of city
> dwellers to the opportunities that Vermont offers for summer
> residents. . . . This does not mean that we should, as a rule,
> displace our productive farms with a non-agricultural class of

residents, but rather that we should utilize the areas where scenery is beautiful and the soil is not very productive. It appears to your Committee that a special effort should be made to interest possible purchasers of summer homes in what Vermont has to offer in this respect.

A great many of these predictions have come to pass in the fifty years that have elapsed. At least fifteen Vermont towns are almost completely "summer-property" towns, though today the season lasts longer. The state has done its best to promote this type of land use, and private developers are not far behind.

Heeding the recommendations of the Vermont Commission on Country Life (1930), the philosophy embodied in *Vermont Life*, and the word-of-mouth "uniqueness" of Vermont, a concerted effort lasting many years has attempted to create New Vermonters. In the spring 1965 issue of *Vermont Life*, the inside back cover carried the message; "For Rent: One Heavenly Summer, Reasonable." Detailed directions were included to help achieve such a goal. In other years the magazine even established a referral bureau, to which those interested in making Vermont their home could write for details. Innumerable real estate brokers search for the person wanting to get away from it all. Choice properties are constantly advertised, often at inflated prices.

Property has been acquired in three forms. Earliest were older homes in scattered villages. Woodstock, Manchester, Weston, Dorset, Craftsbury, Peacham, Grafton, Chester, and Townshend are examples. In these towns and others, many are still "summer people," but others have become year-round residents. And as a result the character of the villages has changed from gradual deterioration to contrived restoration.

A second type of property acquisition has been the rundown and sadly neglected farm. A development of more recent vintage, probably its earliest manifestations were in Peacham and Greensboro. Now many towns are dominated by nonresident property ownership, a help to the tax base to be sure, but sometimes a source of irritation when the land is posted. The biggest native irritant, however, is probably the need for the town to plow a road three miles long for the newcomer who shows up only when the skiing is good. A large amount of old, marginal Vermont farmland is in the hands of new residents, some being used for beef cattle or sheep, but most

The same Vermont farmhouse before and after restoration. Top photograph taken in 1955 by the author, lower one in 1975. In North Shrewsbury.

growing up into marketable timber whose cutting would immeasurably improve game habitat.

The third type of land acquisition has been small lakeshore cottages, and condominiums in the ski-area towns. Many of these recently acquired structures will probably change hands several times before deterioration. Others may be improved and strengthened and may even become permanent residences. This type of nonresident ownership, immeasurably affecting the character of the communities in which they are located, probably even that of the whole state, has less social and economic influence than the first two.

The Ski Industry

Skiers are now the most important type of brief visitors to Vermont, and the greatest source of recreational income. Their existence, besides their hedonistic sliding down the slopes, was described eloquently in an article in *Skiing Magazine* (October 1979).

> In restaurants, normally their bailiwick, they are often seated and served after the local Vermont crowd. In supermarkets, they are glared down by the express lane check-out girl for being one pill of Tums over the ten-item limit while Vermonters whisk through carrying a year's supply of yogurt. They buy a half cord of green firewood for $50; Vermonters pay a third more for twice as much, dry.

Vermont has not always had chic restaurants for the skiing fraternity, and it was many years before a Cortina Inn, a Tyrol Motel, or an Alpenhof appeared on local highways. Woodstock claims the first ski tow in the United States, but the ski tow in the pasture was pretty much a local curiosity. Later developments to the north had far greater influence on the advertising of Vermont as a skiing state.

During the 1920s, wintertime activity in Stowe was built on annual winter carnivals, which had begun in 1921. Although the first ascent of Mt. Mansfield on skis was reported to have been in 1914, it was an activity that had little appeal. But change was coming.

In 1931 a member of the New York National Guard in training at the Fort Ethan Allen firing range in Underhill climbed up, looked down, and thought about skiing as a recreational sport. In such a manner did Roland Palmedo form the Amateur Ski Club of New York City, and in 1932 the first of the annual hordes arrived. Sched-

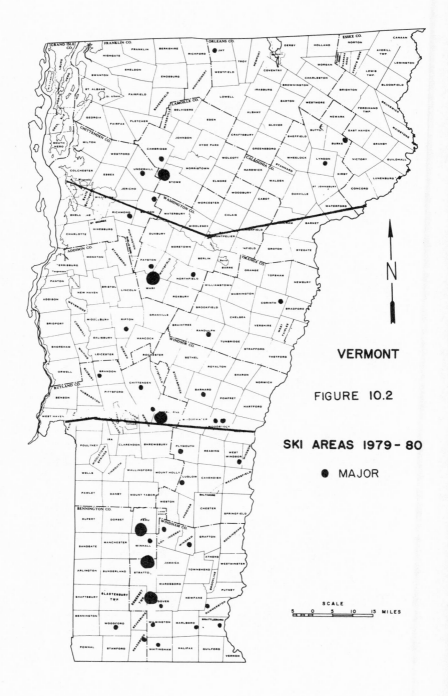

VERMONT

FIGURE 10.2

SKI AREAS 1979-80

● MAJOR

SCALE
5 0 5 10 15 MILES

ules on the railways were not then suited to the ski crowd, which resulted in several dozen New York ski buffs being deposited at the Waterbury station at 4:30 A.M. on a dark, cold, and snowy January day in 1932. Nonetheless, with patience, the electric railway from Waterbury to Stowe got into gear, and downhill skiing was born in Stowe. In 1933, Civil Conservation Corps workers cut the first trail, and during the 1930s others were constructed as labor was available. The first tow was a rope tow on the trail that is now the Toll House slopes near the entrance to the carriage road. The first chairlift in the United States was built in 1940, and Stowe was on its way to becoming the Ski Capital of the East.

Other areas were not far behind. A ski area in East Corinth developed after a rope tow was built there in 1935. Hogback Mountain, just west of Brattleboro, began without a tow in 1931. Fred Pabst, Jr., pioneered the development at Bromley Mountain in 1937 after building many rope tows. In 1939 and 1940, Bromley officially became a ski resort. Other large developments that preceded the great expansion of the 1950s and 1960s were Pico Peak (1937) and Mad River Glen (1947). The remaining ski areas are all more recent and some debate whether Stowe is still the eastern Ski Capital it once was. No count of visitors to the respective areas is available, but the Killington-Pico combined region, with nineteen lifts and eighty trails and with the greatest vertical drop in the State (3,000 feet) probably leads in skier visits. Other major centers include Stowe (twenty-one lifts, twenty-nine trails, 2,150 feet), Sugarbush North and Sugarbush South (twelve lifts, sixty-three trails, 2,645 foot drop), Mt. Snow (thirteen lifts, forty-six trails, 1,700 feet) and Stratton Mountain (eight lifts, thirty-seven trails, 1,750 feet). In skier capacities other Vermont areas are smaller but all have their loyal enthusiasts. Figure 10.2 shows all ski areas operating (or trying to operate) during the almost snowless winter of 1979–1980. The larger circles represent areas that had a total combination of trails and lifts exceeding forty.

Vermont ski areas fit well into a northern, central, and southern regionalization, using Route 2 to separate north and central, and Route 4 to divide central from south. Those divisions are drawn approximately on the map of ski areas. Of the major resorts, then, one is in the northern region (seven ski areas), two in the central (fourteen ski areas), and three in the southern region (seventeen areas). The geographic pattern of the regions should not come as a surprise. Southern Vermont has more snow than the north and is also closer to large urban centers. Stowe, in splendid isolation, will have an increasingly hard time resting on its early reputation because, geographically, it is the most poorly situated major ski region for an American market.

Where skiers come from clearly reflects the advantages of a major ski area's being close to a large market. During the 1983–1984 season, skiers from New York were most important, representing 20 percent of skier visits. Following New York in out-of-state skiers came Massachusetts with 15 percent, Connecticut with 14 percent, and New Jersey with 12 percent. Five percent were from Canada, and the remaining 14 percent were from scattered locations, including Pennsylvania, Ohio, Maryland, and the District of Columbia. Table 10.1 shows this information for both the 1983–1984 season and the 1977–1978 season. Some noteworthy shifts have appeared in the origin of Vermont's skiers, partly reflecting the cost of fuel and the lower value of the Canadian dollar.

TABLE 10.1

	Northern Region		Central Region		Southern Region		Statewide	
	1977–78	1983–84	1977–78	1983–84	1977–78	1983–84	1977–78	1983–84
State								
New York	6%	4%	5%	15%	16%	14%	9%	20%
Vermont	30	31	19	16	9	17	17	20
Connecticut	7	7	16	11	40	23	23	14
Mass.	12	16	18	19	15	9	16	15
New Jersey	NA	4	NA	15	NA	14	NA	12
Canada	35	18	3	2	—	—	9	5
Other U.S.	10	14	39	17	20	12	26	14

State of Origin of Vermont Skiers, 1977–1978, 1983–1984

Source: Vermont Agency of Community and Development Affairs.

Northern Vermont contains the state's fastest-growing urban region and greatest college population and is closest to Quebec. The high percentages of Vermont and Canadian participation reflect this position. Southern Vermont, at the other extreme, is closest to Connecticut and New York, and Massachusetts skiers, coming over the Interstate from Boston, are geographically close, at least in time, to all three Vermont regions. If gasoline costs increase appreciably, many skiers are going to begin thinking of miles of travel rather than hours and it seems likely that southern ski regions will continue to grow at the expense of those located in the north.

Economic and Social Effects of Skiing

The direct influence of skiing is felt more locally than it is throughout the state. Although all Vermont residents receive some benefit from skiers' spending, the visiting downhill skier makes his or her presence felt close to the ski area itself, and along the major access highways. Something dramatic happened in the Mad River Valley, in the towns of Warren, Waitsfield, and Fayston. Between 1960 and 1980, the permanent population of the towns combined increased from 1,285 to 2,917. In 1968 they had 568 vacation or seasonal dwellings. Five years later the number had increased to 895. In 1973 these seasonal dwellings were paying a good share of the real estate taxes in the towns. In Fayston, where vacation homes far outnumbered permanent residences, 46 percent of the taxes came from this source. Warren and Waitsfield, with more commercial property, took 35 percent and 18 percent respectively. All this growth has been accompanied by inflating land values as more customers competed for the acreage. In Warren, the grand list of $6 million in 1960 had grown to more than $451 million in 1976.

Commercial activity grew along with population and housing. In 1957 no "professionals" (doctors, architects, engineers, etc.) lived in either Warren or Waitsfield. In 1976 the two towns had twenty-five firms in that category. Similarly, the number of places offering accommodations increased from five to thirty-three, restaurants from two to nineteen, building contractors and services from three to twenty-six, retail stores from fourteen to forty-nine, and gas stations from one station in Waitsfield to the present seven. Real estate offices have sprouted like weeds. In 1957, one small agency was located in Waitsfield; by 1976 there were twenty-two. In about twenty years the Valley has been changed forever. Population has doubled, the grand list has increased astronomically, and the number of commercial services has gone from twenty-eight to 210. And this action is going on in a small Vermont valley with little land that's flat, and with few native people left.

The story here is not unique. All ski regions in Vermont have seen extraordinary growth. Of the ten towns leading in number of

Only eight miles apart and separated by the bulk of Roxbury Mountain, Roxbury and the ski area town of Warren are in *different* worlds. The Warren Store (above) sells "Provisions" and has a Wine Shop. The Roxbury Country Store (below) specializes in kerosene heaters.

vacation homes in 1973, seven were ski towns. In order, these were Wilmington (Mt. Snow and Haystack), 665 vacation homes; Sherburne (Killington), 550; Winhall (Stratton Mountain), 473; Stowe (Mt. Mansfield), 470; Warren (Sugarbush and Mad River Glen), 433; Ludlow (Okemo Mountain), 425, and Dover (Mt. Snow), 389.*

The ownership of condominiums and other ski-area vacation homes reveals where an area's clientele comes from. From the 1973 inventory, the most recent available, Table 10.2 shows where those who own vacation property in selected ski areas come from. Surrounding towns close to and oriented toward each downhill area are included. Manchester is included in the totals for Bromley, Mendon for Killington-Pico, Montgomery for Jay Peak, and Jamaica for Stratton Mountain. As we'd expect, Connecticut dominates in southern Vermont, Quebec in the north. New York owners are generally found in the central and southern parts, as are New Jersey owners. The number of Vermont owners is surprising, especially in Killington and Stowe, but many of these may be newcomers who claim Vermont as their permanent residence.

In 1973 more than 5,700 vacation homes were directly associated with the seven ski-resort regions covered in Table 10.2. If we add the vacation homes in some of the smaller areas like Ludlow (Okemo Mountain), Bolton Valley, Magic Mountain, Burke Mountain, Timber Ridge, and Round Top, the number of second homes closely connected with skiing in 1973 was approximately 7,200, or about a quarter of the units of this type in the state. Because these 7,200 vacation havens were located in only thirty-one towns in which the economy is primarily ski-oriented, their effect on restricted areas is significant.† Direct out-of-pocket expenditures are great; taxes on vacation homes are another contribution. The ski industry has become a mainstay of the economy, and without it many would be looking for work. Even if employment is highly seasonal in the

---

*Expansion in these since 1973 has been tremendous, but unfortunately there has not been another count of second homes since that date. Though it is very much needed, the state has not been willing to appropriate funds for such a study.

†For those interested, I consider these thirty-one towns to be mainly ski-area oriented (many might well disagree): Jay, Montgomery, Richford, Cambridge, Stowe, Fayston, Warren, Waitsfield, Mendon, Sherburne, Pittsfield, Jamaica, Peru, Winhall, Manchester, Londonderry, Landgrove, Stratton, Dover, Wilmington, Wardsboro, Burke, Ludlow, Chittenden, Randolph, Plymouth, Bolton, Whitingham, Duxbury, Sutton, and Moretown.

TABLE 10.2

Vacation-Home Ownership in Selected Vermont Ski Areas, 1973

Ski area	Vacation homes	CT	MA	NY	Quebec	NJ	VT	NH	Other
Jay Peak	295	6%	8%	11%	35%	3%	29%		6%
Smugglers	162	9	15	21	6	2	36		12
Stowe	470	10	13	17	10	9	26		14
Sugarbush-Mad River	895	16	21	27		9	18		8
Pico-Killington	781	12	15	15		12	36		8
Stratton-Bromley	1,756	29	10	29		10	15	1	7
Mt. Snow-Haystack	1,355	35	13	24		8	13	1	6

Source: Vermont Vacation-Home Inventory, 1973. Although the numbers now are considerably higher, the geographic pattern of ownership is probably still valid.

TABLE 10.3

Vermont Travel Industry Estimates

	1978	1979	1980	1981	1982
Estimated visitors (millions)	7.4	6.6	6.8	7.2	7.2
Summer	4.8	4.2	4.5	4.7	4.5
Winter	2.6	2.4	2.3	2.5	2.7
Estimated visitor expenditures[a] (millions)	$420	$430	$480	$510	$650
Summer	$220	$230	$270	$270	$320
Winter	160	160	160	180	260
Annual vacation-home taxes	40	40	50	60	70
Persons per trip	2.8	2.8	2.7	2.6	2.6
Days stayed per trip	2.5	2.6	2.6	2.5	2.6
Expenditures per visitor per day	$20.70	$22.80	$24.60	$25.60	$31.50
Summer	18.20	20.90	23.10	22.90	29.00
Winter	26.70	26.20	27.60	31.00	36.00

[a]Trip expenditures by out-of-staters for food, lodging, gasoline, activities, and incidentals. Major equipment purchases and travel expenditures by Vermonters are not included.

Source: Division of Research and Statistics, Agency of Development and Community Affairs (July 1983).

major ski-area towns, it provides income for many who would otherwise be doing little except drawing unemployment checks.

According to the Agency of Development and Community Affairs, annual skier expenditures have fluctuated widely, depending mostly on snow. In recent years the lowest was the $80 million spent in 1976–1977, the highest the $230 million of 1983–1984. In 1982–1983, an average snow year, expenditures were $165 million, averaging $64 a day for nonresidents and $18 a day for residents. The rise and fall of skiing relates directly to the white gold that falls upon the Green Mountains; no wonder more and more highly capitalized ski areas are installing snowmaking equipment!

Summer Recreation

Skiing is the most important recreational activity in Vermont, but it is not the only reason people come to the state. In fact, the summer recreation season is more important, but that is a season of multiple-purpose activity compared to single-purpose skiing.

Distinguishing between winter and summer values of recreation is difficult. Table 10.3 displays the best estimates available. In 1982, winter expenditures were about $260 million, and summer tourist expenditures were $320 million, but though the calendar year spans two ski seasons, the fiscal year (July 1–June 30) cuts into a summer recreation season.

Most information on the behavior of tourists is from registrations at thirty information booths, reports from selected motels and campgrounds, and attractions such as the Shelburne Museum, Maple Grove Museum, Santa's Land, and the Mt. Mansfield Gondola. All data are collated by the Agency of Development and Community Affairs and published in monthly Vacation Travel Indicators, which have annual summer and winter summaries. For many years the peak months for visitors have been August, July, October, and June, in that order, and the origin of Vermont summer tourists has changed little, although compared to the 1960s, some now come from a greater distance (Table 10.4).

Summer recreation pursuits are so varied as to make it far harder to categorize than single-purpose skiing. Touring, however, is probably most important—families who spend a few days driving

TABLE 10.4

State of Origin of Vermont Tourists, Summer Months

State	1966–67	1976	1980	1984
New York	21.3%	20.5%	21.3%	19.7%
Massachusetts	19.6	14.4	12.9	14.5
Quebec	12.6	8.5	8.0	7.6
Connecticut	10.8	9.0	9.6	9.5
New Hampshire	7.1	3.8	3.7	4.3
New Jersey	6.0	7.9	8.5	7.0
Pennsylvania	3.4	4.4	4.2	4.2
	80.8	68.5	68.2	66.8

Source: Agency of Development and Community Affairs.

through the state, visiting attractions, perhaps playing a game of golf or tennis on the way, and stopping to use the Alpine Slide at Bromley or Stowe. Tourers are also those, usually more elderly, who drive at a snail's pace looking at fall foliage in October, often missing the peak of the season in late September.

This type of recreational activity has been a Vermont mainstay for fifty years or more. The state has few real resorts like those in New Hampshire or Maine, which are blessed, the one with more lakes and spectacular mountains, the other with an unsurpassed seacoast. Complete resorts in Vermont are few, and Vermont has never been a resort state in the same class as Michigan, Minnesota, Wisconsin, or even New York.

Besides looking at quaint villages, contented cows, tree-shaded commons, and white churches, the modern meanderer is attracted to a wide variety of man-made attractions, and a visit or two to tourist places is often an important part of any sightseeing trip. In summer 1976, these were the favorite stopping spots:* Shelburne Museum in Shelburne (142,000); Maple Grove Museum in St. Johnsbury (86,000); Rock of Ages in Barre (78,000); Bennington Museum (73,000); Santa's Land in Putney (71,000); Vermont Marble Exhibit in Proctor (61,000); and St. Anne's Shrine on Isle LaMotte (56,000). The Mt. Mansfield and Killington gondolas hauled 50,000 visitors

---

*These figures are no longer collected by the Agency of Develpment and Community Affairs.

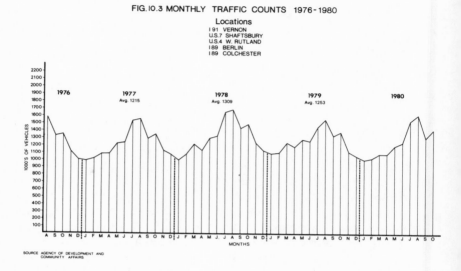

FIG. 10.3 MONTHLY TRAFFIC COUNTS 1976-1980

Locations
I 91 VERNON
U.S.7 SHAFTSBURY
U.S.4 W. RUTLAND
I 89 BERLIN
I 89 COLCHESTER

SOURCE AGENCY OF DEVELOPMENT AND
COMMUNITY AFFAIRS

each, and the Bennington Battle Monument, the Morgan Horse Farm, and the President Coolidge Birthplace in Plymouth were popular attractions.

Touring is inevitably a multiple-purpose activity, hard to measure for regional effects. In summer 1980, 4.5 million people visited Vermont. More than a million touring visitors spent at least one night in a Vermont motel, which is estimated to have generated $105 million, mainly in motel and hotel receipts. Four hundred and fifty thousand persons stayed in private and public campgrounds, and their estimated expenditure was $20 million. Other components of the 1980 summer tourist trade included 250,000 visiting relatives and friends, spending $13 million; 200,000 renting a cottage or a condominium, spending $28 million including rentals. Another 200,000 visited their own vacation homes and were estimated to have parted with another $21 million in so doing. In numbers, though, the typical tourist was the one-day variety who wandered, stopped at gift shops, and visited the Bromley Slide. More than 2.7 million fell into this category, but they were not the big spenders by a long shot. Day trippers, numerically the most common type of Vermont tourist, spent $33 million during the summer season, averaging $13.10 per day per person.

Traffic counts are a good measure of recreational travel. Figure 10.3 shows how summer travel dominates, and that the winter ski season is the time of least activity. The October foliage season shows up well.

Hunting and Fishing Recreation

Most of the outdoors types who come to Vermont in large numbers have been coming to their favorite spot for many years. Even though the trout get smaller regardless of stocking programs, and the deer herd gets smaller, Vermont Legislature or no, hunting and fishing have been and continue to be a major part of Vermont's total recreational mix.

In 1970, a year in which visitors to Vermont had expenditures of approximately $200 million, the Agricultural Experiment Station of the University of Vermont did a thorough study of nonresident sportsmen and women. In that year the estimated expenditure for this type of tourist was more than $25 million or 14 percent of recreational income in Vermont. A follow-up study was completed in 1975; expenditures had risen to $47 million, and $63 million was reported in 1980. This figure can be compared to the approximately $180 million that skiers spent in 1980–1981. Probably, after skiing and "touring," hunting and fishing is Vermont's third most important recreational activity.

In 1970, nonresident sportsmen mirrored the distribution of most Vermont visitors. Massachusetts residents comprised 38 percent of the 70,000 persons involved. Connecticut followed with 25 percent, New York with 11 percent, and then came New Jersey with 7 percent. People in general are not going to go as far to hunt and fish as they are to ski and see attractions, as we see in the size of Massachusetts participation.

Notwithstanding the recent success of turkey hunting in southwestern Vermont, the diminishing deer herd, combined with other perceived problems, has led to a decline in hunting and fishing activ-

A somewhat unusual No Trespassing sign at a hunting camp in Middlesex.

A rather typical, probably Vermont-owned hunting camp along the East Branch of the Nulhegan River in Ferdinand Township.

ity. This drop is reflected in license sales, which, since 1973, have shown a downward trend in both resident and nonresident purchases, while costs remained about the same. In 1982 15,000 fewer nonresident hunting licenses were issued than in 1973, and nonresident licenses of all types fell off. When we translate this change into its effect on Vermont's economy, the consequences may be serious. The decline in nonresident fishing is as large as that in hunting. The trout, if one can find them, are getting smaller. In some towns natives keep a round-the-clock watch for the stocking truck and clean out the trout even before they have a chance to leave the pool into which they were dumped.

A parallel decline in resident license sales has been registered, but here the reasons are different. Because cost is not really a factor, part of the reason is naturally the greater difficulty in getting a deer or landing a twelve-inch brook trout. But another and perhaps more important reason is that with Vermont's many new residents, the deer season is foreign and strange. Fishing continues in popularity; nearly everyone has fished at one time or another, but many newcomers have never held a rifle in their hands or the idea of deer hunting has rarely entered their minds.

University of Vermont studies show that sportsmen are frustrated with less success over the years, but they also perceive less accessibility to hunting lands because of increased posting of land. Posting has been increasing, and few acts will raise the ire of hunters more than to come across a "No Trespassing" sign during the third week of November.

Until 1961, when the law was repealed, posting of land was informal, and no filing with the Town Clerk was required. Now according to Vermont Statutes (10 VSA, Chapter 119, Section 5201), posted land has to be legally signed and recorded. In 1973, approximately 325 square miles were posted in that fashion (about 4 percent of the privately owned land in Vermont). Windsor and Orange counties were areas of maximum posting, as were a few towns in the Taconics of southwestern Vermont. The amount of land posted today is probably considerably greater than in 1973, but no statewide study has been done.

Geographically, areas of No Trespassing correlate well with towns that have more than average numbers of new residents and high percentages of vacation homes, especially of Connecticut ownership. Much of the large amount of posted land in northern Wind-

In 1974, this sign greeted travelers outside Bethel. The sign is now gone, perhaps because many travelers took the advice, or perhaps because gasoline costs more. Whatever the reason, the sign symbolizes what has been happening in Vermont.

Rising tier upon tier, condominiums have become common in many ski areas. These are at Mt. Snow in West Dover.

sor County is in towns with large numbers of beef cattle. You can read into that observation anything you like.

Vacation Homes and Camps

No study has been specifically focused on how many new residents first owned a vacation home in Vermont before they became permanent residents. The number is probably considerable, for from the 1930s on, heeding the recommendations of the Commission on Country Life, the state and private interests have made a concerted drive to sell Vermont as a second home location. Today the effect is staggering in the areas of major concentration, and because these often provide to a potential newcomer an introduction to "Vermont Life," there are cultural implications as well.

The first accurate count of vacation homes was made in 1968, followed by a second survey in 1973. Since then no statewide inventory has been made, but the increase between 1968 and 1973 was certainly equaled in 1980. In 1968 there were 22,599 second homes. By 1973 the number was 29,605, and in 1980 it was more than 36,000. The vacation-home space was enough to house 108,000 people or 20 percent of the 1980 population.*

As long ago as 1973, forty Vermont towns had more than two hundred vacation homes each, as shown in Figure 10.4, which also shows statewide distribution. There are more homes now, but the same attractions persist. Water and slopes draw people. Leicester and nearby Salisbury in Addison County reflect cottages around Lake Dunmore. Lakes Hortonia, Bomoseen, and St. Catherine in Rutland County are indicated by the large numbers of vacation homes in Hubbardton, Castleton, Poultney, and Wells. The same is true in Woodbury, Greensboro (Caspian Lake), Westmore (Lake Willoughby), Morgan (Seymour Lake), Barnard (Silver Lake), Maidstone (Maidstone Lake), and the large numbers in towns along Lake Champlain. Stowe, Warren, Fayston, Sherburne, Ludlow, Winhall, Wilmington, and many other towns show the effect of the nearby ski areas.

---

*The 1980 U.S. Census of Housing estimated that 12.21 percent of the dwelling units in Vermont were seasonal—a total of 27,244, but this figure is not compatible with other estimates.

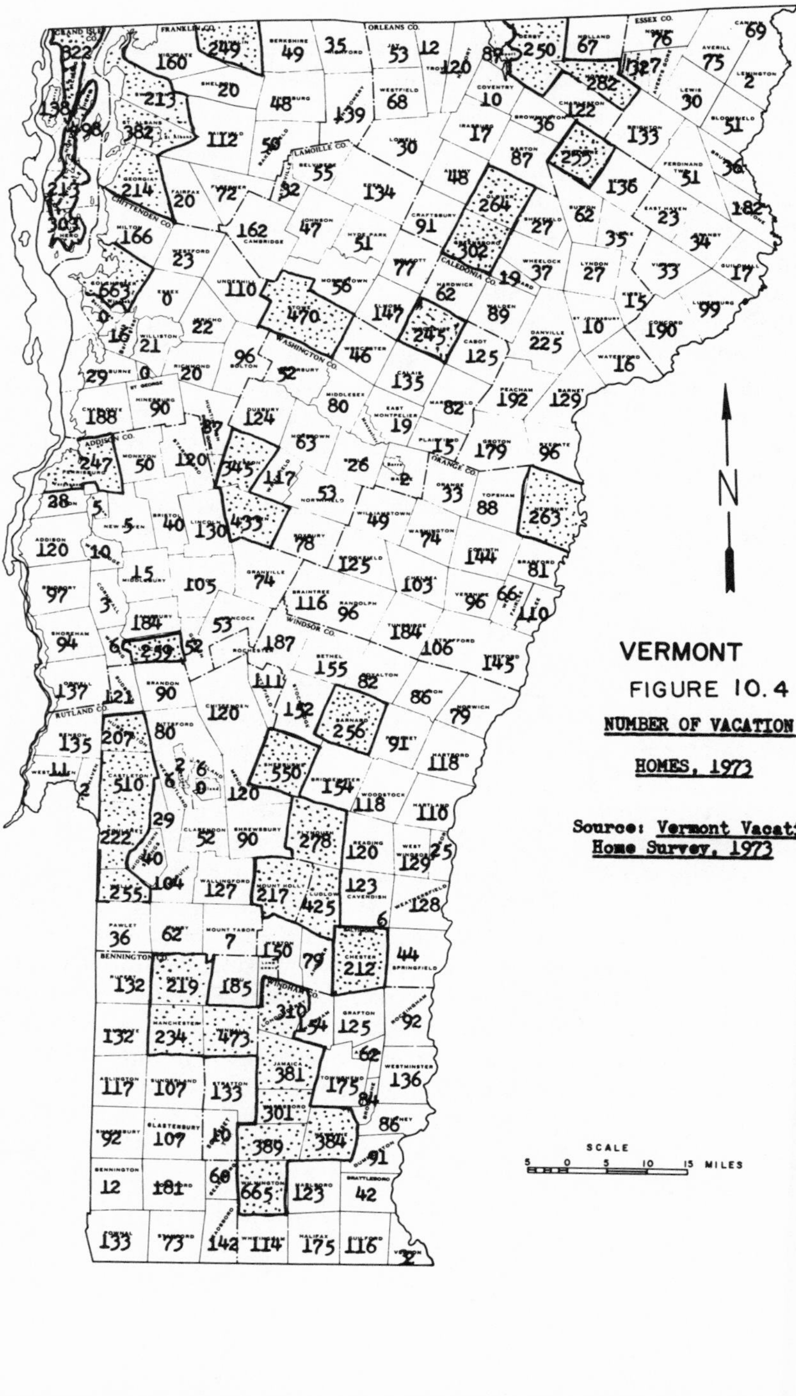

VERMONT

FIGURE 10.4

NUMBER OF VACATION

HOMES, 1973

Source: Vermont Vacation
Home Survey, 1973

SCALE

5   0   5   10   15 MILES

GRAND ISLE CO. 322

FRANKLIN CO. 249 49 35 53 12 ORLEANS CO. 87 250 67 75 ESSEX CO. 69

180 20 48 68 120 282 327 73 30 2

213 112 56 30 17 36 122 133 31

382 58 48 87 222 136 51 36

214 20 72 32 134 264 27 62 35 23 182

166 162 47 51 91 302 37 27 33 34 17

23 110 58 77 19 99

65 0 470 147 62 245 89 225 10 190

16 21 22 96 46 125 16

29 0 20 52 135 192 129

188 90 87 124 80 82

247 50 120 345 63 19 15 179 96

28 5 147 53 26 2 33 88 263

120 10 5 40 130 433 78 49 74 81

97 3 105 74 125 116 103 144

184 53 96 184 106 66 110

94 66 259 52 187 155 82 86 145

137 121 90 120 152 256 91 79

135 207 80 2 550 154 118

11 2 510 6 120 118 110

222 29 52 90 278 120 129

40 104 127 217 425 123 128

255 36 62 7 130 79 6 44

132 219 185 212 92

132 234 473 310 154 125

117 107 133 381 175 136

92 107 10 301 84 86

12 181 60 389 384 91

133 73 142 114 665 123 42 175 116 2

Not all vacation homes are owned by nonresidents. In 1968, 42.1 percent were owned by Vermonters, although by 1973 that figure had become 37.9 percent. Resident ownership is nearly all in the northern half of the state. Concentrations include the inevitable "hunting camp" in northeastern Vermont, and many Lake Champlain summer camps maintained by Burlington-area people. Colchester had the second greatest number of vacation homes in Vermont, and 63 percent of the lakeshore cottages in South Hero were owned by local residents. Most other resident-owned vacation properties were close to Barre-Montpelier and in the northern Green Mountains.

Acreage owned by nonresidents is considerably higher than the number of second homes would suggest, although the last study on the subject was done back in 1969. At that time, using thirty sample towns, it was found that 53.3 percent of the state's privately owned land area was probably owned by out-of-state interests. These include not only the summer-property person, but lumber companies and developers. In the sample towns, Bloomfield was 96.8 percent out-of-state ownership, almost entirely the St. Regis Paper Company. The two towns lowest in outside ownership were the Addison County farm communities of Cornwall and Panton. The sample towns in agricultural communities generally show much less nonresident ownership, and forested, poor farmland and ski-area towns have far more.

Nonresident ownership of second homes is similar to nonresident participation in skiing, recreational travel, and even hunting and fishing. In 1973, 16.3 percent were owned by Connecticut residents, followed by New York (14.7 percent), Massachusetts (10.6 percent), New Jersey (5.8 percent), and Quebec (3.6 percent). Figure 10.5 provides a regional breakdown of ownership in the thirteen state Regional Planning and Development Commissions. The distribution reflects accessibility to those areas closest in time and distance to the home state or province of nonresident owners.

Second-home owners, many of whom become permanent residents, range over the entire social and economic spectrum, but in many ways those who have best melded into the state are the longtime summer people. One old center has been the West River Valley, which has a regional identity all its own. One of the first studies of the summer-person syndrome was done here in the middle 1950s by Robert M. Carter, Rural Sociologist with the University of Vermont

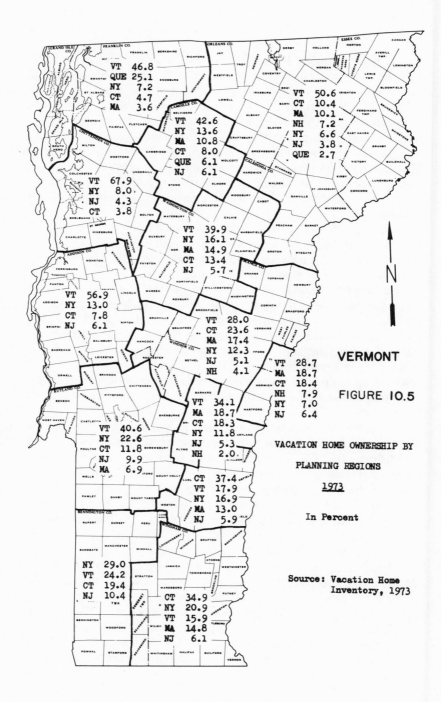

VERMONT

FIGURE 10.5

VACATION HOME OWNERSHIP BY

PLANNING REGIONS

<u>1973</u>

In Percent

Source: Vacation Home
Inventory, 1973

Agricultural Experiment Station (Bulletin 591).

Some interesting observations came from Carter's pioneer study. Among other things, he discovered that newcomers to the area tended to be younger than the native population, were politically and socially more active, attended church less, owned more land, and, in proportion to numbers, paid more in taxes. The newcomer was also, overall, a bit better in the social standings than the native and was more willing to see more nonnatives come into the valley. The latter sharply contrasts with a now rather prevalent philosophy (the "moat theory"), whereby most newcomers want to be the last to come into the Green Mountain state and would like to raise the drawbridge behind them.

Until recently, the newcomer and summer person settled in a small village and purchased a rundown farm or simply acquired equally rundown land. Skiing was in the future and the new Vermonter was looking for peace and tranquility: a stream to fish in, an acre to hunt on, a general store to buy groceries in, and an opportunity to enjoy that nebulous thing called open space and to enjoy it in an unhurried environment providing the opportunity for peaceful retirement.

The modern summer person and new resident is often younger than the person of twenty or so years ago but the same aspirations are there.* The skier is often a different breed entirely, drawn to Vermont for reasons other than its image. But whether it is the first-time skier, or the person carefully sanding the wide floorboards of an 1840 farmhouse, the effect on a rather conservative and traditional state is indelible. One of the clearest expressions of this influence has been on Vermont farming.

*My friend, Garrison Nelson, of the UVM Political Science Department in 1985 coined the buzzword MARPYS—Middle-Aged Rural Professionals. This group contrasts to the YUPPIES—Young Upwardly Mobile Urban Professionals, who seem to have become a major force in Burlington politics.

11

Farms and Farmland

With Vermont's population increasing by a third between 1960 and 1980, and with more than 36,000 second-home properties using up many acres, pressure has been mounting on the state's land resources. The most direct result has been an increase in land prices, which in turn makes it harder for low-value uses like forestry and farming to compete in a growing suburban environment. West Windsor was a town made accessible by interstate highways. According to the Conservation Foundation's Rural Land Project, between 1953 and 1976 the number of privately held parcels more than doubled, to 533. Property transfers averaged about eighty a year. Average size of holdings went from fifty acres to only twenty-six, and by 1976, 43 percent of the land was owned by nonresidents.

Ironically, it is mainly newcomers who are most vocal about preserving Vermont farmland and farming, yet their existence is one of the major reasons for its disappearance. But probably abandonment of the stony hillsides was inevitable; recent growth has only hastened a natural process and, economically speaking, perhaps recreational and residential use is the highest and best use for marginal Vermont farmland. Surely the best use is not commercial agriculture.

Pressure on the land resource is greatest where urbanization is growing, or where environmental quality is perceived as suitable for residential and recreational uses. Thus, different parts of the state reflect such perceptions as reflected in what one is willing to pay for a piece of Vermont. Table 11.1 gives the average value of farmland and building per acre as reported by Vermont farmers.

Table 11.1 does not show that the value of Vermont farmland has gone up at a rate far greater than the national average, which in

TABLE 11.1

County Farmland Values and Inflation of Land Value

County	Dollar value per acre[a]					% by which land value exceeded agricultural productive value, 1969[b]
	1954	1969	1974	1978	1982	
Addison	78	235	530	669	802	17%
Bennington	86	318	554	782	1033	176%
Caledonia	42	180	382	541	623	49%
Chittenden	94	276	500	799	1129	58%
Essex	36	130	365	465	542	20%
Franklin	66	186	409	563	742	1%
Grand Isle	128	291	541	872	958	48%
Lamoille	48	257	582	772	1188	62%
Orange	44	195	421	603	869	65%
Orleans	47	185	384	559	702	34%
Rutland	58	181	413	523	768	68%
Washington	53	281	488	689	932	128%
Windham	77	322	574	903	1105	115%
Windsor	56	269	537	742	988	176%
State	61	224	462	663	842	53%

[a]Includes land and buildings: *U.S. Census of Agriculture*, various years.
[b]Benjamin Huffman, *The Vermont Farm*. Vermont State Planning Office, 1973.

1978 was only $628 an acre. By no stretch of the imagination can much Vermont agricultural land be thought of as above average in quality, but that is not reflected in its reported value. Values of more than $2,700 an acre are common through much of Iowa and Illinois, and that reflects only *agricultural* value!

In 1973, Benjamin Huffman calculated (for 1969), the effect of the artificial inflation factor on farmland value for Vermont and its counties. The figure he came up with, and it may be conservative, was that more than half the value of Vermont farmland was set by nonfarm demand for that land. Using the census values in Table 11.1, the $224 per acre worth of farmland was actually worth only about $112 for its agricultural quality, but its value was doubled because of buyers wanting to get a piece of Vermont. The extremes show up well. The poorer-farmland counties in southern Vermont (Bennington, Windham, and Windsor) show a greater inflation factor, but Class I counties (Addison, Chittenden, Franklin, Grand Isle, and Orleans) show less, although Chittenden is higher because of

Views of Mount Mansfield from Underhill taken fifty years apart. The top photograph was taken by the U.S. Army in 1924, the lower by the author in 1975. The loss of farmland is striking. Notice the road at the bottom of each photograph. U.S. Army Photo courtesy of Noel Ring.

Burlington. The same applies to the high inflation rates in Washington County.

The Vermont Agricultural Experiment Station has made two studies of recent changes in prices of rural land. Robert Sinclair analyzed the situation in 1968 (Bulletin 659), and this analysis was updated through 1973 in a study by Neil Pelsue, Jr. (Bulletin 682). Over five years, the average cost of an acre of rural Vermont land increased from $239 to $580; an increment of about $68 a year. In both the years studied the highest prices prevailed in the southern parts of the state ($638 an acre in 1973), which is in line with the value of agricultural land given in Table 11.1. A review of northern-Vermont newspaper advertisements through 1984 indicates that an average price of $1,200 an acre for undeveloped rural land is not uncommon.

Besides higher land prices affecting Vermont agriculture, other factors promote rapid change in local farming. One of these is the greater availability of off-farm work, whereby more farmers become part-time operators, so that part-time farming becomes the norm rather than the exception.

Vermont Farms

One might think it would be easy to define a farm, but it is not. Before 1925 the census taker, probably on a horse, might simply ask, "Is this place a farm?" Between 1925 and 1945, any rural place with three acres or more was automatically so classified. For 1945, 1950, and 1954 the enumerator, now probably in an automobile, would ask, "Did you produce more than $150 off this place?" The place also had to have three acres or more. The $150 also included the food consumed by the family! The number of farms was certainly being inflated.

The system worked reasonably well in an era when practically every person not living in a town or village was growing food, fiber, or milk. But as the rural "nonfarm" population began to grow, chances were that many of the isolated rural places that had once been farms were no longer farms. The census began to differentiate between rural farm and rural nonfarm population in 1920 (Chapter 9), but nothing much was done about determining a census-defined farm until the 1959 Census of Agriculture.

In 1959 a farm was defined more quantitatively. That is, the rural place had to meet specific standards. At the time, with the prevailing prices for farm products, the definition that was used had considerable merit. Its use resulted in a decline of more than 25 percent in the number of farms in five years. This definition, first used in 1959, was also used in 1964 and 1969. It was changed for 1974, 1978, and 1982.

From 1959 through 1969 a rural place was a farm if: (1) it had fewer than 10 acres, more than $250 worth of agricultural products were sold; and (2) it had more than 10 acres, and more than $50 worth was sold. This definition still allowed many rural landowners to be classified as farmers even though they worked in Montpelier or St. Johnsbury for 90 percent or more of their annual income. Even so, the definition was an improvement. In the 1970s these standards were dated, and the U.S. Bureau of the Census redefined a farm so that the definition would apply only to those operations which sold more than $1,000 worth annually, regardless of size. This is the current definition, used in 1974, 1978, and 1982.

Over the years, then, and especially after 1959, a changing definition of the farm has been partly responsible for the large decrease in the number of farms. Yet this newly defined farm is probably still overstated, and the 5,852 reported in 1978 was certainly too high a figure. In that year, Vermont Town Listers counted only 3,330 dairy herds of more than five cows, and because most farms are dairy farms the number of farms was certainly fewer than that reported by the U.S. Bureau of the Census. The place that is a farm to the local Town Lister usually bears no relation to the place that the U.S. government says is a farm.

Farms can be divided into several economic classes by their sale of farm products. Table 11.2 shows the up-to-date Vermont situation, according to the U.S. Census of Agriculture.

The table shows several interesting developments, most obvious of which is the decrease in census-defined farms up to 1978, and the unexpected increase after that date. In truth, we are seeing the evolution of hobby farms.* Some of these owners may be business people

---

*The magnitude of the difficulty in defining the farm was illustrated when the 1978 Census of Agriculture was being taken. In that year, in addition to the normal mail survey on which the census is based, direct enumeration was made of *all* households in sample rural areas. In Vermont, the mail survey counted 5,852 farms, which is the figure used throughout this book. But when the direct-enumeration sample was added to that figure, 7,304

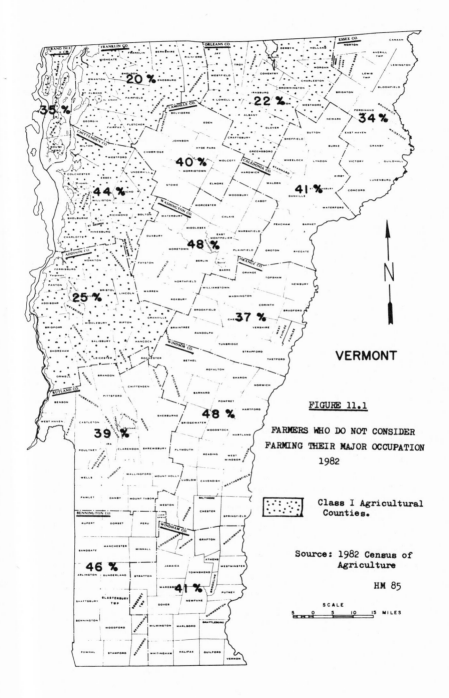

VERMONT

FIGURE 11.1

FARMERS WHO DO NOT CONSIDER
FARMING THEIR MAJOR OCCUPATION
1982

Class I Agricultural
Counties.

Source: 1982 Census of
Agriculture

HM 85

with a small herd of beef cattle, and some are probably young people setting up a small self-sufficient farm. Nearly all the recent increases in farms are in the lowest economic class, and in fact the number of dairy herds continues to shrink, for the newer farms are usually oriented not toward dairying, but toward vegetables, beef, and even horses. The number of farms in the top economic classes continues to increase, as do those at the bottom. The ones in the middle, the smaller dairy farms, continue to disappear.

A 1979 analysis of some larger Vermont dairy farms found that an average 66-cow farm had sales of $115,000 and expenses of $100,000, with a resulting net income of $15,000. Inventory changes added $11,000 to that figure, for a total of $26,000. In other words, 66 cows were producing a family cash income of around $15,000 annually, which, when we consider labor, responsibility, and inhuman hours, was very little return. Table 11.2 shows that only 737 farms were selling more than $100,000 worth of product in 1978.

Part-Time Farming

In 1974, 6.6 percent of United States farms were in Economic Class I and II; that is, they sold more than $100,000. For all of New England, the figure was 9.1 percent, and Table 11.2 shows Vermont at 5.7 percent, suggesting that many local farmers were not making an adequate income. Certainly they were not making an adequate income from their farm operations, a major reason why part-time farming has become so important. As the overall Vermont economy improves, it creates more jobs for rural nonfarm and rural farm people. Because of large cowherd responsibilities, some farmers cannot work at Colt Industries in St. Johnsbury, IBM in Essex, or Globe Battery in Bennington. But in these days the spouse can hold such a job. So too can the children, some of them contributing to the farm income. Thus, because of off-farm opportunities in a growing industrial state, part-time farming has become common.

Nearly all Vermont farmers at the lower end of the economic

"farms" were listed for the state. In 1982 the census did not conduct an area sample.

Table 11.2 reports only the mail-survey enumeration for 1978, and is therefore comparable to both 1974 and 1982. If 7,304 farms are considered, however, the figures look considerably different. Most noteworthy would be the fact that 2,443, or 33.4 percent showed gross sales of less than $2,500, and would be considered Economic Class VI operations. Most of these are not serious farm operations.

class scale have some income from nonfarm sources. For the older farmers the source may be Social Security payments; others may drive a school bus; still others may do rough carpentry work or work on an assembly line. Some may even combine farming with a job as an account executive with a brokerage firm or as a college professor. Most farms selling less than $100,000 a year have outside sources of income to maintain the family.

The U.S. Bureau of the Census no longer has a category for part-time farms, but back in 1969, 65 percent of Vermont farms were considered part-time. Instead, the census now asks farm operators their primary occupation. In 1974, more than 27 percent of the state's "farmers" reported that farming was not their major business. By 1982 the figure was 35 percent, and in that year, 42 percent were working off their farms more than 100 days a year. Furthermore, *no* farm operators with gross sales of less than $20,000 claimed to be farmers; at least they did not list farming as their major occupation.

The conclusion that more farmers are not farmers may seem paradoxical, but the trend continues. One unfortunate result is that many of these small operations in which farming is a sideline are cutting into the sales and income of those Vermont farmers whose entire livelihood consists of agriculture. This change may hasten the demise of the serious farm as the hobby farm evolves.

One should be aware that part-time farming has a regional pattern, as shown in Figure 11.1. The least important counties for extended off-farm work are those in which large-scale dairying is most important; Addison, Franklin, Grand Isle, and Orleans are among the lowest of these, all Class I counties as defined by their natural productivity. Chittenden, also a Class I county, shows much higher off-farm employment because it has jobs, and also because innumerable new gentleman farmers are associated with the growing manufacturing and service base of the county. The least-productive counties, Bennington, Washington, Windham, and Windsor, all have a high percentage of part-time farming.

In future years, the number of farmers holding down two jobs, one on the farm and the other in town, may continue to increase as Vermont becomes less of an agricultural state and more of an exurban, industrial, and recreational piece of real estate.

As Vermont has become more suburban, escalating land prices have made it hard for farming to expand. Furthermore, with the

TABLE 11.2

Vermont Farms, by Economic Class,

Economic class	Gross sales	1969	1974	1978	1982
I	200,000+	11 (0.1%)	66 (1.0%)	135 (2.3%)	346 (5.5%)
II	100,000–199,999	69 (1.0%)	289 (4.6%)	632 (10.8%)	987 (15.6%)
III	40,000– 99,999	833 (12.1%)	1,596 (27.0%)	1,655 (28.3%)	1,444 (22.9%)
IV	10,000– 39,999	2,933 (34.9%)	1,759 (29.8%)	1,149 (19.6%)	832 (13.2%)
V	2,500– 9,999	924 (13.4%)	766 (13.0%)	916 (15.7%)	1,037 (16.4%)
VI[a]	1,000– 2,499	2,092 (30.4%)	1,418 (24.0%)	1,350 (23.1%)	1,661 (26.3%)
		6,874	5,906	5,852	6,315
Number of dairy herds with more than 5 cows		4,760[b]	3,750[b]	3,330[b]	3,200[c]

[a]In 1969, included places with sales of $250 or more.
[b]Dairy herds from Vermont Town Listers.
[c]Dairy herds registered with Vermont Department of Agriculture.

Source: U.S. Census of Agriculture for 1969, 1974, 1978, and 1982.

This small hill farm in Chelsea has low quality farmland, but land which is probably worth a great deal for other uses.

accompanying economic prosperity, part-time farming and hobby farming are rapidly tending to dominate Vermont farm operations, and small to medium-sized dairy farms continue to disappear.

Yet this change does not imply that Vermont will cease to be an agricultural state. Some large dairy farms will survive and even prosper in more favored areas with less pressure on the land resource. Furthermore, agriculture will become more varied in its products, for new small farms are seldom oriented toward dairying, and a larger population demands a greater variety of locally produced farm products. In Chapters 12 and 13 we examine the present status and future of dairying, and the trend toward more agricultural diversification.

12

Dairy Farming

The Cow
As Seen by an Automation Expert

A cow is a completely automated milk-manufacturing machine. It is encased in untanned leather and mounted on four vertical, movable supports, one at each corner. The front end of the machine, or input, contains the cutting and grinding mechanism, utilizing a unique feedback device. Here also are the headlights, air inlet and exhaust, a bumper, and a foghorn. At the rear, the machine carries the milk-dispensing equipment as well as a built-in flyswatter and insect repeller. The central portion houses a hydrochemical-conversion unit. Briefly, this consists of four fermentation and storage tanks connected in a series by an intricate network of flexible plumbing. This assembly also contains the central heating plant complete with automatic temperature controls, pumping station and main ventilating system. The waste disposal apparatus is located to the rear of this central section. Cows are available, fully assembled, in an assortment of sizes and colors. Production output ranges from two to 20 tons of milk per year. In brief, the main external visible features of the cow are: two lookers, two hookers, four stander-uppers, four hanger-downers, and a swishy-wishy. There is a similar machine known as a bull. It gives no milk, but has other uses. (*Source:* Anonymous)

In Vermont a cow graces the State Seal, the only one so honored in the United States. Alongside the cow stands a pine tree. The Vermont Seal Pine in Arlington blew down a few years ago, and one wonders how long the cow is going to last.

In southern New England one has a hard time finding a dairy farm, the result of urbanization and the fact that using an acre for cows returns less than using it for a product of higher value like nursery stock or a housing development. As Vermont increases in population, as cities spread, land becomes more valuable for other uses. Artificial controls such as land-development rights may slow or perhaps temporarily stop such trends, but history has shown the inevitability of change in agricultural land use with change in population so long as the natural environment is such that alternative land uses are possible.

With the decrease in farms and farmers since World War II, the number of cows in Vermont has gone down, but not at the rate as the decrease in farms, because the remaining farms have gotten larger and the economic ten-cow herd of 1950 is now the economic sixty-cow herd of 1980. As recently as 1953, only 3.8 percent of the 10,790 dairy herds in the state had more than sixty milking cows. In 1977, 34.4 percent of the herds were of sixty cows or more, although there were only 3,500 herds in that year. Total number of cows went from 276,000 to 194,000. The average herd increased from twenty-five cows in 1953 to fifty-five cows in 1977, and to more than sixty in 1982.

Fluid Milk

In Vermont the present emphasis on dairying stems from two causes. One is an environment that is ideal for dairy farming: rough land, cool summers, and adequate rainfall for hay crops. The other is a demand for fluid milk, 87 percent water, which because of transportation costs and perishability has historically been produced close to where it is consumed. Earlier, most milk went into cheese and butter, but as the demands of southern New England grew, so too did the market for fresh milk (Chapter 7).

The Boston "milkshed" first penetrated Vermont after draining New Hampshire. In the 1880s the first milk trains were running from Concord to Boston, and Massachusetts farmers close to Boston were growing vegetables instead of milk and cream. As the thirst mounted with the growth of the market, Vermont became a supplier, beginning first in Windham and Windsor counties and then covering much of eastern Vermont. In 1905 the tendrils of Boston thirst had reached as far as Bristol, Vermont, some 213 miles away, and in that year six depots were shipping cans of fluid milk to "the Hub." Fluid-milk shipping from Vermont was Boston shipping, and not until after 1925 did Vermont milk begin to go to other destinations.

264   *Modern Vermont*

Wilson in his *Hill Country of Northern New England* comments, "By the early twenties Vermont was in the unique position of being the only state in the Union in which the number of cattle was larger than the number of people, and its cattle were for the most part dairy animals." His source is cited as the Report of the Commissioner of Agriculture, 1924–1926. This is where the favorite myth of "more cows than people" got started. At this time, 50 percent of the fluid milk and 62 percent of the cream shipped to the Boston market came from Vermont. In 1925 190 types of dairy plants were exporting milk, cream, cheese, and butter from the state.

In the 1930s, Vermont was sending milk to Rhode Island, New York, and Connecticut as well as some destinations in central Massachusetts. For the first time some was moving by truck, a prelude to today's complete dominance by that form of transportation. Also, competition was being felt from western producing areas, just as Vermont had competed with New Hampshire at an earlier time. Production costs were lower in places like Indiana, Ohio, and Wisconsin for several reasons. One was that the average growing season, depending upon where one was, is up to a month longer than in most of Vermont. That, of course, meant that more grain could be grown and less had to be purchased. Then, of course, the land was flatter. By central Indiana standards the "flatlands" of Addison county are virtually mountains. Calculations made in 1929 showed the following costs for the production of 100 pounds of milk per cow per year. A sample of fifty-two Iowa and Minnesota farms gave a figure of $141.50. Similar New England costs were: northern Vermont, $157.69; southern Vermont, $176.79; and Maine and New Hampshire, $188.40. Production costs today have the same general relationship, except that they are higher. In 1975 the average "blend price" received by farmers in the Chicago Regional Market was $8.53 per hundredweight, compared to the $9.85 received by most Vermont producers.*

*Prices received by farmers are an average of Class I (drinking milk) prices and Class II (manufacturing milk) prices prevailing in a Federal Milk Marketing Region. In Vermont, in 1980, the Class I price was $12.10, the Class II price $10.91, and the "blend price" about $11.60. A higher percentage of Vermont milk goes into Class I uses than Class II because of the nearby large fluid-milk market. The opposite prevails in Wisconsin. As a general rule, production costs are higher close to large population markets; therefore, prices received by farmers tend to be higher, offsetting the higher cost.

One example of higher production costs closer to markets: In 1973 only New York, Massachusetts, Rhode Island, and New Jersey had higher farmland taxes than Vermont.

Nearly all milk produced in Vermont, regardless of where it ends up, is priced according to the New England Region price system, which came into existence in 1933 as the Boston Regional Market. Perhaps a half dozen or fewer farmers in Bennington County still send milk to New York and receive a slightly different price, but Vermont milk is for all intents and purposes "New England" milk. This arrangement has not always applied, and origin and destination patterns for milk have changed many times over the years.

The path of milk from milking parlor to consumer is as confusing as the pricing structure, and today, because of bulk tanks and trucks, it is even more complex (although more economic) than it used to be. In the 1950s some milk never left the farm, being consumed by the family and, in some of the smaller operations, being fed to the livestock. The remaining milk went into four channels. By far the largest quantity would go to milk-receiving plants, which would weigh the milk received from farmers, sample it, sometimes process it, and then send it on its way to Boston and milk plants close to that city. In 1950, seventy-six plants were handling milk in this way. The only county with no Boston plants was Bennington, which shipped to New York. Of these seventy-six plants (many at that time located along the rail lines), twenty-one corporations, cooperatives, or individuals were owners and operators. Some of these milk receivers would go to the farms and collect the milk (for a price); others would have the farmers deliver to them.

In 1950, another twenty-two handlers of milk were associated with the secondary market; that is, the market for non-Boston or non-New York destined milk. Some of these, like the Boston plants, collected the milk, some processed it, some just weighed it, but all sent it. The same was true of the seven plants that shipped to the New York pool. To add to the confusion, some milk receivers, then as now, had no plants in the state but simply trucked the milk directly from the farm to their New York or Connecticut or Boston plant, thereby completely bypassing a milk-receiving station. Whatever the method, every farmer, again varying a bit based on location, received the same blend price for milk, no matter who collected, shipped, or processed it.

The remaining bit of Vermont milk, now from 5 to 7 percent of what was produced, went to local plants for ultimate consumption by Vermont consumers. In the early 1950s, fifty-five plants were purchasing milk directly from local farmers and an additional 113

The change from rail to truck shipment of milk is shown in these views of a milk-shipping plant in New Haven Junction. The top photograph was taken in 1955, when milk was delivered in cans. (Notice the wheeled conveyor belt for the return of empties.) In 1975, two doors to accommodate milk-truck tankers had been cut into the building. The railroad is just out of both pictures to the left.

dealers purchased from the fifty-five primary plants. Some of the milk went into local cheese, some to butter, but most into bottles.

Today it is much harder to figure out what is happening to Vermont milk because of bulk tanks and widespread use of truck transportation. As mobility (and fluidity) has increased, so too has flexibility in marketing. Milk cans lent themselves to easy counting. The mass of milk in a large, temperature-controlled bulk tank on a large Vermont dairy farm can go in one of several directions, depending upon who changes a valve setting at a large milk processing plant. All milk is now handled in bulk tanks. Here, after milking, often in new automated milking parlors, the milk goes to where it is stored under controlled temperature, weighed, and tested prior to shipment. Depending on the size of the herd and the tank, it may be picked up only two or three times a week. It is pumped into a stainless-steel truck and from there transported to the local collection plant, or sometimes directly to the southern market. One farm economist told me in 1980 that if the can system were still in operation, it would be about 40 percent more expensive for transportation than the bulk system. The farmer has additional costs, but on the larger farms the savings in transportation render the present system cheaper.

In 1980, Vermont produced 2.1 billion pounds of milk, of which 8 percent remained in the state as Class I fluid milk consumed by local customers. This milk was handled by eleven dairies. The rest went into the New England pool, where, depending upon supply and demand, it was allocated as Class I or Class II milk. Some ended up in a dairy store in Rhode Island in bottles, some in a cottage-cheese plant in Maine, and some perhaps in ice cream made in Massachusetts (which may ultimately have been consumed by people living in Vermont).

Probably a great deal more Vermont-produced milk remains in the state than the small amount sold as Class I milk. This notion is mainly conjectural, because we have no way of knowing precisely what happens. In 1980 the New England Region (including some New York counties east of the Hudson River) produced 5.5 billion pounds of milk (with 2.1 billion coming from Vermont). Of this production, 2.6 billion pounds were marketed as Class II (manufacturing) milk, or about 47 percent. Vermont's cheese factories and creameries, the latter not too important, used more than half of the pooled Class II milk produced in the New England market. Therefore, Vermont milk-manufacturing plants are large consumers of Vermont milk. On any given day or in any given season it's entirely possible that practically all milk produced in Vermont is consumed locally, or at least a product is made from it in the state, later to be shipped to supermarkets in New Jersey, Ohio, or even California. Without question, the most important dairy product manufactured in Vermont is cheese, though smaller quantities of butter are churned, along with lesser amounts of other products like ice cream and powdered milk.

Cheese Manufacturing

Vermont cheesemakers over the last forty or fifty years have remained in business because of a high-quality product and judicious advertising of that product as "Vermont." To argue whether cheese from Grafton, Plymouth, East Wallingford, Cabot, or Mt. Holly is any better than identical cheddar or Colby from Wisconsin is an exercise in futility. Many consumers strongly *think* the cheese is superior, and buy it at prices often higher than comparable New York or Wisconsin products. As a result, production of hard cheese has survived and even prospered. In the mid-1970s, Vermont produced more than thirteen million pounds of American cheese, ranking it nineteenth in the country, just slightly behind Michigan. Wisconsin was first with 720 million pounds, New York a distant fifth with 61 million. Vermont's production far surpassed that of homemade and factory cheese of the nineteenth century.

Cheesemaking has also prospered on other fronts. The nearness of Vermont to large ethnic markets has helped, and recently more than 20 million pounds of Italian types of cheese have been produced, giving the state a sixth-place national ranking. Also, because soft cheese like cottage cheese is perishable, its manufacture has recently been important.

In 1975 the largest cheese plant in the state opened in Middlebury, manufacturing Swiss cheese and other dairy products. Each year more than 20 million pounds of cheese are manufactured in this plant. In the early 1980s, Vermont's production of cheddar, Colby, Italian varieties, and Swiss cheese amounted to approximately 60 million pounds. Because it requires on the average 10 pounds of milk

The modern Kraft cheese plant in Middlebury is Vermont's largest milk consumer.

As upland Vermont has become nonfarm Vermont, most commercial dairy farms have concentrated around Newport in Orleans County, or on the clay lands of the Champlain Valley. The rest are widely scattered, as here in the upper White River Valley in Rochester.

to manufacture one pound of cheese, milk requirements for the state's hard cheesemakers alone are more than half a billion pounds. Add to that the milk requirements for the 30 million or so pounds of cottage cheese that are made, and another 200 million pounds of milk are utilized. Therefore, cheesemaking alone has an appetite of around 700 million pounds of milk annually, probably a conservative estimate.

Cheese manufacturing has been growing rapidly and production today is higher than at any other time in the state's history. Yet in 1980 only eight plants were making cheddar and Swiss cheese; they were in Swanton, Troy, Cabot, Middlebury, Plymouth, Mt. Holly (Healdville), East Wallingford, and Grafton. Italian cheeses were being produced in Hinesburg, Swanton, Richmond, and Wells River.

The recent growth in Vermont cheesemaking is astounding when one realizes that in 1946, total production of hard cheese was only 185,000 pounds. In 1954 cheddar and Italian cheese totals were a little more than 8 million pounds, and now production is more than 50 million pounds and a national ranking. Manufacturing for years was kept alive by the recreation industry and a small but steady demand for Vermont cheese from Healdville and a few other small factories. The main reason for this growth has been the increase in milk supply, rapidly growing even with the decrease in cows. Another is the flexibility of the milk supply, stemming from widespread use of bulk tanks and truck transportation. Thanks to the lower Class II prices (in 1983 only a dollar more than those in Wisconsin), local manufacturing plants are attracted by the large amount of available milk, reasonably priced, close to a large number of consumers. Assuming production costs on a par with large Midwest plants, the transportation costs from Vermont to Boston or New York, lower than shipment from Minnesota, ensure a good market for locally manufactured cheese. Shoppers now can find Vermont-made cheese on grocery shelves at the same price, or sometimes less, than competing brands from America's Dairyland. The trend is bound to continue, for it is expected that the milk supply will continue to increase, even with fewer producers.

Dairy Farming and Quality of Land

With fewer cows, fewer farms, and far less land in farming, still production of milk has grown. The output per cow has risen dramatically because of better breeding and improved feeding. In 1920, the peak year for cows (290,000, depending upon how one counts), milk production was 122 million gallons, or approximately 1.4 billion pounds. By 1963, 251 million gallons were produced by 51,000 fewer animals concentrated on fewer farms, and projections are that 2.3 billion pounds will be produced in the 1980s as the present production of pounds per cow increases to 13,000 or more.

A major reason for greater milk production has been that dairy farming has retreated from poorer lands to concentrate where soils are better, land is flatter, and summer temperatures are higher. All this change translates into higher-quality feed and pasture, which further translates into more milk produced by fewer animals. Commercial dairy farming in Vermont is gradually becoming located in areas of highest agricultural quality.

In 1964, the Vermont Agricultural Experiment Station devised a system for ranking counties and towns according to their agricultural productivity (Sykes, 1964). Class I, II, and III agricultural counties and towns were identified, but the method was more valid with larger areas than with individual towns.

According to index numbers developed with this system, Grand Isle County, with a rating of 134, is far ahead of Addison and Franklin, both with 81, and Orleans, with 74. The last three counties have large acreages of hilly, infertile land. Grand Isle has few hills, fertile limestone soils, a temperature climate moderated by the lake, and only one problem: encroachment upon farmland by lakeside vacation cottages. Because it is small (106 square miles, of which only 83 are land), Grand Isle does not always show up as the excellent agricultural county that it is. Rounding out the Class I counties is Chittenden, with a ranking of 72.

Secondary agricultural counties (Class II) are Caledonia (63), Orange (61), Washington (52), Lamoille (46), Windsor (42), and Rutland (40). At the bottom of the natural-resource barrel are Class III Bennington (24) and Windham (32) in southern Vermont.

The retreat from the hills and the evolution of commercial dairy regions has been long and slow. At the end of the nineteenth century, cows were rather evenly distributed throughout the state (Figure 7.1). Compare that map with the density of 1977, eighty years later (Figure 12.1). Although there were twenty-four cows per square mile in 1897, and twenty-one per square mile in 1977 (almost the same density), the pattern is now very different. Figure 12.2 summarizes this long-term trend in redistribution of dairy farming.

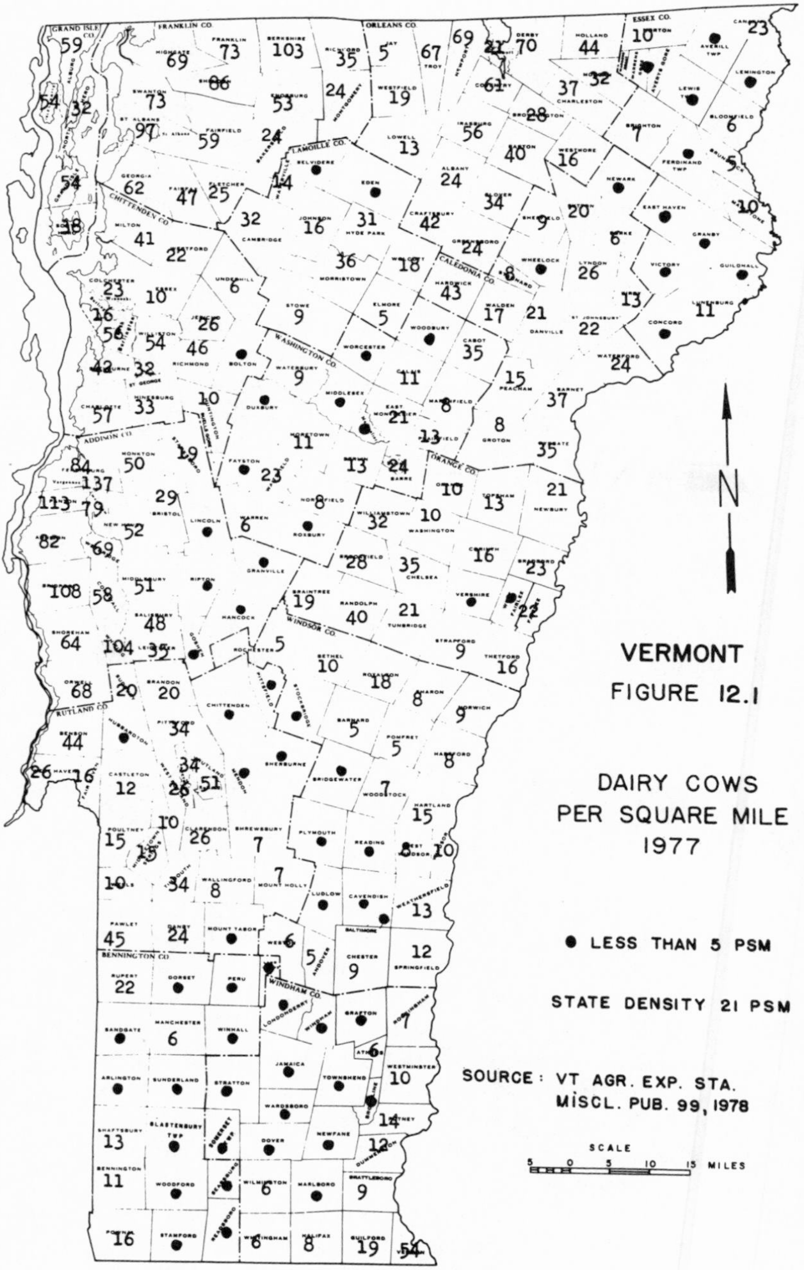

VERMONT
FIGURE 12.1

DAIRY COWS PER SQUARE MILE 1977

● LESS THAN 5 PSM

STATE DENSITY 21 PSM

SOURCE: VT AGR. EXP. STA.
MISCL. PUB. 99, 1978

SCALE
5   0   5   10   15 MILES

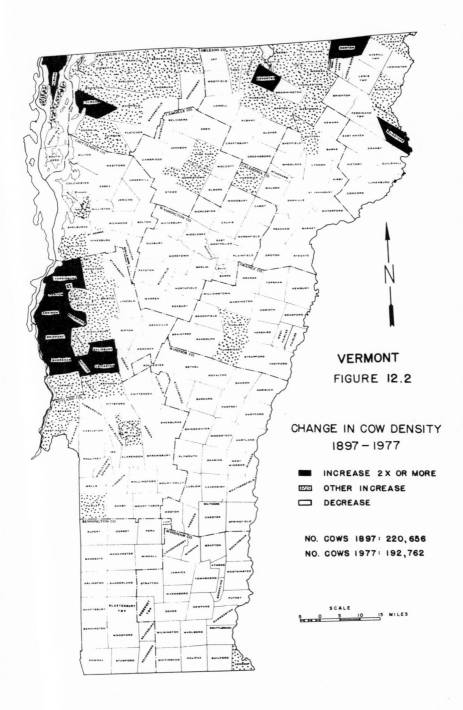

VERMONT
FIGURE 12.2

CHANGE IN COW DENSITY
1897 – 1977

■ INCREASE 2X OR MORE
▨ OTHER INCREASE
☐ DECREASE

NO. COWS 1897: 220,656
NO. COWS 1977: 192,762

SCALE
5   0   5   10   15 MILES

All over Vermont, however, are small pockets of reasonably good land, which no index of agricultural quality dealing with county-size units can reveal. Commercial agriculture has retracted into the counties with high land quality, but it has also become concentrated in local areas where the land is better.

Figure 12.3 maps the distribution of dairy cows as of 1977, using the same method as in Figure 4.4, which showed the pattern in 1840. Though approximately 1,200 more dots appear on the 1977 map (because there were 35,000 more cows), the concentration of farming in specific locations is clear.

Small areas of important dairy farming show up associated with the Lamoille Valley in northern Vermont as well as with the White River tributaries through Randolph, Brookfield, Chelsea, and Tunbridge. Most other river valleys have some good farms remaining; that is clear in the valley of the Passumpsic in St. Johnsbury and Lyndon, along Otter Creek in Pittsford, Brandon, Clarendon, and other places. Farming along the Connecticut River is still significant, as it is in the Mettawee and Poultney valleys in the Taconics of southwestern Vermont.

To see real cowtowns one has to go to the areas with the densest pattern on the maps. At the top of the heap is the incredible pasture congestion that one finds in Panton, just outside of Vergennes. There 113 dairy cows per square mile are competing with 450 beef cattle in probably the most purely agricultural town in Vermont.

Cows in the Future

By the early 1980s, Vermont agriculture was responsible for only 5 percent of the gross state product, which means that farming alone, measured in dollars and cents, counted little. The importance of farming can be measured in other ways, however, some of them nonmonetary. Nearly all nonforested land is in active farm ownership. What would happen to the recreation business if visitors could not find the picturesque valley with open fields and contented cows? And what would the tourist do if maple sugar and Vermont cheese were not available at the countless roadside stands and gift shops? And how about the sportsmen who are usually allowed to hunt and fish on Vermont farmland?

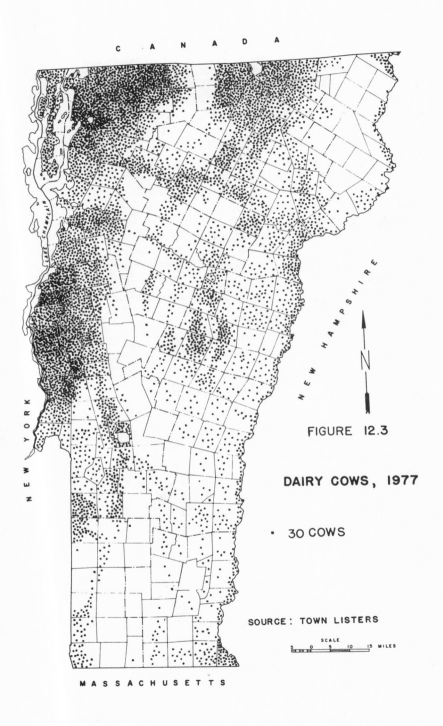

FIGURE 12.3

DAIRY COWS, 1977

• 30 COWS

SOURCE : TOWN LISTERS

SCALE

5 0   5   10   15 MILES

Economically, farming is more valuable than the $250 million or so in gross receipts received by the farmers themselves. Farm-supply retailers sell more than $200 million annually to farmers. The processing and wholesaling of agricultural commodities produces values of about $500 million. These activities employ about 4,200 workers, with a payroll in excess of $30 million. The figures are impressive, but still this is less than skiers spend.

It seems inevitable that there will be fewer cows and more milk production for the foreseeable future. Vermont, the dairyland of New England, is not about to change drastically, although less land will be devoted to the state's major agricultural system. Fewer commercial farmers will be around, but the declines may be less rapid than during the last twenty-five years. More diversification will probably occur. Besides the normal economic forces creating fewer and larger farms, less land in agriculture, and higher milk production per cow, Vermont's agriculture is changing because of the location of the land itself.

13

Changing Agriculture

In recent years, Vermont agriculture has been directly contributing approximately 5 percent to the gross state product. In 1983 Vermont's gross cash receipts from farm marketings amounted to $427 million, placing the state forty-second in the country. In New England, Vermont is the most important agricultural state, followed by Maine ($413 million), Massachusetts ($367 million), and Connecticut ($321 million). More than 6,000 farms remain, but half had sales of less than $10,000, and many are part-time operations.

Farming is not what it used to be. Pressures for alternate land uses have been mounting, taxes and land costs are high, dairy-product receipts have not always grown along with expenses, and younger farmers are often unable or unwilling to continue or even to start farming. The amount of Vermont used for commercial farming continues to shrink as agriculture becomes concentrated on the best lands. Prime farmland in the state (Class I and Class II) occupies only 10.6 percent of Vermont's area, and the distribution of commercial farms conforms to these lands. The comparable amount nationwide is about 15 percent.

We must realize by now that Vermont farmers are a difficult group to generalize about. Thirty years ago there were no hobby farms and most rural Vermonters were on a serious farm of some sort, although most farms were not paying them a decent income. Now those who are listed as farmers in the U.S. Census run the spectrum from full-time commercial dairy operators to a state employee in Montpelier who lives in Worcester and sells some cordwood and maple syrup and grows three acres of sweet corn. We can find

277

absolutely no way of breaking down the statistics so that serious commercial farms can be separated from others. In 1900, farming was one of many economic activities, but by the 1980s it had become both an economic and a *social* activity. Thus one wonders if those who look at their fifty acres and five beef cows as a "farm" should be classified as "farmers." Many would probably love to be given that designation, and the U.S. Census definition ($1,000 or more in sales) certainly does not help. This is what makes it so difficult to categorize Vermont farming in the 1980s.

A historic trend in agriculture seems to be continuing in the northeastern United States. As population increases, less land is available for commercial farming, and we see the clear result: larger and fewer commercial farms. A lower proportion of state income is derived from the farm sector as other land uses dominate. Depressed incomes tend to characterize the remaining "commercial" farmers as hobby farms evolve. Part-time farming and increased agricultural diversification become normal as suburban pressures mount.

Vermont is not unique in undergoing these changes, but because it has some reasonably good land and awareness of the resource value of open space has recently become visible, the inexorable trends, at least in Vermont, may not continue to their conclusion. In very recent years the rate at which agricultural land is being abandoned has slowed, some farm incomes have improved, and in many Vermont towns legislation has been passed to reduce burdensome farm property taxes. Off-farm employment is allowing many farmers to keep going as part-timers. The numbers of dairy cows, if not of herds, may decrease at a slower rate, and more of the abandoned farmlands are grazed with herds of sheep and beef cattle. These practices are not always commercial agriculture, but they show a continuing desire to keep the land open and producing something besides brush and trees. Table 13.1 and Figure 13.1 summarize Vermont farm changes during the twentieth century.

Even though the decline in farms, farm population, and land area in farms has been great, the decline in number of cows and acres of cropland has been far less, as reflected in figures on increasing farm sizes (at least up to 1974, after which the hobby farm is affecting the picture). Fewer farms with better land resources are producing more with larger dairy herds. Some of these trends are reflected in the maps and graphs and indicate those places in Vermont where commercial agriculture is becoming more concentrated.

TABLE 13.1

Vermont Agricultural Changes, 1900–1982

	1900	1920	1940	1950	1959	1974	1978	1982
Number of farms	33,104	29,075	23,582	19,043	12,099[a]	5,906[a]	5,852	6,315
Number of cows	270,194	290,122[a]	279,141	261,370	250,928	202,735[b]	184,860[c]	191,089
Average farm size (acres)	143	146	156	185	243	282	279	249
Percentage of land in farms	NA	73	69	59	50	28	27.5	26.5
Acres of cropland	NA	NA	1,487,066	1,155,668	983,564	779,344	806,244	772,055
Farm population	NA	124,445	105,515	81,132	55,591	19,489[d]	18,079[e]	19,700[d]

[a]Change in definitions. For numbers of farms, see Chapter 11.
[b]From U.S. Census of Agriculture. Vermont Listers reported 200,187 cows in 1974.
[c]U.S. Census of Agriculture. Vermont estimate of 183,257.
[d]Estimated.
[e]U.S. Census of Population, 1980.
NA-Not available

Source: U.S. Bureau of the Census. Census of Agriculture, U.S. Census of Population. Washington, D.C.: U.S. Govt Printing Office, appropriate years.

CHANGE OF LAND IN FARMS
1910–1974

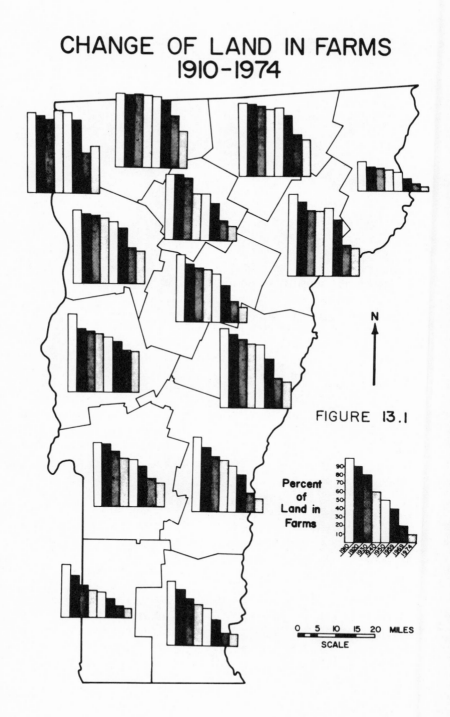

N

FIGURE 13.1

Percent of Land in Farms

90
80
70
60
50
40
30
20
10

1910 1920 1930 1940 1950 1960 1974

0   5   10   15   20   MILES
SCALE

General Decline of Agriculture

The trend of fewer and larger commercial farms and fewer people engaged in producing food and fiber is a national phenomenon. Its causes are two, both stemming from a technological revolution in agriculture after World War II. One is mechanization, the other is often called scientific farming. The effect these changes are having on a place like Vermont has been particularly severe because of land resources poorer than the national average, and closeness to major urban areas. Vermont's land capability for farming is below national averages and it has precious little prime agricultural land. Willing buyers are plentiful for Vermont's poorer farmlands, however, because of proximity to large numbers of people, a problem that many other places in the United States do not have. Thus, as we have seen, the state is very sensitive to nonfarm demands upon farmland.

Mechanization of agriculture involves substituting machinery for hand labor: tractors instead of horses, milking machines instead of hands, and automatic barn cleaners instead of shovels and brooms. Mechanization alone does not always create a greater output per acre of land, but it increases the capital and technical know-how that a farmer must have to be able to compete. Its influence upon Vermont land use is probably best seen in the decrease of grain farming. Land that once had to provide the fuel for draft horses could now produce the fuel for dairy cattle to produce milk, and the decline of grain farming correlates closely with greater numbers of tractors.

Mechanization not only changed Vermont cropping patterns, releasing more land to feed cows; it also increased capital requirements for farming and required that farmers who used the new helpmate become mechanics as well as veterinarians. The capital requirements necessitated by modern equipment have had tremendous influence in forcing farmers out of agriculture. As late as 1954, only 66 percent of Vermont farms had tractors, and only 11,000 trucks were distributed among the almost 16,000 farms of the period.

Scientific farming involves commercial fertilizers, pesticides, and improved crop strains. It also requires capital. For the same reasons many farmers were unable, or were unwilling, to join the technologic revolution. Milk yields per cow and hay and corn yields per acre have increased, and attrition of farmers has been constant.

The representative yield figures given were calculated from U.S. Census of Agriculture data for appropriate years.

Yields per Acre

	1920	1940	1974	U.S. Yields/Acre 1974
Grain corn (bu)	44.2	37.8	81.5	86.2
Silage corn (tons)	9.7(1924)	9.9	14.2	10.7
Hay (tons)	1.3	1.4	1.8	2.1
Potatoes (bu)	94.2	127.0	302.0	344.0
Oats (bu)	NA	35.2	45.6	46.5

Note: Other crops are not listed because of their minor importance. In 1982, yields per acre of grain corn were 94.4 bushels an acre on 12,000 acres. Hay was 1.9 tons an acre. Silage corn yield was 14.3 tons per acre. Otherwise, only 305 acres of potatoes, 424 acres of wheat, and 3,024 acres of "other" grains were grown in Vermont. Interestingly, 1,128 acres of sorghum were grown, and two farms were reported to be growing soybeans.

The costs of achieving increases in output per animal or per acre have been enormous. In 1983 the production expenses on Vermont farms were more than $375 million, an increase of $199 million since 1969. Commercially mixed feeds alone went from $32 million to $106 million and the value of machinery on farms increased from $73 million to $324 million during the same period.

Sad as it may seem, one factor leading to increased net income *per farm* has been that over the years there have been fewer farmers to share a somewhat static agricultural income. The net income for all the farms in Vermont in 1949 amounted to $27.7 million, which averaged out to $1,425 per farm. Twenty years later (1969), the Vermont net farm income had increased only to $46.2 million ($6,372 per farm). During this period the number of farms went from 19,043 to 6,874, or a loss of more than 12,000 farms. Thus the individual farmer's net income increased mainly because there were fewer farmers to share the slowly growing agricultural dollar. Since 1969 the rate of attrition of farms has slowed, and the commercial farms remaining are larger, more efficient, and concentrated on the best lands. Farm prices have been improving, so that between 1969 and 1983 the net income to Vermont agriculture went from $46.2 million to $68.1 million and the net income per farm, after all production expenses and taxes, was up to $9,086, still an inadequate figure. And, as pointed out in Chapter 11, an increase in noncommercial farms may cut into full-time farmers' incomes, further accelerating a decline in farms that were once viable.*

Production expenses keep mounting, and farmers do not receive income comparable to that of their urban counterparts. A further decline in commercial farms is inevitable, although the rate will slow. Notwithstanding tax abatements, less land will be under farm ownership, for land costs now make it prohibitive for most remaining farmers to acquire more acreage.

Diversification

Vermont agriculture, as it has developed since the early 1900s, has hardly been diversified. With greater emphasis on dairying, and with rapid disappearance of the smaller, less-specialized farm, farming is now nearly monocultural. In 1983, cash receipts of Vermont farmers were $427 million, of which $337 million came from dairy products. In other words, about 79 percent of farm income in Vermont was based on dairying. That is the highest percentage in the United States. Wisconsin derives only 60 percent of its farm income from milk.

Table 13.2 shows how Vermont and New England farming has been changing over the last fifty-five years. Vermont has become more specialized in dairying, from 69 percent of cash receipts from that source in 1929 to 79 percent in 1983.

As Vermont has become a premier New England dairy state, agriculture in most other parts of the region has further diversified. That is clearest in Connecticut, Massachusetts, and Rhode Island, where the greatest number of people are. As Vermont's population grows, and the state becomes more suburban than rural, changes in farming are to be expected.

Nursery and greenhouse products will probably gain importance, as will vegetables and other market garden crops. As greater diversity comes, farmland may decline further because nearly all other agricultural systems require less land to return as much profit.

---

*Interestingly, as reported in *Economic Indicators of the Farm Sector* for 1983, net income per farm had risen to $13,122 in 1978, only to decline to the $9,086 reported for 1983. Between 1978 and 1982 the number of farms reported by the U.S. Bureau of the Census *increased* from 5,862 to 6,315.

TABLE 13.2

Cash Receipts for Farm Products, New England, 1929

	Vermont	Maine	N.H.	Mass.	Conn.	R.I.
Millions of $	42	90	22	70	52	9
Percentages:						
Dairy products[a]	69.0	14.4	40.9	32.9	34.6	55.5
Chickens/eggs	7.1	7.7	27.2	17.1	15.4	15.1
All vegetables	6.9	64.4	10.5	13.2	8.1	10.8
Fruits	4.1	3.9	5.9	9.8	3.8	5.9
Nursery/greenhouse	.7	.9	1.8	14.7	9.4	15.1
Tobacco	——	——	——	6.9	24.4	——
Forest products[b]	11.7	8.9	14.1	5.3	3.5	3.5
Honey	1.4	.4	.8	.3	.6	.3

[a]Includes cattle and calves.
[b]Includes maple syrup.

Source: U.S. Bureau of the Census, 1930, Agriculture, Second Series, 1931.

Cash Receipts for Farm Products, New England 1983

	Vermont	Maine	N.H.	Mass.	Conn.	R.I.
Millions of $	427	413	114	367	321	31
Percentages:						
Dairy products	78.9	26.0	48.2	24.9	29.4	21.2
Cattle/calves	10.3	4.5	7.1	2.0	4.4	1.7
Eggs	1.3	9.1	9.1	5.5	25.4	12.9
Apples	1.7	3.3	6.6	4.0	2.3	2.8
Maple products	1.8	.1	1.6	.1	——	——
Nursery/greenhouse	.7	1.9	10.5	27.3	17.3	36.4
Potatoes	.1	22.9	——	.6	.4	8.7
Misc. vegetables	.6	1.4	4.1	9.3	4.7	6.8
Cranberries	——	——	——	17.7	——	——
Broilers	——	9.3	2.8	2.4	.7	.3
Tobacco	——	——	——	1.2	6.8	——
Other[a]	4.6	8.5	10.0	5.0	7.5	9.3

[a]In Vermont, includes wool, beeswax, honey, sheep, lambs, hay, other fruits, forest products, other field crops, including grains.

Source: *Economic Indicators of the Farm Sector*, State Income and Balance Sheet Statistics 1983, Economic Research Service, U.S. Department of Agriculture, January 1985.

The only exception would be cattle and sheep raising, but these systems of land use yield a small return per unit of land, which means that they may normally be at all significant only in part-time hobby farming. Interestingly, 1983 data showed that though dairy farming retains its place, cash receipts for vegetables, maple products, and nursery and greenhouse products have all increased relatively since 1977.

Figure 13.2 presents the major sources of farm income, county by county. Although 79 percent is from dairying, major differences distinguish one county from the next. Most of the counties poor in land resources show greater diversity. Windham, Bennington, and Caledonia are good examples. The category Crops in the graph includes grain, hay, corn, and potatoes but excludes poultry, vegetables, nursery stock, apples, maple products, wool, honey, and forest products, which are included in the Other category. Chittenden County, with its Burlington-area growth, shows more diversification because the press of people stimulates various nondairy alternatives. The same happened years ago to Connecticut dairy farming. The strength of egg production in Caledonia County (Hardwick) shows up well.* Grand Isle has greater diversity because it is close to Burlington and because apples have a big share in its farm economy.

Dairy farming has become synonymous with Vermont. Of 1,574,441 acres of farmland, only 10,000 were being used for non-dairy-related uses in 1982. Of this nondairy land, 305 acres were used for potatoes, 1,633 for other vegetable crops, 237 for strawberries, 2,845 for other crops, 4,980 in apple orchards, and even 401,000 square feet in greenhouses! These uses are presently negligible in the agricultural economy, but their local standing is significant. Also, as farming developed, some played an important part in the history of Vermont land use, and may do so again in the future.

Fruit Production

The first apples introduced into Vermont were of the Fameuse variety, or "Snow Apple." They were planted by the French in the Champlain Valley in the 1730s. The presently popular mackintosh belongs to the same family. From this small beginning, apple trees

---

*In 1982, the production of eggs in Hardwick ceased.

FIG. 13.2 SOURCES OF FARM INCOME

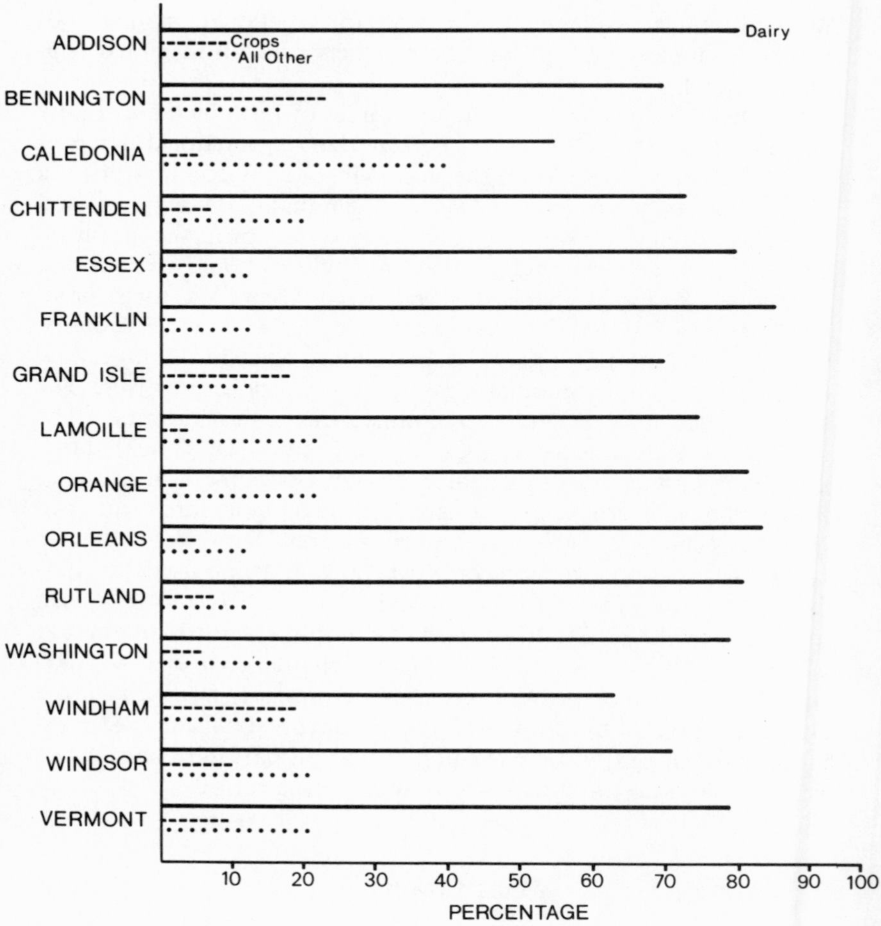

SOURCE: U.S. CENSUS OF AGRICULTURE

Large trucks carry Addison County apples from Shoreham for distribution throughout the eastern United States.

followed Johnny Appleseed across Vermont until by 1900 nearly
every farm had a few trees. Apples were raised easily, but no widespread success attended pears, peaches, or other small fruit.

Apple production passed through three distinct stages. Until the
1870s apples were grown primarily for cider and cider brandy, and
several local distilleries reflected this orientation. After 1870, production of cider brandy declined, for hard liquor could easily be obtained from outside sources. Cider making continued in a small way,
but many small farm orchards were cut for firewood and others fell
into decay. Growers soon began to regret this step. Expanding markets again directed Vermont land use, and a demand appeared for
apples from the north country. By 1900 apple growing became profitable, and nearly every farm with an orchard was shipping some fruit
to market.

Articles in agricultural journals and Reports of the Vermont
State Board of Agriculture suggested that much of the rougher hill
land might profitably be put into large orchards, and that the crop
might become a worthwhile specialty for some farmers disenchanted
with sheep or milk cows. The advantages of air drainage on hillsides
was often cited as a reason. Larger orchards began to take shape,
fortunately avoiding higher mountainous land, specific varieties of
eating apples were planted, and the cider apple became a thing of the
past. In 1928, 35 percent of the trees in commercial orchards were
less than nine years old. The 1.7 million trees of 1899 produced

1,176,822 bushels; ten years later, 1.2 million trees were yielding 1,459,689 bushels of better fruit. Greatest production was in 1910; after that year came a gradual decline in both trees and harvest, but because of better trees and better management, the decrease in bushels was far slower than the disappearance of the old orchards. By 1940, 288,792 trees were yielding 898,583 bushels, or a little more than three bushels per tree. Back in 1910, the average yield was 1.2 bushels.

The number of apple trees reported steadily declined to a low of 153,563 in 1959 but since then, trees and acres devoted to the crop have steadily increased. Changing definitions of the farm make year-to-year comparisons awkward, but by 1970 the state had 55 orchards with 200,000 bearing trees, and production was increasing. The 1974 Census of Agriculture reported 161 farms growing and selling apples, but only 112 of these were selling more than $2,500 worth of fruit. These more commercial farms had 278,738 trees (215,804 or 77 percent were of bearing age), and produced 50,991,322 pounds, or 1,062,319 bushels.

TABLE 13.3

County	Number of trees, 1910	Number of trees, 1959	Number of trees, 1970	Number of trees, 1982[a]
Addison	93,947	40,422	100,652	157,868
Bennington	66,053	20,859	16,661	27,898
Chittenden	91,375	5,994	5,094	14,905
Grand Isle	52,908	11,674	7,451	13,280
Rutland	85,541	18,891	18,443	25,124
Windham	152,627	27,519	43,266	74,116
Windsor	177,913	9,580	6,155	15,784
All others	463,165	5,806	2,021	15,559
Vermont	1,183,529	153,563	199,743	344,522

Vermont Apple Trends: 1910–1982

[a]Farm definition was different in 1970 than in 1982.

Note: In 1982 the Extension Service of the University of Vermont reported 81 apple growers with 4,541 acres. The U.S. Census of Agriculture reported, for the same year, 243 farms and 4,952 acres.

Source: U.S. Bureau of the Census, Census of Agriculture. Washington, D.C.: U.S. Government Printing Office, various years.

By 1982, 240 farms were reported as selling apples. On these, 4,963 acres were in orchards, with 344,522 trees, and they produced 51,692,679 pounds (1,332,526 bushels). Yield per tree in both 1974 and 1982 was about five bushels, far above those of an earlier era.

Addison County, especially in Shoreham, Orwell, and Cornwall, has become the center of production. The Shoreham Cooperative has had much to do with this regional concentration. Outside of Addison County, commercial apple production counts heavily in Monkton and Shelburne in Chittenden County, in South Hero and Isle La Motte in Grand Isle County, in Poultney and Castleton in Rutland County, Bennington and Shaftsbury in Bennington County, Putney and Dummerston in Windham County, and Springfield in Windsor County.

As you may have noticed in the footnotes to Table 13.3, there are real problems in figuring out, at least statistically, trends in apple production. One apparent conclusion is that a greater number of rural people are planting a few apple trees, calling these an orchard, and selling fruit. Of 6,494 acres in orchards reported in 1978, 1,861 acres were reported *after* the original census questionnaire form was mailed to those most likely to be considered "farmers."

Commercial apple production in Vermont continues to be relatively healthy, though year-to-year output is influenced greatly by weather.

Maple Products

In 1893 the Vermont Maple Sugar Makers Association was organized to improve and increase the production and marketing of maple products. The Association was successful in protesting against labeling of blended products as "Pure Vermont," and was a strong force behind the passing of the Federal Pure Food and Drug Act of 1906.

Maple sugaring was a common occupation on all New England farms during the colonial period, and like the few apples and the bushels of home grown grain, early maple production had to do with seeking self-sufficiency. It rose to leading status in Vermont mostly because of interest in the commercial production championed by the state Board of Agriculture. Early reports are full of advice on sugaring.

When the railroads came, they brought refined sugar, obtained very cheaply. Production decreased in the 1860s for the sweet sugar and syrup were no longer needed. Nonetheless, with some prodding, many Vermont farm families began to make commercial syrup; after all, it was something to do during the mud season, and sugar on snow could be enjoyed at the annual town meeting if the sap run was early enough.

People outside the producing areas generally did not care for the sweet, light flavor of maple syrup, and demand for the product, regardless of cost, declined even as population increased. In 1922, the output of sugar and syrup was less than that of 1860, though national population had tripled, and per capita consumption of cane and beet sugar had nearly quadrupled. Strong marketing by the state of Vermont promoted attractive packaging, and developed a major outlet for commercial syrup in the tobacco industry, where the poorer grades found a use in sweetening chewing tobacco. By 1910, more than 3 million pounds of maple sugar and syrup ended up in that product. Notwithstanding such efforts, the production of most sugar and syrup, after the period of self-sufficiency, was very definitely for a luxury market, and that has been the trend in Vermont production to this day. Production had long been in decline, first because it was hard to secure a market, and until recently, because of the decrease in number of producers. Now many new landowners with a sugarbush are producing syrup, an occupation once strictly a farm-related activity.

As smaller dairy farms disappeared, remaining farmers were reluctant to keep a sugar operation. A herd of 80 or 100 cows requires so much year-round labor that one place where work can be reduced is in making syrup. As early as 1928, the Vermont Agriculture Experiment Station advised that any farmer hanging fewer than 450 sap buckets was suffering a loss of nearly forty cents a gallon on the syrup produced. With more than 1,200 buckets, a slight profit might be realized. With an average (1980) retail price of $15 a gallon, relatively few farmers can make much profit in tapping maple trees. As prices increase, more people will purchase a commercial brand of maple-flavored cane syrup.

Although the future of commercial maple sugar and syrup may be a bit bleak, there will always be a market for Vermont maple syrup, no matter what the cost. In recent years production seems to have stabilized, with variations from year to year, more because of local weather conditions than anything else. The 465,000 gallons of March 1979 came on the heels of only about 410,000 gallons in the year before. Both look good in comparison to the 304,000 gallons produced in 1959, but pale to insignificance with the 545,000 gallons of 1981. That year brought an excellent sap run, which makes it difficult to determine if production reflects weather or more new nonfarm producers.

As long as records have been kept, Vermont has led the United States in producing maple products. In 1909 the state was responsible for about 30 percent of national output, followed by New York and Ohio. In 1980, Vermont's production was 38.1 percent of syrup production, with New York at 25.8 percent. After New York, Ohio, Wisconsin, and Michigan were about the same, followed by New Hampshire and Pennsylvania. Maple orchards are still around and are a favored tourist attraction at a time of year when nothing else has much appeal. Over the years the making of maple products has had its ups and downs, but consistently, thanks to emphasis on maple research and promotion, Vermont has maintained its leadership. Within the state, Franklin County leads, being responsible for about a quarter of production.

Many Vermonters carried their knowledge of the sugarbush West, and the concentration of production of maple products in the northeastern part of the country partially reflects that long migration. Today, Vermontville, Michigan, a few miles south of Lansing, has its annual Maple Sugar Festival.

Poultry and Eggs

Just as the self-sufficient nineteenth-century farm produced a few apples, a few bushels of grain, and some milk and maple products, so too it raised both chickens and eggs for the family table. Once a vital part of general farming in Vermont this diversification has become a thing of the past. Eggs are now mainly produced on a few large specialized farms, and only a few local chickens and turkeys find their way to the roasting pan. It is amusing when restaurants feature "Young Vermont Tom Turkeys." Town Listers in 1977 reported only forty-two in the whole state, though in all fairness the 1982 U.S. Census of Agriculture listed 4,675 turkeys sold by seven turkey farms.

The Vermont sugar house is a celebrated institution. This one in Fairfield is unique.

This operation in Salisbury is one of Vermont's largest egg producers.

Egg marketing now accounts for only about 1 percent of Vermont's agricultural cash receipts (Table 13.2). Since the beginning of the century the number of chickens has steadily declined, and the major trend has been toward large egg factories and away from the small barnyard flocks that produced hen money. Vermont produces almost as many eggs as it consumes, and because poultry production does not require good land (nearly all feed comes from the Midwest), it is a part of Vermont agriculture that could take expansion. It is even possible that broiler production could take hold, at it has in Maine and other naturally poor farm areas.

With ups and downs, the number of birds has dropped, but egg production has generally been increased by mechanization and scientific farming, a trend that has also helped milk production.

According to Vermont Town Lister records, poultry numbers remained reasonably constant for the first fifty years of the century. In 1900, 806,451 birds were reported, and 759,913 in 1950. After 1950 the numbers decreased to a low of fewer than 300,000 hens in 1967, except for an unexplainable high of 823,000 in 1960, when well over 8 million dozen eggs were also produced. Since 1967, the number has erratically but constantly increased to the 500,000 of 1982.

At one time the distribution of poultry would have mirrored that of all farms. Today more than 800 farms report egg-laying chickens, but most of these are small operations. In 1982, only sixty-seven Vermont farms were classed by the census as poultry farms, and only ten had more than 10,000 birds.

Beef Cattle, Sheep, and Horses

Many new property owners, especially if their land includes old pasture, will graze some animals, especially if the old barn remains more or less intact. One geographer has called this habit the "cowboy complex," and it is widespread throughout the country. Most of these new farmers have outside income in excess of what they might make from a few steers, but the popularity of this type of land use has increased markedly in recent years.

Sheep farming has been growing. In 1967, Town Listers reported 269 farms with 4,959 sheep. Ten years later, 418 places had 7,550 and the trend appears to be continuing. It will have to continue strong to reach even the 36,000 sheep reported as late as 1940. Vermont is no longer much of a sheep state, but a few flocks still use the hillsides, and land is being kept open that otherwise would revert to brush. In 1977 the most important towns for sheep were Tunbridge, Shaftsbury, Ryegate, and Greensboro, but none of these had more than 500 animals.

The 1982 Census of Agriculture reported 527 farms with sheep and lambs, but only 25 had more than 100 animals. The total number of sheep and lambs in that year was 12,840.

As the home of the Morgan horse, Vermont has had a long tradition in breeding and showing fine horses. As riding enjoys more popularity, stables, riding camps, and stock farms keep increasing. When machinery began to replace horses early in the century, the number of horses in Vermont plummeted. The Census Bureau even stopped listing them. In 1960 the state had only 9,351, a far cry from the 80,000 and more of 1910, and in 1967 Town Listers counted only 7,585. Ten years later (1977), 3,229 farms and stables had 10,239 animals.

The distribution of horses has little relationship to the quality of farmland. In fact, Addison County, with some of the best agricultural land in Vermont, has very few. Weybridge is an exception, for the Morgan Horse Farm of the University of Vermont is there.

More than 3,200 farms in Vermont had horses in 1977. This figure, as reported by the Town Listers, is remarkably high, but the definition of a farm differs from that of the Census Bureau, and in Vermont towns it is often very subjective. Standing out among towns with large numbers of horses (and horse farms) is Woodstock, with 64 farms and 195 horses, tops in the state. Not far behind are Manchester, with 34 and 120 respectively; Strafford, 28 and 140; Norwich, 32 and 106; Charlotte, 34 and 136; Shaftsbury, 24 and 133; Warren, 21 and 140; and Stowe with 28 and 95. All these towns have higher-than-average per capita incomes, some with a significant number of nonresident owners, and all are in areas where dairy farming has lessened, as other land uses, especially recreational or suburban, have grown. Stowe also has one of the highest numbers of hogs reported, for reasons that are not clear.

There seems to be some relationship among newer residents, more horse farms, higher incomes, and poorer agricultural land. The same general observations hold true for beef cattle: few old-style farmers are raising Herefords, Polled Herefords, Aberdeen Angus, and other breeds. Rather, beef herds have a good correlation with nondairy regions.

The raising of beef breeds is new in Vermont. In the old days the worn-out cow would often end up as local hamburger. Many still do, but it is just recently that Town Listers have tabulated "beef" cattle as opposed to animals kept mainly for dairy purposes. In 1971, one of the first counts of Herefords and their relatives showed 591 farms and 6,973 cattle. By 1977 the number had grown to 1,263 farms (more than doubling), and the number of beef animals had reached 13,022.* Almost a fifth of Vermont "farms" now have beef cattle, and today the state has more of these animals than of either sheep or horses. Their numbers are approaching 7 percent of the dairy cows in the State. This remarkable trend will probably continue so long as abandoned dairy farms can be acquired, and as enough jobs with sufficient off-farm income are available to compensate for the low return per unit of land represented by grazing. Some agricultural people have suggested that the day will come when local cattle may be fattened on locally produced grain corn.

If that day comes, more beef cattle will have to be pastured on the good dairy lands of Addison and Franklin counties. Now the farms with a beef cow or two are widely distributed. Panton and Sudbury have the greatest numbers, but the activity is also important in Chittenden County and in the Woodstock-Hartland-Pomfret area of Windsor County.

Except for a few serious beef producers, the pattern of farms and animals, as with horses and sheep, has little relationship to quality of land. Other factors matter more, especially off-farm jobs. These changes contribute to a greater number of secondary animals in Vermont agriculture, a diversification similar to earlier trends in Massachusetts and Connecticut, as those states changed from a dominantly agrarian to a mostly urban life-style. Thus, the increase in numbers of different animals and different crops is rooted more in social causes than in the natural environment. Whether the changes away from the dairy cow are economic is a moot point. Those who have changed are generally those who could afford to change, but one expects that it might be some time before the black-and-white cow disappears from the Vermont countryside.

*As remarked previously, the last complete inventory on a town basis was in 1977. In 1982 the U.S. Census of Agriculture reported 1,136 farms with beef cattle, and 18,481 animals.

A large beef cattle enterprise in Sudbury uses what was once a dairy farm.

Throughout its history nearly all economic activity in Vermont has been based on the raw materials of the environment, be it soil for agriculture, rocks for quarrying, wool for sheep, trees for lumber, or even scenery for recreation. But now things are changing. Vermont is suburban America, and its change in relative location has lastingly affected the character of farming. It also has influenced Vermont in other ways, both social and economic. Economically the state is more prosperous than at any other time in its history, with the recent growth in high-technology industries. Socially the state has become far more complex, with newcomers and natives often having different views and interests. These are the topics of Chapters 14 and 15.

14

Manufacturing and the Vermont Economy

The interstate highways changed the location of Vermont with respect to the rest of the Northeast. Once an isolated corner of New England, the state became an integral part of its region because it was now accessible with rapid and convenient transportation. At the same time, many locational factors that once drew industrial activity lost importance, and immeasurable amenity factors such as recreational and cultural advantages began to be considered. Furthermore, high-technology industries requiring a low volume of raw materials and producing light, high-value products were free to locate practically anywhere they chose. Finally, the Vermont labor force had a reputation for high quality, as well as willingness to accept lower wages than workers in other areas, and it was predominantly non-union. The result has been significant industrial growth. Translated into jobs, this expansion meant that no longer did the young Vermonter have to leave to find work; it meant that people could actually *come* to Vermont and find work. Between 1975 and 1980 alone, 12,000 new jobs were created in Vermont industries.

Each year the Agency of Development and Community Affairs attempts to calculate Vermont's gross state product, or the value of all goods and services produced. In recent years, because of expanding recreation, the portion of the economy derived from the tourist industry has been estimated. Table 14.1 compares the components of the gross state product for 1974 and 1982. Recreation affects all aspects of the economy, and the share of each major activity that directly or indirectly results from the industry is estimated. Recrea-

298

TABLE 14.1

Estimated Gross State Product, 1974 and 1982,
in Millions of Dollars and Percentages

Economic sector	Amount and percentage				Amount and percentage due to recreation			
	1974		1982		1974		1982	
Manufacturing	598	26%	1,419	27%	30	5%	70	5%
Retail-wholesale trade	396	17%	837	16%	95	24%	210	25%
Services	327	14%	807	15%	105	32%	280	35%
Finance, insurance, real estate	284	12%	639	12%	43	15%	100	15%
Government	273	12%	599	12%	14	5%	30	5%
Transportation and public utilities	211	9%	415	8%	21	10%	40	10%
Construction, mining	146	6%	274	5%	12	8%	20	8%
Agriculture	103	4%	247	4%	5	5%	10	5%
	$2,340		$5,237		$325		$760	

Percentage of Vermont economy due to recreation: 1974—13.9%
1982—14.5%

Source: Agency of Development and Community Affairs. Material for 1982 compiled in July 1984 by George A. Donovan, Chief of Research.

tion is responsible for approximately 15 percent of the gross state product. This figure is lower than some would believe, but it still indicates that tourism is probably Vermont's third greatest source of income.

Clearly, manufacturing is the most important part of the economy. It is paramount whether measured by its share of the gross state product, or, as measured until recently, by the number of persons employed. And only about 5 percent of manufacturing is tied to the recreation industry, compared to much higher amounts in services and trade. In 1984, more than 48,000 were employed in manufacturing occupations, or about 24 percent of the nonagricultural workforce.

Table 14.2 sketches historic trends in Vermont employment; it is long and involved, but shows the weight of various types of economic activity since 1850, when detailed figures were first collected. The footnotes explain significant changes in definitions. The table also gives periodic counts of individuals employed, rather than percentages, which better show overall trends. Figures given in 1930 and

TABLE 14.2

Vermont Employment, 1850–1984,
in percentages

Year	Agriculture	Manufacturing	Trade	Personal services / Services	Govt.	Mining	Quarrying / Constr.	Transportation, communications, public utilities	Other
1850[a]	52.5%	14.2%	3.0%	27.3%			1.1%	.7%	1.3%
1880	46.6	19.9	4.3	23.7			2.2	3.3	
	(55,260)	(23,598)	(5,099)	(28,104)			(2,609)	(3,913)	
1900	36.6	21.8	8.8	22.3			5.3	5.2	
1920	30.2	30.2	7.9	19.8			4.9	7.0	
	(41,822)	(41,803)	(10,940)	(27,420)			(6,786)	(9,694)	
1930[b]	27.0	28.4	11.5	18.6			1.9	9.4	3.2
1940[c]	—	37.9	18.3	12.4	13.8	1.4	4.1	9.3	2.8[d]
1950[e]	—	38.0	17.1	13.2	14.1	1.1	4.1	9.3	2.9
		(36,900)	(16,600)	(12,800)	(13,700)	(1,100)	(4,000)	(9,000)	(2,800)
1960	—	31.6	19.1	15.6	15.0	1.2	5.6	7.0	3.6
1970[f]	—	25.5	20.0	20.5	18.4	.7	6.2	5.4	3.9
		(37,800)	(29,700)	(30,100)	(27,200)	(300)	(9,200)	(8,000)	
1980[g]	—	25.5	20.6	21.7	17.9	—	6.0	4.4	4.0
1984	—	23.5	21.5	24.0	17.6	—	5.8	3.9	3.7
		(48,100)	(44,100)	(49,300)	(36,100)		(11,900)	(8,000)	(7,500)

[a] Data for 1850–1920 calculated from material in U.S. Census of Population, appropriate years.

[b] Data for 1930 from *New England's Prospect*, American Geographical Society, 1933.

[c] Beginning in 1940, data from U.S. Department of Labor. New definitions and classifications. Agricultural employment not listed, and not figured in the percentages. Thus only nonagricultural employment.

[d] Beginning in 1940, "Other" is largely "Finance, Insurance and Real Estate."

[e] Agricultural employment estimated at 24,984, or 18.2 percent.

[f] Agricultural employment estimated at 13,000, or 8.0 percent.

[g] Agricultural employment estimated at 8,500, or 5.3 percent. Manufacturing employment in 1980 was reported as 51,600.

Note: Data on employment are also collected by the Vermont Agency of Development and Community Affairs and the Vermont Department of Employment Security. These usually differ from the data published by the Federal Reserve Bank of Boston, which used the U.S. Department of Labor figures. The Federal Reserve Bank figures have been used to provide consistency. The U.S. Bureau of the Census also provides material in its County Business Patterns series.

earlier are not exactly comparable to those from later years.

Even a quick glance shows the major events. In early years most people lived and worked on farms, or provided personal services. Manufacturing was relatively unimportant. As textiles and wood industries developed, manufacturing employment began to dominate as agriculture had before. By the 1940s almost 40 percent of Vermonters were engaged in various types of manufacturing. Since then, industrial employment has relatively decreased as activities that economists call tertiary have come to dominate.

These activities generally include occupations that provide necessary support to the manufacturing worker, including stores, barbershops, colleges, banks, real estate agencies, telephone workers, and a host of other occupations. As manufacturing workers receive higher disposable income, activities multiply to service those workers. These services themselves spawn other workers with disposable income, who seek additional services. As these workers multiply, they normally exceed those who gave them birth. This sequence has happened in the United States, and today is happening in Vermont.

If we look closely at Table 14.1 and want to do a little mental arithmetic, we find that something with profound ramifications shows up. Although the gross state product increased by about 124 percent over the eight years shown (leaving aside inflation), the "Service" category increased by nearly 147 percent, growing more than any other.

The U.S. Chamber of Commerce has estimated that for every 100 new manufacturing workers employed in a community there will be one more retail store, 68 more employees in various nonmanufacturing occupations, close to $2 million in bank deposits, and nearly that in annual retail sales. On the other hand, it may not seem as desirable to some that there will be 300 more people and 70 more schoolchildren to educate. Still, most places regard industry to be beneficial, especially if it is nonpolluting.

For this reason, nearly all states are trying to attract industry; preferably clean light manufacturing. The ripple effect of an industrial plant brings far more jobs than just that of the individual worker in the plant. Today a battle is on between the Sunbelt and the Old Northeast for more industry, and to a lesser degree the same battle is being waged between the northern New England states and the old industrial states in the southern part of the region. Between 1975 and 1980 Vermont's manufacturing employment went up by 30

As Vermont becomes a suburban and industrial extension of southern New England, marginal farmland suddenly becomes an industrial park.

Vermont's single largest industrial employer is the International Business Machines plant in Essex Junction. Photo courtesy of IBM Corporation.

percent, and nonmanufacturing employment by 22 percent. These growth rates were twice the national average, and in New England were exceeded only by New Hampshire. Between 1950 and 1975 the gross state product of Vermont increased by 417 percent, again exceeded only by New Hampshire, with 454 percent. For comparison, Connecticut went up by 416 percent, Rhode Island 275 percent, Massachusetts 334 percent, and Maine 330 percent.

Although still the least important manufacturing state in New England, Vermont, from all this activity, has developed a respectable industrial base. Many communities would like to see more manufacturing jobs come their way, and local industrial parks have sprung up like weeds.

Manufacturing

Just as Table 14.2 showed how Vermont's employment structure has changed since 1850, Table 14.3 illustrates what has happened to manufacturing (industrial) employment over the same period. Though definitions have changed through the years, and new categories (such as "electrical machinery") have been established, in a general way the table shows how the character of Vermont industry has been changing. Nineteen thirty was the first year for which we have a fairly complete tabulation of where people were working. In that year 84 percent of those employed in manufacturing were in four industries: textiles, machine tools, stone products, and wood-related occupations. Jobs mirrored dependence on native raw materials, the traditional staple of Vermont industry.

The most up-to-date material on current Vermont manufacturing appears in the monthly *Economic Indicators*, published by the Federal Reserve Bank of Boston, and in *Vermont County Business Patterns*, 1982, published by the Bureau of the Census in March 1984. The results of the 1982 Census of Manufacturers are not available at this writing.

Using these sources, we find that Vermont's average manufacturing employment is now about 48,000, up from 42,800 in 1977, but down a bit from the high of more than 51,000 in 1980. Employment in all areas is about 205,000, compared to only 148,000 in 1970, which amounts to a gain of 38 percent, compared to a population increase of only 17 percent. This figure reflects not only more work-

TABLE 14.3

Vermont Manufacturing Employment, 1850-1982

Year	Apparel and textiles	Lumber & wood	Machinery	Printing & paper	Other
1850[a]	5.0%	29.4%	—	—	65.6%
1880	17.7 (4,648)	23.6 (6,181)	—	—	58.7
1900	19.9	21.1	10.0	6.1	42.9
1920	16.2 (7,845)	20.2 (9,805)	13.0 (4,970)	4.0 (1,530)	46.8

Year	Apparel and textiles	Lumber & wood	Machinery	Elect. mach.	Paper	Printing & publishing	Stone products	Other
1930[b]	18.3 (6,459)	17.7 (6,256)	3.6 (1,265)	2.0 (703)	26.2 (9,247)	2.6 (9.8)	7.4	

Year	Apparel and textiles	Furniture	Lumber & wood	Machinery	Elect. mach.	Paper	Printing & publishing	Stone products	Food	Other
1947	18.1 (7,400)	4.4 (1,800)	16.4 (6,700)	17.9 (7,300)	1.5 (600)	5.4 (2,200)	3.2 (1,300)	9.6 (3,900)	9.3 (3,700)	14.2
1955	12.9	3.8	13.7	21.6	4.3	5.1	4.0	10.0	8.6	16.0
1960	9.1 (3,200)	4.8 (1,700)	12.2 (4,300)	19.3 (6,800)	9.3 (3,300)	5.9 (2,100)	5.9 (2,100)	9.1 (3,200)	9.3 (3,300)	15.1
1965	5.8	5.2	10.0	18.4	13.1	5.6	6.9	8.8	7.9	18.3
1970	3.8 (1,550)	5.1 (2,050)	7.2 (2,900)	14.9 (6,050)	23.8 (9,650)	5.7 (2,300)	8.5 (3,450)	6.4 (2,600)	6.2 (2,500)	18.4
1977[c]	4.4 (1,900)	5.6 (2,400)	8.2 (3,500)	14.5 (6,200)	21.4 (9,500)	6.1 (2,600)	8.2 (3,500)	4.7 (2,000)	5.1 (2,200)	21.8
1982[d]	4.1 (1,950)	4.3 (2,050)	6.7 (3,200)	15.0 (7,200)	22.9 (10,950)	5.3 (2,500)	8.6 (4,100)	3.3 (1,600)	4.8 (2,300)	25.1

[a] No standard classification, 1850–1920. Calculated from occupations listed in U.S. Census.
[b] From Industrial Survey of Vermont, 1930. From 1930, data are reasonably comparable to the present. Sources 1947–1977 from various U.S. Census's.
[c] U.S. Census of Manufacturers, 1977.
[d] County Business Patterns, Vermont, 1982. Bureau of the Census, March 1984.

ing women, but also the strength of the Vermont economy in absorb-
ing new workers. In 1978 and 1979 alone, fifty-five new companies
located in the state, employing more than 1,000 new workers, and
689 firms underwent some expansion, resulting in an increase of
approximately 7,000 employees.

Growth in manufacturing employment has not been uniform.
Figure 14.1 shows for each county the trend in industrial employment since 1954. Chittenden County, which in that year had only 14
percent of the manufacturing production workers, was, by 1982,
accounting for more than 32 percent. A decline in Windsor County
is related to problems of the machine-tool industry. Otherwise, most
Vermont counties have remained stable, or have grown at a small,
steady rate. Most recent trends have shown great expansion in electrical machinery, printing and publishing, and the apparel industries.
Declines have characterized raw material–based industries such as
lumber and wood products, furniture manufacturing, and stone.

As manufacturing has grown, the number of manufacturing
plants has changed, both numerically and geographically. Between
1955 and 1975 there was a decrease of 270 plants, mostly small
operations. Average employment increased from 37 to more than 45
workers. Since 1975 the number has grown from 844 to the 1,001
reported in 1982, and average employment has stabilized at about
48. This change reflects the smaller handicraft industries offsetting
the large-employment firms such as International Business Machines
and General Electric. Fifty-eight percent of Vermont's plants employ
fewer than ten people.

It is these small plants that are widely distributed throughout
the state, but larger employers are concentrated in central places. As
population has become dispersed (Chapter 9), jobs have become
more concentrated, which means that more people are commuting
greater distances to their places of work. This statement may be
difficult to quantify, but a little statistical manipulation shows that in
relation to manufacturing jobs, some Vermont counties are much
worse off than others. Take Grand Isle, which had *no* manufacturing
employment for the 4,613 residents in 1980. Thus, to work in a
manufacturing concern, all workers from that county have to go
someplace else. Lamoille County is similar: it has 651 manufacturing
jobs for a population of 16,767, or 3.9 percent. The worst-off counties, besides Grand Isle and Lamoille, are Washington, Orange, and
Caledonia. One has to remember, however, that Washington County

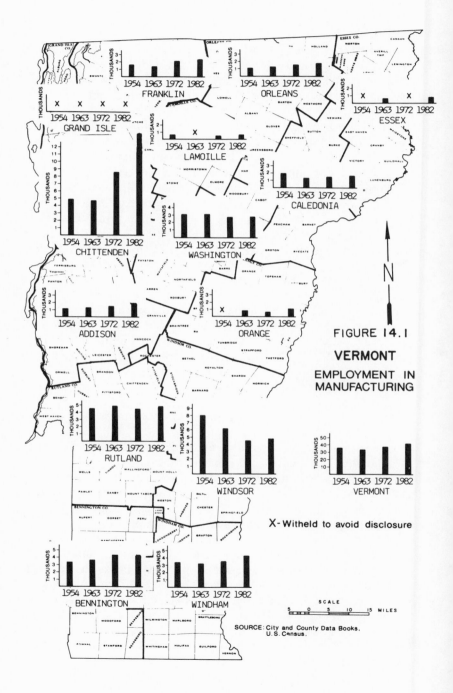

FIGURE 14.1

VERMONT

EMPLOYMENT IN
MANUFACTURING

X-Witheld to avoid disclosure

SCALE

5   0   5   10   15 MILES

SOURCE: City and County Data Books,
U.S. Census.

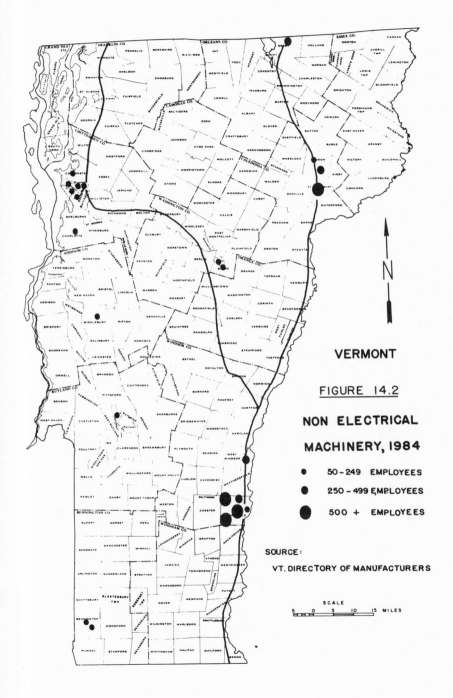

VERMONT

FIGURE 14.2

NON ELECTRICAL

MACHINERY, 1984

● 50 - 249 EMPLOYEES

⬤ 250 - 499 EMPLOYEES

⬤ 500 + EMPLOYEES

SOURCE:

VT. DIRECTORY OF MANUFACTURERS

SCALE
5 0 5 10 15 MILES

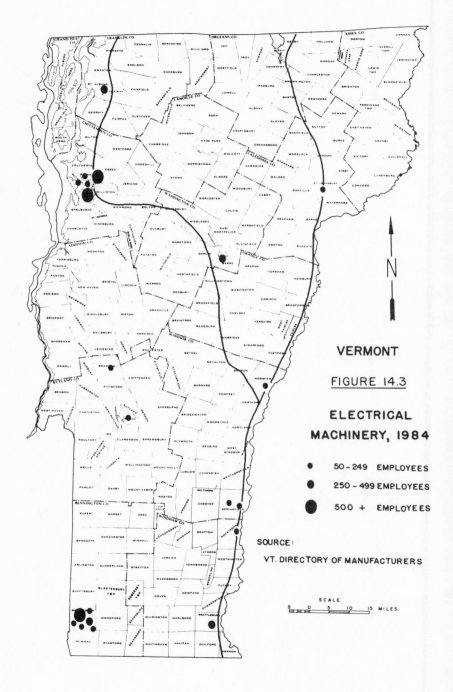

VERMONT

FIGURE 14.3

ELECTRICAL
MACHINERY, 1984

● 50 - 249 EMPLOYEES

● 250 - 499 EMPLOYEES

● 500 + EMPLOYEES

SOURCE:

VT. DIRECTORY OF MANUFACTURERS

SCALE
5 0 5 10 15 MILES

contains Montpelier, meaning that many nonmanufacturing jobs are available. The best counties in ratio of manufacturing employment to population are Essex (furniture manufacturing), Bennington, Chittenden, Windham, and Windsor, in that order.

In employment and wages paid, the biggest Vermont industries are the traditional machine tools, and evolving electronics firms. Figures 14.2 and 14.3 show manufacturing plants in those categories that employed fifty or more people. Nonelectrical machinery shows its traditional strength in Rutland, St. Johnsbury, Lyndonville, and the machine-tool areas of Windsor County, notably Springfield. Electrical machinery (Standard Industrial Classification 36) is represented in Bennington, chiefly by Union Carbide and Johnson Controls; in Chittenden County (IBM and Digital Equipment), and in St. Albans (Union Carbide). Curiously, the large Simmons Precision plant in Vergennes is not considered "electronics," as are the two General Electric plants in Rutland and Burlington. The Burlington GE plant is "fabricated metal products," the Rutland plant, "transportation equipment."

Nonmanufacturing Employment

In 1984, manufacturing accounted for approximately a quarter of the jobs in nonagricultural employment in Vermont (Table 14.2). Therefore, about 75 percent of employed Vermonters are doing something else. Other major occupations are wholesale and retail trade, many types of services, finance, insurance, real estate, government work, transportation, communications, mining, quarrying, and construction. The table has breakdowns by major categories.

Over the years wholesale and retail trade, various types of services, and government employment have increased gradually. Mining jobs have continued to shrink, and transportation and communication employment have stabilized. The increase in trade and service employment are directly related to a growing recreation industry. Table 14.1 shows that about 25 percent of wholesale and retail trade activity can be attributed to tourism, along with 35 percent of services. Growth in government employment has been a national phenomenon.

Except for some government jobs, the lowest-paying positions in Vermont are usually in activities related to the recreation industry.

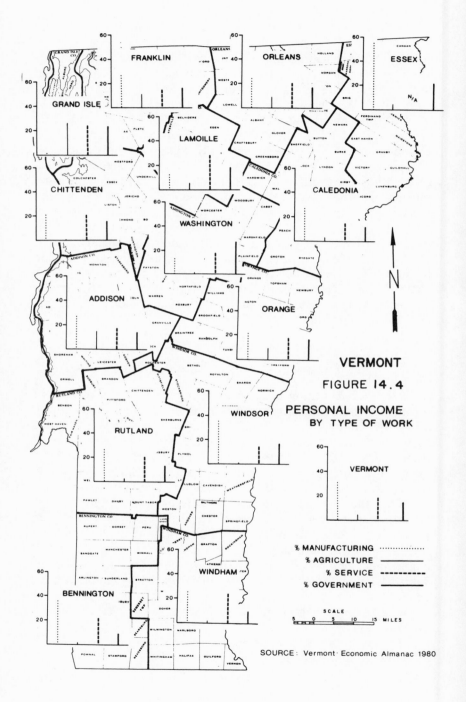

VERMONT

FIGURE 14.4

PERSONAL INCOME
BY TYPE OF WORK

VERMONT

% MANUFACTURING ·············
% AGRICULTURE ⎯⎯⎯⎯
% SERVICE ⎯ ⎯ ⎯ ⎯
% GOVERNMENT ⎯⎯⎯⎯

SCALE
5   0   5   10   15 MILES

SOURCE: Vermont· Economic Almanac 1980

Though tourism may contribute about 15 percent to the state's economic prosperity, wages are low in comparison to those in stabler types of employment.

Figure 14.4 shows the weight of various types of activity, county by county. Wholesale and retail trade are omitted because for every county the percentage of personal income from that source varied little. Only in Essex County was trade activity unimportant, with only 2.8 percent of personal income derived from that source.

The map illustrates how big a part farming occupies in the economy of Franklin, Grand Isle, and Addison counties. In Orleans, it is perhaps less substantial. In manufacturing, Essex County looks like Pittsburgh, Pennsylvania, which shows how misleading some measures of economic activity can be. More than 55 percent of the personal income in the county comes from manufacturing activity, but Essex County is the least important manufacturing county, after Grand Isle. If it were not for the Ethan Allen plants in Canaan (Beecher's Falls) and Island Pond, and the Georgia Pacific paper mill in Lunenberg (Gilman), Essex County would have hardly any manufacturing employment.

Other counties with extensive manufacturing are Bennington; Windsor, with its machine tools; and Chittenden, but the latter, the leading manufacturing county, shows a lower percentage of workers' personal income from that source than three other counties.

The most noteworthy patterns showing in Figure 14.4 relate to government and service activities. In counties with little diversity in economic activity, government employment counts heavily, as illustrated in both Grand Isle and Essex counties. Washington County, home of state government (Montpelier) shows how important public employment is in Vermont economic life.

Service employment covers a wide range of activities, including any person providing a service to another. Therefore it includes service-station employees, ski-lift attendants, motel operators and employees, doctors, lawyers, plumbers, electricians, and sometimes even teachers. Because of problems in collecting data, a teacher at Castleton State College is a government employee, but a teacher at Middlebury College is a service employee. Nevertheless, numbers of most service-employed persons expand and contract depending on the number of people to be served. And that is why service income is so closely tied to the recreation industry.

Some significant differences among Vermont counties appear in

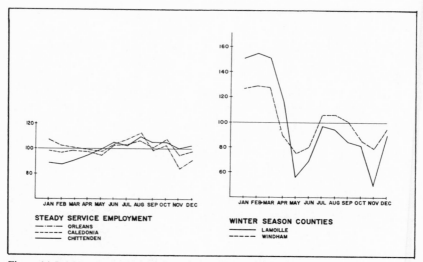

STEADY SERVICE EMPLOYMENT
— · — · — ORLEANS
— — — — CALEDONIA
———————— CHITTENDEN

WINTER SEASON COUNTIES
———————— LAMOILLE
— — — — WINDHAM

Figure 14.5. Monthly Employment in Service Occupations

Sources: *Vermont Social and Economic Characteristics*, Vermont State Planning Office, Montpelier, 1971

service activities. Lamoille County, with recreational ski areas in Cambridge and Stowe, is the most obvious example of tourism's tie to Vermont's economy, but Grand Isle is not far behind. But dependence on recreation for jobs has its disadvantages. Not only are prevailing wages low, but the jobs themselves are highly seasonal; during the off season, many employees are forced to find some sort of public assistance. This seasonality of service employment shows clearly when we compare the monthly job cycle in nonrecreational counties with the cycle in counties that are strongly based on the recreation industry. Figure 14.5 compares the steadiness characteristic of service employment in Chittenden, Caledonia, and Orleans counties (nonrecreational) with the great fluctuations in Lamoille and Windham counties, both of which have major ski areas.

Poverty and Prosperity

The last twenty years have brought remarkable growth in manufacturing jobs, substantial growth in the recreation industry, and an increase in population. Incomes still rank below national and New

England averages, but more people are better paid than at any other time in the state's history.

Prosperity, though, at least as measured by monetary income, has affected neither all areas of the state nor all the people in the state. Wide variations remain in income levels among groups and towns. The Vermont Department of Taxes each year compiles information from income-tax returns filed by Vermont residents. Although this is a good source of material on relative wealth and poverty among the towns, it cannot include many part-time residents whose returns are filed in another state. Towns with large numbers of summer people like Manchester, Weston, Woodstock, and Grafton sometimes therefore show up with lower-than-average incomes. These and other towns, however, often have a few residents with very high incomes. According to 1980 resident tax returns, the towns listed here had more than 5 percent of their taxpayers reporting incomes greater than $50,000. The highest town in Vermont was Landgrove at 13.1 percent. Landgrove was followed, in order, by Norwich, Stratton, Shelburne, Dorset, Charlotte, Weston, Pomfret, Ripton, Peru, Woodstock, Reading, Sherburne, Barnard, West Windsor, and Grafton. Other towns included Warren, Stowe, Rochester, Peacham, Manchester, Mendon, and South Burlington. Many of these are small rural towns in central or southern Vermont.

Unfortunately we have no perfect way of mapping Vermont's rich and poor towns (and the income patterns of Vermont's people). The two sources for this type of information are the Vermont Tax Department and the U.S. Census of Population. The former calculates each year the median and average adjusted gross income of each taxpayer and makes available a figure for each town. The Census of Population, on a sample basis, reports the median family income and a per capita income for each town from material entered on the census questionnaires. In 1980, larger areas were sampled at 15 percent and smaller areas at 50 percent. As would be expected, the differences between the Census and Vermont Tax Department information are considerable. The Census Bureau is also required to report the percentage of residents who are below the current "poverty level."

I must confess to great frustration in working with the statistics available for various years. But nothing compares with the problems of working with material on income on a town basis in Vermont.

Take the small town of Stratton, with a 1980 population of 122.

A rural home in northeastern Vermont.

The blacksmith shop of Orrin Dunn, the only "industry" in the Essex County town of Victory.

The 1980 Census lists 33 families in Stratton with a median family income of $33,153—highest in the state. Back in 1975, however, the Vermont Department of Taxes reported that 55 percent of Stratton's taxpayers reported incomes of less than $6,000—one of the lowest-income towns in Vermont. For 1979 the same source reported that the median adjusted gross income per taxpayer was $9,053, compared to a state average of $11,571.*

Understandably, it is the towns with smaller population that present the greatest problem. Lemington, up in the northeast, had a 1980 population of 108. According to the Vermont Tax Department, Lemington was the fourth "wealthiest" town in Vermont, with a median adjusted gross income per taxpayer of $15,410, exceeded only by Essex, Underhill, and Jericho. For the same year, the U.S. Bureau of the Census reported that the median family income of Lemington was $11,800, the ninth "poorest" town in Vermont. Following are the towns with the highest and lowest income from the two sources for the same year, 1980. The Tax Department data have been slightly modified to reflect town School Districts.

U.S. Census of Population			*Vermont Department of Taxes**	
Population			Returns filed	
		"Wealthy" towns		
1.	Stratton	122	1. Essex Town	1,705
2.	Shelburne	5,000	2. Underhill	949
3.	Norwich	2,398	3. Jericho	1,168
4.	South Burlington	10,679	4. Lemington	28
5.	Essex	14,392	5. Shelburne	1,889
6.	Williston	3,843	6. Williston	1,631
7.	Jericho	3,579	7. Norwich	920
8.	Underhill	2,172	8. St. George	182
9.	Charlotte	2,561	9. Weathersfield	746
10.	Rutland Town	3,300	10. Colchester	4,069
11.	Landgrove	121	11. Stamford	277
12.	Richmond	3,159	12. Essex Junction	3,983
13.	Baltimore	181	13. Waltham	74
14.	Mendon	1,056	14. Georgia	754
15.	Dorset	1,648	15. South Burlington	4,728

*The Vermont Department of Taxes reports two town income figures. One is the *average* adjusted gross income per tax return; the other is the *median* adjusted gross income per tax return. In all towns the median is always lower than the average. In 1979 the average was $13,661, the median, $11,571 for the entire state.

"*Poor*" *Towns*

1.	Maidstone	100	1.	Searsburg	26
2.	Athens	250	2.	Victory	16
3.	Brownington	708	3.	Greensboro	235
4.	Granby	70	4.	Warren	536
5.	Victory	56	5.	Sheffield	145
6.	Halifax	488	6.	Dover	357
7.	Lowell	573	7.	Athens	81
8.	Hardwick	2,613	8.	Montgomery	283
9.	Lemington	108	9.	Stannard	48
10.	Montgomery	681	10.	Plymouth	143
11.	Newark	280	11.	Vershire	146
12.	West Fairlee	427	12.	Waitsfield	691
13.	East Haven	280	13.	Wardsboro	209
14.	Sheffield	435	14.	Hardwick	965
15.	Vershire	442	15.	Alburg	418

*The towns listed in this column represent the *Median* Adjusted Gross Income.

Conclusions? Well, in the first place, depending on the source of the information one uses, one can prove just about anything. But aside from that it is possible to make some generalizations. One is that places of smaller population usually have people with lower incomes than places more urban and suburban. This rule applies nationally. Another is that the Vermont Department of Taxes is probably a better source than the U.S. Census, which is based on a sample.

Third, regardless of the source of data on income, there appear to be clear geographic patterns. Of the fifteen places with highest incomes reported by the Census Bureau, seven are in Chittenden County; of those listed by the Tax Department, nine are in the county. At the other extreme are the low-income towns. Of the Census Bureau towns, eleven are in north and northeastern Vermont. Of those reported by the Tax Department, six are in the same geographic region. Perhaps this pattern of lower-income residents is best illustrated by the census material dealing with poverty-level incomes. Figure 14.6 maps towns with populations high in poverty-level incomes, according to the 1979 definition as listed in the 1980 Census of Population.

Two patterns are very clear. One is the high incidence of low incomes prevailing in northern Vermont, especially in the northeast. The other is that in Orleans, Franklin, and Addison counties, those

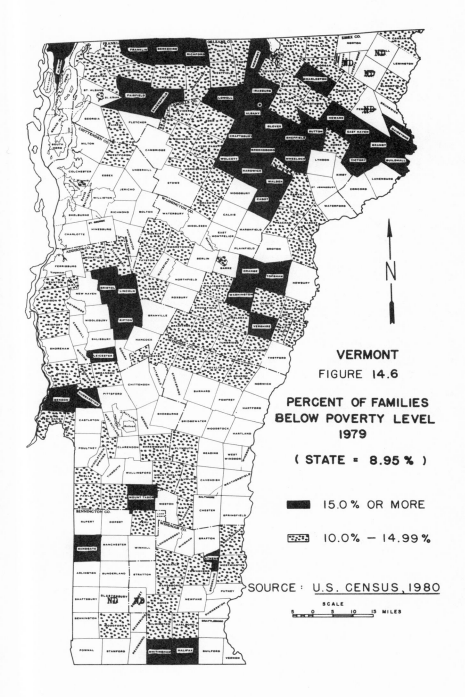

VERMONT

FIGURE 14.6

PERCENT OF FAMILIES
BELOW POVERTY LEVEL
1979

(STATE = 8.95 %)

■ 15.0 % OR MORE

10.0 % – 14.99 %

SOURCE : U.S. CENSUS, 1980

SCALE
5 0 5 10 15 MILES

most important agriculturally, poverty is well above the state average.

Other pockets of poverty are in the hill lands of Orange County, and through the central Green Mountains, frequently in towns that depend heavily on skiing, such as Wilmington, Dover, Warren, and Fayston.

Vermont has matured industrially, and in fact is now entering a period in which manufacturing employment will decline in relation to other occupations. This trend has been national, and though many economists are uneasy about high tertiary employment, it is a fact of economic life.

The outstanding ramification of Vermont's economic growth is that it has stimulated population growth, but growth that is mainly traceable to immigration to a promised land of green hills, quaint villages, and general stores. As the state becomes more of an extension of suburban America, fundamental changes are taking place in its social character. Prosperity can be measured in dollars and jobs, but other aspects of growth are harder to quantify.

15

Changing Vermont

Vermont is changing. Land used for commercial agriculture continues to shrink as smaller commercial dairy farms disappear. At the same time, remaining agriculture is becoming more diverse, although farming continues to lose prominence in the economic mix.

Industrial growth continues, though not all parts of the state benefit equally from the higher incomes and jobs generated. Traditional industries based on raw materials shrink as high-technology activities are drawn to an area with many social and cultural amenities on the fringe of megalopolis.

As more people with higher incomes attain greater mobility, the recreation industry expands and contributes more to the economy. People originally drawn to Vermont by recreation and by promotion of the state's image are becoming permanent residents, and population growth, mostly by immigration, is becoming the norm rather than the exception. State Health Department estimates indicate that the mid-year 1982 population was more than 517,000, some 6,000 more than reported only two years before.

Prosperity inevitably brings problems of congestion, higher cost, and even new people in the old neighborhood. Mobile homes, where allowed, become common. Vermont at the moment is going through the throes of being "discovered" by many whose only previous knowledge came from *Vermont Life* magazine. I hope this chapter sums it all up. Analyzing change in the midst of dramatic change is frustrating at best.

What is happening to Vermont and its culture is complex and has many facets. Change today is rapid and will continue. I know of no better summary than that written by Andrew Nemethy in the

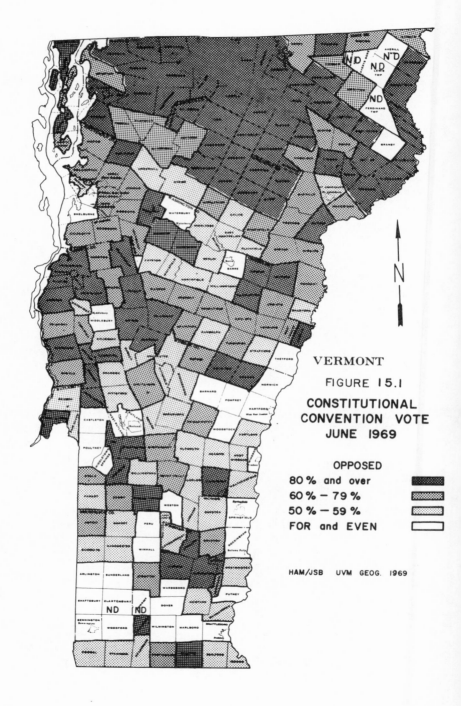

VERMONT

FIGURE 15.1

CONSTITUTIONAL
CONVENTION VOTE
JUNE 1969

OPPOSED

80 % and over

60 % − 79 %

50 % − 59 %

FOR and EVEN

HAM/JSB   UVM GEOG. 1969

Rutland Herald, April 1, 1976, and I quote that discerning and enjoyable analysis almost in its entirety.

Ten years ago the Vermont Development Department launched the "Beckoning Country" campaign to lure out-of-staters to the Green Mountains.

Many of them were urbanites who sought to escape the cities in search of a less hectic life. They sought cleaner air, and a country place to bring up their children. Others brought with them romantic visions of turning back the clock and achieving a self-sufficiency that they hoped would bring them closer to the distant and forgotten roots of our past. . . .

What impact has this had on Vermont? Has Vermont become two states: the rural farmland areas still clinging to traditional ways, and the bustling commercial centers like Rutland, Burlington, Barre-Montpelier and the numerous resort centers that tend to be even more cosmopolitan and urbane than Vermont's cities?

Some state-government agencies have investigated to a degree the impact in environmental and economic terms on Vermont, but there has been virtually no attempt to measure socially and intellectually how Vermont's new residents have changed the state.

The first settlers who wandered . . . up from Connecticut brought with them the sturdy implements and hard-rock courage with which they sought to make an impression on the wild hillsides and valleys of the Green Mountain State. Today settlers come to Vermont bringing with them instead conceptual baggage—preconceptions and ideas which are less concrete than a plow and an axe but equally telling in the impression they carve on the land. The problem is, how to measure their impact. Vermont today is different than it was ten years ago, but it is hard to tell how much of the change, its direction and speed, was influenced by out-of-state residents.

There are subtle changes across Vermont: the altered political tenor of the state, its social attitudes, and the breakdown of tradition.

The influx of out-of-staters in Vermont has its humorous aspects. New Vermonters are stratified, fitted into unfair but inevitable categories. Thus it is better to be from Massachusetts than to be from New York, and better to be from New York than New Jersey, but not by much. On the other hand if one is from Cali-

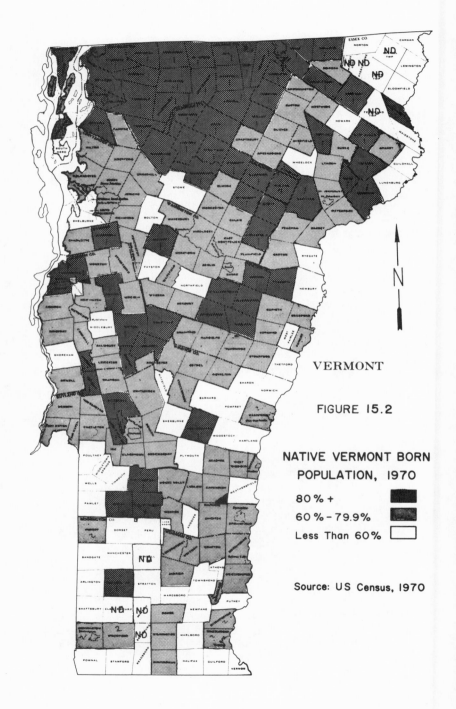

VERMONT

FIGURE 15.2

NATIVE VERMONT BORN
POPULATION, 1970

80 % +

60 % - 79.9 %

Less Than 60 %

Source: US Census, 1970

fornia or Oregon or New Hampshire one slides with relative ease into Vermont. And the preconceptions among persons from the vast middle of America appear so vague as to not even warrant their being categorized.

Those who have moved into the state most recently are often its most rabid supporters, most environmentally conscious, most xenophobic, forgetting their origins with amazing rapidity. As one native put it, they tend to "out-Vermont Vermonters." They want to see a return to the old ways; a step back into the past. "They come to make it the way it was" says a Vermont-born postmaster—an impossible task.

This often produces ironic confrontations. The classic is the dirt-road showdown. Locals, tired of buying new shock absorbers every year and new cars almost as frequently after having their vehicles jostled into oblivion, want to have a paved road; those who recently moved in, perhaps better able to afford the cost, want to preserve the rustic beauty of dirt roads. The conflict assumes hundreds of other shapes, which will determine the form of progress in Vermont. Another obvious source of conflict is the snowmobile. It is mostly Vermonters who enjoy it and out-of-staters who object because it destroys the peace and quiet they came for. The Vermonter has of course always had peace and quiet, but not snowmobiles to make the winter more tolerable.

Another manifestation of the different attitudes . . . is the fact that Vermonters seeking convenience and lower costs for heating tend to move into new ranch houses or trailers, while out-of-staters invariably head in the opposite direction, looking for old rustic farmhouses. What is occurring of course is the confluence of two divergent streams of thought into one often-turbulent river.

Sometimes the river seems to turn to a flood, washing the native way of life with it. A drive through any major ski-resort area on a weekend, be it Stowe or Dover, will reveal mostly cars with out-of-state license plates, and in some places a native Vermonter can find himself almost a foreigner in his own town, assaulted by a barrage of un-Yankee accents from up and down the East Coast. In a very real sense the resort areas of the state form the surfaces where an interaction between Vermonters and newcomers takes place and where the resulting friction wears down custom and tradition and a new fabric of society is created. But to some these areas are also the most artificial and segregated, and represent exaggerated views of what Vermont really stands for or what Vermont is to become.

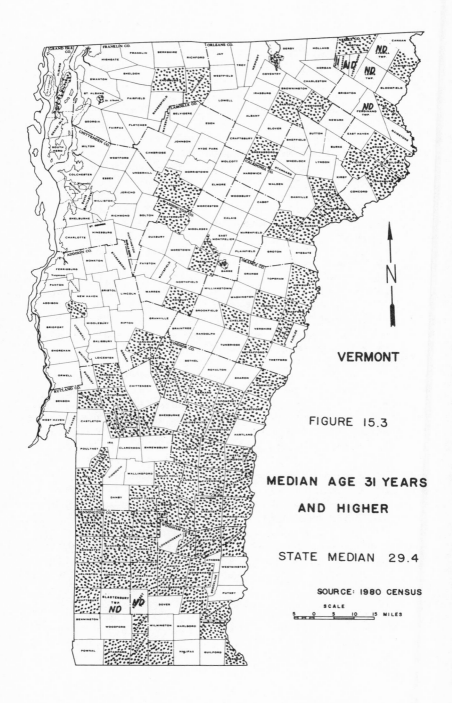

VERMONT

FIGURE 15.3

MEDIAN AGE 31 YEARS
AND HIGHER

STATE MEDIAN 29.4

SOURCE: 1980 CENSUS

SCALE

5   0   5   10   15 MILES

"People come here because it is utopic, and when they get here they bring some of the things with them that they tried to get away from," says a Vermont insurance agent, citing traffic problems, social hierarchy and environmental problems as examples. "Speaking strictly from a selfish point of view I think the out-of-staters have done nothing but good," he adds. "I used to farm fifty Jerseys and now I don't have to do that."

Throughout Vermont new jobs in a wide variety of fields have been created. In resort towns, more sophisticated residents from other states have created a demand for better shops and restaurants and new recreational facilities, which benefit all Vermonters. This has meant more jobs in service fields, and allowed talented craftsmen to set up shops, along with creating a need for such specialized jobs as photography and advertising.

While economic benefits are conceded, for most native Vermonters the impact of in-migration is felt in the more intangible areas such as concern that the traditional way of life in Vermont is fading. A road-crew member in Stowe reflects that people who move to Vermont may espouse rural living but they want the same level of services they had in the city. And at town meetings they can often outvote the natives to get their way, because many Vermonters no longer bother to vote. This means more schools and more taxes.

Vermont has, perhaps conceptually, become two states: the rural farmlands and the bustling resort areas. There is little doubt that if present trends continue, the latter hint the predominant direction the state is headed in. The question remains: Whither Vermont? Will out-of-state influx change the rural character of the state, something neither the new resident nor the native wants? It may be that another decade will be needed to pass before that issue is settled.

The newcomer and the newcomers' philosophy sometimes show up in ways that can be mapped. Many statewide and national elections in the last fifteen years have shown contrasts between two Vermonts, one urban and southern, the other northern and rural. The schism of two states is not as simple as rural and resort, or urban and rural, or something else based on a census definition; rather it is geographic as well as people. One telling representation of this phenomenon was the geographic pattern in the results of a Constitutional Convention vote back in 1969. The issue was whether a convention should be called to review the state's constitution, not necessarily to do anything with it. It was the classic example of a neutral political issue with no political party taking sides; it represented only a vote on possible change or no change. Not too many groups got excited, and fewer than 30 percent of Vermont's registered voters bothered to go to the polls. The results are shown in Figure 15.1, and the pattern is: urban, southern, and ski areas for change; and northern, rural, and agricultural Vermont resisting. The issue went down to defeat by a considerable margin, but the people in areas that voted in favor possibly reflect many more new Vermonters. College students in Castleton, college professors in Norwich, Middlebury, and Shelburne, and new Vermonters in Weston, Woodstock, Wilmington, Winhall, and Marlboro all favored change. Margins of defeat were small in places like Stowe, Fayston, Waitsfield, Sherburne, Manchester, Dorset, and Londonderry. Urban voters in South Burlington, Essex Junction, Bennington, Rutland, and Brattleboro showed liberal tendencies, and those surrounding Montpelier voted the proposition down by only a small margin. Because of the few voters in many towns, the map is naturally biased, but biased equally in both directions. In any event, it is nearly a mirror of Figure 15.2, which shows native and non-native-born population at the same time, in 1970.

In recent years most new Vermont residents have come from nearby areas: about 23 percent from New York, 16 percent from Massachusetts, 11 percent from Connecticut, and 10 percent each from New Hampshire and New Jersey. Many moves have involved local industrial expansion, especially in Chittenden County; others reflect growing state government in and around Montpelier, and these are often young to middle-aged professional people. Others are retirees, usually settling in the more rural regions. Figure 15.3 clearly shows an older population in southern Vermont as well as in scattered areas throughout the northeast. The pattern in the south represents many retired newcomers in such places as Dorset, Manchester, Weston, Woodstock, Landgrove, and Newfane. Of Vermont towns with more than 1,000 people, the oldest populations are, in order, Dorset, Manchester, Woodstock, and Cavendish.

In northern Vermont many of the towns represent an older native-born population, but not in such places as Peacham and Greensboro. Generally, putting the three maps together shows a "Vermont" in the southern and eastern areas very different from the rest of the state.

One of the most interesting ways of trying to get at what residents think about Vermont is the survey. A try was made back in 1977 to decipher what the people thought about the future of the state. Vermont Tomorrow, an organization now long gone, distributed a questionnaire at forty-three town meetings; the governor boosted the idea, and 30,000 were picked up, 7,000 returned. Of those who bothered to send back their opinions, 54 percent were born outside Vermont (40 percent having been residents for fifteen years or less), 48 percent were between ages twenty-five and forty-five, and 60 percent were college graduates. Even though the respondents were not a truly accurate cross-section of the population, the opinions were interesting and are arranged here by major questions.

What Vermonters Want

New energy source (solar)	22%
New energy source (wood)	25%
New energy source (wind)	14%
New energy source (hydro)	14%
New energy source (coal, nuclear)	24%
Money to encourage Vermont businesses	84%
Money to encourage out-of-state business in Vermont	16%
Encourage shopping malls and shopping centers	19%
Encourage shopping in city centers	81%
More light industry	33%
More agriculture and forestry	33%
More recreation industry	9%
More crafts industry	12%
Will you continue to live in Vermont even with low wages	Yes 92%
Will you be willing to pay to preserve open land?	Yes 56%
One of the best places to live in United States	56%
About average place to live	28%
Below-average place to live	4%
Has Vermont improved as place to live?	26%
Has Vermont declined as place to live?	38%
Vermont in future will be more desirable	35%
Vermont in future will be less desirable	35%

The Vermont of the future will be different from the Vermont of the past. Commercial agriculture will continue to occupy less land, although the remaining commercial farms will become more viable. Agriculture will be more diversified, although many involved in that diversification may not be full-time farmers. Recreational use of Vermont land will continue to increase because it is close to large numbers of people seeking the better life. With escalating costs of transportation, areas like Vermont will see more pressure on resources because the state is close to many millions of people. All this change will be translated into population growth.

Vermont will continue to be attractive to industries seeking places on the fringe of megalopolis where the living conditions are attractive. Jobs will increase with population, but the Sunbelt and its equal attractiveness are an ever-present threat.

The State Planning Office published a *People Book* in 1978 predicting future population changes. It projected 503,500 Vermonters in 1980. In that year, the final U.S. Census returns counted 511,456 persons. In other words, predictions made two years before 1980 contained an error of nearly 8,000 people. By 1990 the prediction is for 575,000, but the majority may not have been born in the state. Latest census estimates (for 1982) indicate a population of more than 518,000, or a 1.4 percent increase in two years. This projection represents some slowing of growth and it will be interesting to see if the trend continues.

If new Vermonters become a greater force, the social changes of the 1970s will probably be intensified for the remainder of the century. Many natives will continue to avoid town meetings, knowing that they may be outvoted. Vermont may be more liberal in political philosophy than in the past, and with that, more cosmopolitan in ideology and in outlook. The state, whether for good or for bad, cannot ever be what it was before. It has become, because of its geographic location, an extension of suburban America.

And that is a good place to stop. Vermont is undergoing profound economic and social changes. Traditional industries are giving way to highly specialized occupations. People continue to seek the good life, and Vermont has much to offer. Land-use legislation is an attempt to ensure that the Vermont of the future, though different from that of the past, will continue to have many of those vital environmental attributes. Though changing politically, socially, and economically, the Land of the Green Mountains endures. The winds will continue to sweep across the tracks of the Lamoille Valley Railroad; the Winooski and other rivers will have their inevitable floods, and Vermonters in the future will continue to be blessed with one of the unique and vital pieces of real estate in the United States.

Selected References

Chapter 1

Allen, Richard S. *Covered Bridges of the Northeast*. Brattleboro, Vt., 1957.

Bassett, T. C. Seymour. "Migration to Vermont, 1761–1836." *The Vermont Geographer*, No. 2, 1975. Dept. of Geography, University of Vermont.

Day, Gordon. "The Indian Occupation of Vermont." *Vermont History*, Vol. 33, No. 3, 1965.

Fuller, Edmund. *Vermont: A History of the Green Mountain State*. Montpelier, Vt.: State Board of Education, 1952.

Haviland, William. *Vermont Indians: A Summary and Listing of Selected Sources of Information*. University of Vermont, 1977.

Haviland, William A., and Marjorie W. Power. *The Original Vermonters*. Hanover, N.H.: University Press of New England, 1981.

Kurath, Hans. *Handbook of the Linguistic Geography of New England*. American Council of Learned Societies, 1939.

McHenry Stewart G. "Eighteenth Century Field Patterns as Vernacular Art." *Old Time New England*, Vol. 69, Nos. 1–2, 1978.

Meeks, Harold A. "An Isochronic Map of Vermont Settlement." *Vermont History*, Vol. 37, No. 2, Spring 1970.

Morrissey, Charles T. *Vermont: A History*. New York: W. W. Norton, 1981.

Neudorfer, Giovanna. "Vermont's Stone Chambers: Their Myth and Their History." *Vermont History*, Vol. 47, No. 2, Spring 1979.

Nicholaisen, W. F. H. "Celtic Place Names in America B.C." *Vermont History*, Vol. 47, No. 2, Spring 1979.

Ritchie, William A., and Robert E. Funk. *Aboriginal Settlement Patterns in the Northeast*. New York State Museum and Science Service, Memoir 20, 1973.

Swift, Esther M. *Vermont Place Names: Footprints of History*. Brattleboro, Vt.: Stephen Greene Press, 1977.

Chapter 2

Brown, William H. "John Goffe and the Crown Point Road." *Historical New Hampshire*, New Hampshire Historical Society, September 1948.

Charlton, Mary F. "The Crown Point Road." *Proceedings* of the Vermont Historical Society, 1931.

Cooledge, Guy O. "The French Occupation of the Champlain Valley, 1609–1759." *Proceedings* of the Vermont Historical Society, September 1948.

Jacobus, M. W. "A Canal Across Vermont." *Vermont History*, Vol. 23, No. 4, October 1955.

Lee, W. Storrs. *The Green Mountains of Vermont.* New York: Henry Holt, 1955.

Lee, W. Storrs. "Vermont Turnpikes." *Vermont Life*, Vol. 5, No. 1, Autumn 1950.

McCorison, Marcus A. "The Bayley Hazen Military Road." *Vermont History*, Vol. 37, No. 1, January 1959.

A Short History of Crown Point. Adapted from Notes by Paul Huey. Pamphlet issued by State of New York, Office of Parks and Recreation, no date. Available at Crown Point Historic Site, Crown Point, N.Y.

Wilgus, William J. *The Role of Transportation in the Development of Vermont.* Montpelier, Vt.: Vermont Historical Society, 1945.

Wood, Joseph S. *The Road Network and Regional Interaction in Vermont, 1796–1824.* Masters Thesis, Dept. of Geography, University of Vermont, October 1973.

Chapter 3

Allen, Richard S. "Gores, Grants and Ghost Towns." *Vermont Life*, Vol. 12, Autumn 1957.

Allen, Richard S. "Four Corners of Vermont." *Vermont Life*, Vol. 11, Spring 1957.

Carpenter, Warwick S. *The Summer Paradise in History.* General Passenger Department. Albany, N.Y.: Delaware and Hudson Railroad, 1914.

Fuller, Edmund. *Vermont: A History of the Green Mountain State.* Montpelier: Vermont Dept. of Education, 1952.

Joint Report Upon the Survey and Demarcation of the Boundary Between the United States and Canada from the Source of the St. Croix River to the St. Lawrence River. International Boundary Commission, Washington, D.C.: U.S. Govt. Printing Office, 1925.

Jones, Matt B. *Vermont in the Making, 1750–1777.* Cambridge: Harvard University Press. Reprinted 1968, Anchor Books.

Lates, Richard, and Harold Meeks. "The Line Which Separates Vermonters from Canadians: A Short History of Vermont's Northern Border with Quebec." *Vermont History*, Vol. 44, No. 2, Spring 1976.

Parks, Joseph. *Pownal: A Vermont Town's Two Hundred Years and More.* Pownal Bicentennial Committee, 1977.

Schwarz, Philip J. *The Jarring Interests: New York's Boundary Makers, 1664–1776*. Albany: State University Press of New York, 1979.

Swift, Esther M. *Vermont Place Names; Footprints of History*. Brattleboro, Vt.: Stephen Greene Press, 1977.

Van Zandt, Franklin K. *Boundaries of the United States and the Several States*. Geological Survey Bulletin 1212, Washington, D.C.: U.S. Govt. Printing Office, 1966.

Chapter 4

LeBlanc, Robert G. *Location of Manufacturing in New England in the 19th Century*. Geography Publications at Dartmouth, No. 7, 1969.

Malmstrom, Vincent H. "When Vermont Went West." *The Vermont Geographer*, No. 2, 1975.

Steponaitis, Louis W. *The Textile Industry in Vermont, 1790–1973: Its Development, Diffusion and Decline*. Unpublished Master of Arts Thesis, Dept. of Geography, University of Vermont, October 1975.

Stilwell, Lewis D. "Migration from Vermont." *Proceedings of the Vermont Historical Society*, Vol. 5, 1937. Also, *Migration from Vermont*, Montpelier, Vt.: Vermont Historical Society, 1949.

"Vermonters Abroad." *Vermont History News*, Vol. 30, No. 2, March–April, 1979.

Wilgus, William. *The Role of Transportation in the Development of Vermont*. Montpelier: Vermont Historical Society, 1945.

Wilson, Harold P. *The Hill Country of Northern New England*. New York: Columbia University Press, 1936.

Chapter 5

Baker, George P. *The Formation of the New England Railroad System*. New York: Greenwood Press, 1968.

Barlow, James M. *The St. Johnsbury and Lamoille County Railroad in Northern Vermont*. Unpublished Master of Arts Thesis, Dept. of Geography, University of Vermont, 1975.

Bassett, T. D. Seymour. "500 Miles of Trouble and Excitement: Vermont Railroads, 1848–1861." *Vermont History*, Vol. 49, No. 3, Summer 1981, pp. 133–154.

Caldwell, R. S. "Short Line Railroads of Yesterday." *Vermont Life*, Vol. 5, No. 1, Autumn 1950.

Carman, Bernard R. *Hoot, Toot and Whistle: The Story of the Hoosac Tunnel and Wilmington Railroad*. Brattleboro, Vt.: Stephen Greene Press, 1963.

Gove, William G. "The Bristol Railroad." *Vermont Life*, Vol. 26, No. 1, Autumn 1971.

Gove, William G. "Railroad up the Mountain." *Vermont Life*, Vol. 23, No. 2, Winter 1968.

Gove, William G. "The Troublesome Addison Branch." *Vermont Life,* Vol. 28, No. 1, Autumn 1973.

Heslin, Thomas. "The Irish in Vermont." *Barre Times-Argus*, September 19, 1976.

Herwig, Wes. "Whistle up the Valley." *Vermont Life*, Vol. 18, No. 1, Autumn 1963.

Jones, Robert C. *The Central Vermont Railway: A Yankee Tradition*, 5 vols., Silverton, Colo.: Sundance Books, 1981.

Kendall, John S. *History of the St. Johnsbury and Lake Champlain Railroad*. Boston: Railway and Locomotive Historical Society, 1942.

Lewis, Edward A. *Vermont's Covered Bridge Road: The Story of the St. Johnsbury and Lamoille Country Railroad*, The Baggage Car, Strasburg, Pa. 1974.

Mead, Edgar T. "Over the Hills to Woodstock." *Vermont Life*, Vol. 32, No. 2, Winter 1967.

Morse, Victor. *36 Miles of Trouble: The Story of the West River Railroad*. Brattleboro, Vt.: Stephen Greene Press, 1959.

Northfield Town History Committee. *Green Mountain Heritage: The Chronicle of Northfield, Vt*. Northfield, Vt.: Phoenix Publishing, 1974.

Official Railway Guide. New York: National Railroad Publication Company, various dates.

"Railroad Centenary." *Vermont Life*, Vol. 2, No. 4, Summer 1948.

Shaughnessy, Jim. *Delaware and Hudson*. Berkeley, Calif.: Howell North Books, 1967.

Shaughnessy, Jim. *The Rutland Road*. Berkeley, Calif.: Howell North Books, 1964.

Spaulding, Albert C. "Trolleys." *Vermont Life*, Vol. 18, No. 3, Spring 1964.

Stevens, G. R. *History of the Canadian National Railway*. New York: Macmillan, 1973.

Wilgus, William. *The Role of Transportation in the Development of Vermont*. Montpelier: Vermont Historical Society, 1945.

Chapter 6

Lee, W. Storrs. *The Green Mountains of Vermont*. New York: Henry Holt, 1955.

Meeks, Harold A. "Stagnant, Smelly and Successful: Vermont's Mineral Springs." *Vermont History*, Vol. 47, No. 1, Winter 1979. This article contains a complete bibliography.

Roomet, Louise B. "Vermont as a Resort Area in the Nineteenth Century." *Vermont History*, Vol. 44, No. 1, Winter 1976.

Chapter 7

Alvord, Henry E. "Dairy Development in the United States." *Yearbook of the U.S. Dept. of Agriculture, 1899*. Washington, D.C.: U.S. Govt. Printing Office, 1900.

Annual Reports. Vermont State Board of Agriculture, various years.

Annual Reports. Vermont State Dairymens Association, various years.

Firk, Walter W., and Charles Thom. *The Book of Cheese*. New York, 1918.

Latimer, W. J. *Soil Survey (Reconnaissance) of Vermont*. U.S. Dept. of Agriculture, Bureau of Chemistry and Soils, Washington, D.C.: U.S. Govt. Printing Office, 1930.

Meeks, Harold A. "Favorite Vermont Myth in Need of Debunking." *Vermont Life*, Vol. 35, No. 4, Summer 1981, p. 56.

Mitchell, Edwin V. *It's an Old New England Custom*. New York, 1946.

1978 Dairy Producer Highlights, National Milk Producers Federation, 30 F Street NW, Washington, D.C., 20001. This booklet is published annually and is a good survey of United States dairy trends.

Roswenc, Edwin C. *Agricultural Policies in Vermont, 1860–1945*. Montpelier: Vermont Historical Society, 1981.

Rural Vermont: A Program for the Future, Vermont Agricultural Experiment Station Brieflet 1002, RV 461, no date, probably 1964. This publication accompanies a series of fourteen individual reports on each of Vermont's counties, Brieflets 794–807.

Russell, Howard S. *A Long Deep Furrow: Three Centuries of Farming in New England*. Hanover, N.H.: University Press of New England, 1976.

Tremblay, R. H., and C. H. Bigelow. "Vermont Livestock, 1977." *Vermont Agricultural Experiment Station Miscellaneous Report 99,* July 1978.

U.S. Census, various years.

Wilson, Harold F. *The Hill Country of Northern New England*. New York: Columbia University Press, 1936.

Chapter 8

"Birth of the Modern Scale." *Vermont Life*, Vol. 3, No. 2, Winter 1948–1949.

Chapin, Miriam. "The French Vermonter." *Vermont Life*, Vol. 22, No. 4, Summer 1958.

Chittenden County Historical Society. *Look Around Winooski, Vermont.* Burlington, Vt.: Heritage Pamphlet Number Three, 1972.

Crosby, George M. "The Fabulous Fairbanks Family of St. Johnsbury." *Vermont History*, April 1953.

Follett, Muriel, "Vermont's Machine Tools." *Vermont Life*. Vol. 1, No. 1, Autumn 1946.

Picher, Robert. "The Franco-Americans in Vermont." *Vermont History*, Vol. 28, No. 1, January 1960.

The Shires of Bennington: A Sampler of Green Mountain Heritage. Bennington, Vt.: Bennington Museum, 1975.

Steponaitis, Louis W. *The Textile Industry in Vermont, 1790–1973. Its Development, Diffusion and Decline.* Master of Arts Thesis, Dept. of Geography, University of Vermont, October 1975.

Vicero, Ralph D. *Migration of French Canadians to New England, 1840–1900*, Ph.D. Dissertation, Dept. of Geography, University of Wisconsin, 1968.

Wilson, Charles M. "Valley of Precision." *Vermont Life*, Vol. 13, No. 1, Autumn 1958.

Wilson, Harold F. "Population Trends in Northwestern New England." *New England Quarterly*, Vol. 7, 1934.

Woolfson, Peter. "The Rural Franco-American in Vermont." *Vermont History*, Vol. 50, No. 3, Summer 1982.

Chapter 9

Anderson, W. A. *Population Change in Vermont, 1900–1950.* University of Vermont, Agricultural Experiment Station, Bulletin 585, September 1955.

Bright, Graham M., ed. *The Vermont Economic Almanac, 1980.* Bellows Falls, Vt.: Vermont Business World.

Conant, Edward, and Mason Stone. *Conant's Vermont: Geography, History, and Civil Government of Vermont.* Rutland: Tuttle, 1905. Contains a town listing of population figures from the earliest census through 1900.

Maher, Frederick J., Jr. *Population Change and State Planning in Vermont.* Dept. of Sociology, University of Vermont. Mimeo., no date. Probably 1965.

Population, State of Vermont. A Report prepared for the Central Planning Office by Sargent, Webster, Crenshaw and Folley, Architects, Engineers and Planners, Syracuse, N.Y. May 1963.

U.S. Bureau of the Census. *United States Census of Population.* Washington, D.C.: various years.

Vermont Social and Economic Characteristics, Vermont State Planning Office, June 1971.
Vermont Postcensal Population Estimates, 1971–1979, Division of Public Health Statistics, Vermont Dept. of Health, November 1980.
Wells, George F. *The status of Rural Vermont*. Vermont State Agricultural Commission, 1903.

Chapter 10   .

Carter, Robert M. *Summer and Country Homes in the West River Valley*. University of Vermont, Agricultural Experiment Station, Bulletin 591, June 1956.
Canfield, Dorothy. *Vermont Summer Homes*. Montpelier, Vt.: Vermont Bureau of Publicity, 1935 (One of many "Vacation Booklets" published by this agency in the 1930s.) Other topics included *Vermont Lakes and Mountains, Hotel and Resort Directory, Vermont Agriculture, Cottages and Camps for Rent, Farms and Summer Homes for Sale, Vermont Bridle Paths, Vermont Tours*, and *Golfing in Vermont*.
Crane, Charles Edward. *Let Me Show You Vermont*. New York: Alfred A. Knopf, 1937.
Gilbert, A. H. *Vermont Hunters: Characteristics, Attitudes and Levels of Participation*. Miscellaneous Publication 92, Agricultural Experiment Station, University of Vermont, December 1977.
Gilbert, A. H., and S. M. Khayami. *Expenditure Patterns of Nonresident Sportsmen in Vermont, 1970*. Miscellaneous Publication 78, Vermont Agricultural Experiment Station, University of Vermont, October 1973.
Huffman, Benjamin. *The Vermont Farm and a Land Reform Program*. Montpelier: Vermont State Planning Office, June 1973.
Merrill, Perry H. *Vermont Under Four Flags*. Montpelier, 1975.
Official Automobile Blue Book, 1920, vol. 11. New York and Chicago: Automobile Blue Book Publishing, 1920.
Pelsue, Neil H., Jr. *Trends in Rural Land Prices in Vermont*. University of Vermont, Agricultural Experiment Station, Bulletin 682, December 1977.
Pitt, Albert. *Geography of the Vermont Deer Herd*. Unpublished Master of Arts Thesis, Dept. of Geography, University of Vermont, 1973.
Progress Report. Montpelier: Vermont State Planning Board, 1936.
Rural Vermont: A Program for the Future, by Two Hundred Vermonters. Burlington: Vermont Commission on Country Life, 1931.
Sinclair, Robert O. *Trends in Vermont Land Prices*. University of Vermont, Agricultural Experiment Station, Bulletin 659, October 1969.

Sinclair, Robert O., and Stephen B. Meyer. *Nonresident Ownership of Property in Vermont*. Bulletin 670, Agricultural Experiment Station, University of Vermont, May 1972.

Vermont: The Land of Green Mountains. Vermont Bureau of Publicity, Office of the Secretary of State, Guy W. Bailey. Essex Junction, 1913.

Vermont Vacation Home Survey, 1968. Montpelier: Vermont Development Department.

Vermont Vacation Home Inventory, 1973. Vermont Agency of Environmental Conservation, Montpelier. Produced by Action Research, Inc., Burlington, Vt.

Chapter 11

Economic Handbook for Rural Vermont. Extension Service, University of Vermont. Publication Q212, November 1978.

1978 ELFAC Dairy Farm Analysis. Cooperative Extension Services of the Northeastern States, Publication NE 232, June 1979. Authored by Raymond H. Tremblay, Agricultural Economist, University of Vermont. This report is published each year and current issues are valuable in depicting what good commercial dairy farms are like.

U.S. Bureau of the Census. *U.S. Census of Agriculture*. Washington, D.C.: U.S. Govt. Printing Office, various years.

Chapter 12

Balance Sheet of the Farm Sector. Washington, D.C.: U.S. Dept. of Agriculture. This annual publication contains a wealth of statistical material on national and state farming trends.

Bigelow, Charles W., and Raymond H. Tremblay. *Projections of Dairy Farm Numbers in Vermont*. Bulletin 657, Agricultural Experiment Station, University of Vermont, December 1968.

An Economic Analysis of Agriculture in the State of Vermont. A report prepared for the Central Planning Office, May 1964, by Sargent, Webster, Crenshaw and Folley, Consulting Engineers and Planners, Syracuse, N.Y. 61 pp, mimeo.

Land, Bread and History: A Research Report on the Potential for Food Self-Sufficiency in Vermont. Center for Studies in Food Self-Sufficiency, Vermont Institute of Community Involvement, 1976.

Lough, Harold L. *The Cheese Industry*. U.S. Dept. of Agriculture, Economic Research Service, Agricultural Economic Report No. 294, July 1975.

1978 ELFAC Dairy Farm Business Analysis. Cooperative Extension Services of the Northeastern States, NE-232, June 1979.

Sykes, James H. *Trends in Vermont Agriculture.* Vermont Resources Research Center, Report 7, Agricultural Experiment Station, October 1964.

Sykes, James H. *Vermont Land Classes.* Vermont Resource Research Center, Report 6, Agricultural Experiment Station, June 1964.

Tremblay, Raymond H. *Dairy Farming in Vermont.* Vermont Agricultural Experiment Station, Bulletin 617, November 1960.

Tremblay, Raymond H. *Farming Trends in Vermont.* Miscellaneous Publication 52, Vermont Agricultural Experiment Station, University of Vermont, August 1968.

Tremblay, Raymond H. *Large Dairy Farms in Vermont.* Vermont Agricultural Experiment Station, Bulletin 643, March 1966.

Tremblay, R. H. and C. H. Bigelow. *Vermont Livestock, 1978.* Vermont Agricultural Experiment Station Miscellaneous Publication 105, 1979. See also the 1977 tabulation, Miscellaneous Publication 99, which is the last complete listing available.

Webster, Fred C., ed. *Milk Marketing.* A newsletter published monthly by the Extension Service, University of Vermont.

Wilson, Harold F. *The Hill County of Northern New England.* New York: Columbia University Press, 1936.

Chapter 13

Community Facts and Figures: People—Income—Taxes. Town Officers Educational Conference, 1977. Prepared by Malcolm Bevins, Extension Economist, University of Vermont.

Economic Handbook for Rural Vermont. Extension Service, University of Vermont, Publication Q212, November 1978.

Economic Indicators of the Farm Sector: State Income and Balance Sheet Statistics, 1983. Economic Research Service, U.S. Department of Agriculture, January 1985. This is an annual publication and very helpful in showing agricultural trends.

New England Fruit Tree Survey. Boston, Mass.: New England Crop Reporting Service, U.S. Department of Agriculture, 1972.

U.S. Bureau of the Census. *U.S. Census of Agriculture.* Washington, D.C.: U.S. Govt. Printing office, various years.

Chapter 14

Note: There are problems with material dealing with industry and employment. The Census of Manufacturers is best, but is taken only every five years. County Business Patterns are published by the Census Bureau but list only employees covered by Social Security and omit government employees, self-employed persons, farm workers, and domestic-service workers. Also omitted are railway workers, who are covered under the Railway Retirement Act. The Vermont Department of Employment Security publishes employment estimates, as does the Federal Reserve Bank of Boston. Both differ from material reported in census publications. The *Vermont Directory of Manufacturers* relies upon voluntary filling out of forms and probably understates the industries in Vermont.

Annual Reports. Vermont Council of Economic Advisors, 1974, 1975, 1976, and 1980.

Bevins, Malcolm I. *Community Facts and Figures.* Prepared for Town Officers Educational Conference, 1977. Cooperative Extension Service, University of Vermont.

Bright, Graham M., ed. *The Vermont Economic Almanac, 1980.* Published by Vermont Business World, Bellows Falls, Vt. 1980.

County Business Patterns, 1976. U.S. Dept. of Commerce, Bureau of the Census. Issued April 1979. *County Business Patterns*, 1982, issued March 1984.

Leinbach, Thomas R. "Non-Metropolitan Industrial Growth in Vermont." *The Professional Geographer*, Vol. 30, No. 1, February 1978.

New England Economic Almanac. Issues published in 1961 and 1977 by the Federal Reserve Bank of Boston.

New England Economic Indicators. Published monthly by the Federal Reserve Bank of Boston, Boston Mass.

New England's Prospect, 1933. New York: American Geographical Society, 1933.

1977 Census of Manufacturers. U.S. Dept. of Commerce, Bureau of the Census, issued September 1979. The 1982 Census is expected to be issued in 1985.

Potentials for Industrial Development in Vermont. A Report Prepared for the Central Planning Office, December 1963 by Sargent, Webster, Crenshaw and Folley, Syracuse, N.Y.

State of Vermont Economic Indicators. Compiled and published monthly by the Agency of Development and Community Affairs.

Tear, Jacqueline D. *Vermont Industrial Changes, 1945–1975.* Unpublished Master of Arts Thesis, Dept. of Geography, University of Vermont, 1981.

Vermont Directory of Manufacturers. Published annually by Vermont Agency of Development and Community Affairs.

Vermont Facts and Figures. Volumes published in 1973 and 1975 by Vermont Department of Budget and Management, Office of Statistical Coordination, Montpelier.

Vermont Social and Economic Characteristics. Vermont State Planning Office, June 1971.

Chapter 15

Daniels, Robert V., et al. "The Vermont Constitutional Referendum of 1969." *Vermont History*, Vol. 38, No. 2, Spring 1970.

The People Book: Vermont Population Projections, 1980–2000. Vermont State Planning Office, 1978.

U.S. Bureau of the Census. *U.S. Census of Population.* Washington, D.C.: U.S. Govt. Printing Office, appropriate years.

Index

bridges
  covered, 19, 21, 22
  iron, 23
  patent, 21, 22
  stringer, 21
  toll, 128
Bridgewater, textile mills, 194
Bridport
  settlement, 17
  town grant, 63
Brighton, population growth, 185
Bristol
  dairy industry, 263
  wool factory, 192
Bristol Railroad, 132
Bromley Mountain, 223
  Alpine Slide, 241, 243
  development, 233
  vacation homes, 237, 238
Brookfield, dairy farming, 274
Brownington, town incomes, 316
Brunswick
  fields, 14
  mineral springs, 146, 147, 150, 152–
    53
Bryant Chucking Grinder Company, 188
Bryant, William, 188
buckwheat production, 87, 175
Buel, 70
Buel, Major Elias, 60
Buel's Gore, 60
Burke Mountain, vacation homes, 237
Burlington, 44, 70
  climate, 1
  cotton industry, 103, 189, 196, 197
  electrical machinery, 309
  immigration, 179
  manufacturing, 197
  population growth, 185, 188, 210, 213
  and railroads, 107, 139
Burlington and Lamoille Valley Railroad,
  122
Burr Arch, 21, 22
Burr, Theodore, 21
butter
  production, 166, 167, 169–75
  and railroad shipping, 133, 139, 172,
    173

C

Cabot
  cheese manufacturing, 270
  settlement, 17, 41

Cabot Plains, 38
Caledonia County
  dairy industry, 94, 95, 162, 165
  sheep raising, 94
  twentieth-century employment, 305,
    306, 310, 312
  twentieth-century farming, 253, 259,
    271, 286
  twentieth-century population, 209
  wool factories, 101, 194
Caledonia Mineral Springs Hotel, 151
Camel's Hump
  early accommodations, 141
  vacation homes, 228
Canaan
  and Kenebeki Indians, 8
  furniture plant, 213, 311
  name origin, 18
  population growth, 213
  state North East Corner Witness
    Marker, 75
Canadian National, 135
canals, 43–46, 87, 89, 106
Carter, T. J., 112
Carter, Robert M., 249, 251
Caspian Lake, vacation homes, 247
Castleton
  apple production, 289
  Constitutional Convention vote,
    326
  Dutch influence, 14
  population, 213
  vacation homes, 247
cattle, 157–58, 294–96 (*see also* cows)
Cavendish
  Amsden settlement, 36
  John Coffeen, 35
  population, 186, 326
  textile mill, 194
  town grant, 63
cemeteries, 18–20
Central Vermont Railroad, 107, 112, 121,
  124, 127, 131, 132–35
Chace Mill, 197
Champlain and Connecticut River
  Railroad, 114
Champlain Canal, 5, 89
  construction, 39, 44
Champlain Glass Company, 179
Champlain Lowland (*see* Champlain
  Valley)
Champlain Mill, 195
Champlain, Samuel de, 8, 12
  and Lamoille River, 11

town grant, 63
town incomes, 315
Rutland and Burlington Railroad, 36, 106–7, 110, 111, 114, 147
Rutland and Canadian Railroad, 134
Rutland and Noyan Railroad, 134
Rutland and Washington Railroad, 116
Rutland and Whitehall Railroad, 116
Rutland County
    apple production, 288, 289
    cheese factories, 173
    dairy industry, 94, 162
    Italian population, 178
    sheep raising, 94, 95
    twentieth-century employment, 306, 310, 312
    twentieth-century farming, 253, 286
    twentieth-century population, 209
Rutland Railroad, 114–19, 132–35, 147
Rutland Railway Company, 115, 116, 119, 135
Rutland Transit Company, 134
rye production, 87, 176
Ryegate
    cemetery, 18
    settlement, 17
    sheep farming, 294

S

Sadawga Pond, name origin, 9
St. Albans, 70
    creamery, 173
    electrical machinery, 309
    French Canadian population, 179
    knitting mill, 101
    population growth, 185, 188, 210
    and Vermont and Canada Railroad, 112, 113
St. Anne's Shrine, 241
St. George
    town grant, 63, 64
    town incomes, 315
St. John, Hector, 11
St. Johnsbury
    dairy farming, 274
    and Fairbanks Company, 189, 191
    Maple Grove Museum, 241
    name origin, 11
    nonelectrical machinery, 309
    population growth, 185, 210
St. Johnsbury and Lake Champlain Railroad, 121, 123–24, 189

Maquam Branch, 121, 124
Victory Branch, 124
St. Johnsbury and Lamoille County Railroad, 124–25
St. Regis Paper Company, 249
Salisbury
    town grant, 63
    vacation homes, 247
Salisbury, Connecticut, and settlers, 15
Sanatoga Springs, 132, 150
Santa's Land, 241
Searsburg, town incomes, 316
services, personal and public
    employment, 299–301, 209, 310, 311, 312, 325
    and grow state product, 299, 309
Shaftsbury
    apple production, 289
    horses, 294
    sheep farming, 294
Sharon, settlement, 17
Shatterack Mountain, name origin, 9
sheep farming, 92–95, 158, 159, 161, 166, 293–94, 295 (*see also* textile industry)
Sheffield
    charter, 68
    town incomes, 316
Shelburne
    apple production, 289
    Constitutional Convention votes, 326
    French-Canadian population, 179
    town incomes, 313, 315
Shelburne Museum 135, 241
Sheldon, mineral springs, 144, 147, 148, 152
Sherburne
    Constitutional Convention vote, 326
    town incomes, 313
    vacation homes, 237, 247
Shoreham
    apple production, 289
    Captain Ephraim Doolittle, 35
    covered bridge, 19
    settlement, 17
    town grant, 63
Shoreham Cooperative, 289
Shrewsbury
    settlement, 17
    town grant, 63
silo, first, 164
Silver Lake, vacation homes, 247
Simmons Precision, 189, 309
Sinclair, Robert, 255

West Windsor, town incomes, 313
Weybridge, horses, 294
wheat production, 87, 175, 176
Wheelock
    bottling works, 144, 151
    mineral springs, 144, 147, 148, 150, 151
Whitehall and Plattsburg Railroad, 118, 119
Whitelaw, James, 38
White River, and cross-Vermont canal, 45
White River Junction
    cotton industry, 103
    population growth, 186
    and railroads, 111
White River Railroad, 132
White River Valley
    dairy farming, 274
    and settlement, 17
Whitingham
    settlement, 17
    town grant, 64, 68
Wild Branch, mineral spring along, 144
Wilder, Jonas, 133
Williams, Colonel Israel, 29
Williston
    French Canadian population, 179
    town incomes, 315
Wilmington
    Constitutional Convention vote, 326
    cotton industry, 103
    dependence on skiing, 318
    and railroad, 130
    vacation homes, 237, 247
Wilson, Harold F., 89, 264
Windham County
    apple production, 288, 289
    cheese factories, 173
    dairy industry, 94, 95, 162, 263
    settlement, 17
    sheep raising, 94
    twentieth-century employment, 306, 309, 310, 312
    twentieth-century farming, 253, 259, 271, 286
    twentieth-century population, 209
Windsor
    emigration, 214
    machine-tool industry, 186
    meeting in, 67
    population change, 186

Windsor Armory, 187
Windsor County
    apple production, 176, 288, 289
    beef cattle, 295
    cheese factories, 173
    Connecticut towns, settlement, 17
    dairy industry, 94, 162, 263
    machine-tool industry, 305, 309
    posting of land, 245, 247
    sheep raising, 94, 95
    twentieth-century employment, 305, 306, 309, 310, 311
    twentieth-century farming, 253, 259, 271, 286
    twentieth-century population, 209
Windsor Machine Company, 187–88
Winhall
    Constitutional Convention vote, 326
    vacation homes, 237, 247
Winooski, 70
    name origin, 9
    1850 manufacturing employment, 103
    French-Canadian settlement, 182
    1980 population, 210
    textile industry, 189, 194, 195
Winooski River
    cross-Vermont canal, 45
    valley, settlement, 17
Winooski Worsted Company, 195
Winter, Royal, 148, 151
Witness Marker
    North East Corner, 75
    southeast corner, 72
Wolfe, General Sir James, 26
Woodbury
    and quarrying, 4, 124
    vacation homes, 247
Woodford, Vermont's highest church, 4
Woodland culture, 7
wood products industry, 139, 304, 305
Woodstock
    beef cattle, 295
    Constitutional Convention vote, 326
    first ski tow, 231
    horses, 294
    mineral springs, 132, 147, 150
    population growth, 214
    residents, 229, 313, 326
    and Rockefellers, 141

T-5830

330
.9743
M47t

VERMONT STATE COLLEGES

0 0003 0409354 5

DATE DUE

JUL 2 9 2002	
APR 2 9 2011	

DEMCO, INC. 38-2931

DISCARD
VTC TC Library
Hartness Library
Vermont Technical College
Randolph Center, VT 05061